The Internet Today

Thomas J. Fallon
Southern Polytechnic State University

Prentice
Hall

Upper Saddle River, New Jersey
Columbus, Ohio

Library of Congress Cataloging-in-Publication Data

Fallon, Thomas
    The Internet Today / Thomas Fallon.
        p.   cm.
    ISBN 0-13-010139-7
    1. Internet (Computer network)   I. Title.

TK105.875.157   F354   2001
004.67´8–dc21

99-048941
CIP

Vice President and Publisher: Dave Garza
Editor in Chief: Stephen Helba
Assistant Vice President and Publisher: Charles E. Stewart, Jr.
Production Editor: Alexandrina Benedicto Wolf
Production Coordination: Custom Editorial Productions, Inc.
Design Coordinator: Robin G. Chukes
Cover Designer: Rod Harris
Production Manager: Matthew Ottenweller
Marketing Manager: Barbara Rose

This book was set in Garamond by Custom Editorial Productions, Inc. It was printed and bound by R.R. Donnelley & Sons. The cover was printed by Phoenix Color Corp.

10   9   8   7   6   5   4   3   2   1
ISBN: 0-13-010139-7

This book is lovingly dedicated to my two best friends,
my wife, Lauren, and my daughter, Katie.

Preface

The rise of the Internet is not a random occurrence within the timeline of human events. Rather, it is a logical coalescing of technologies, services, and human interactions. To many, the Internet is a mysterious "ether" through which requests are transmitted and from which responses are received. Fortunately, the mystery can be dispelled. This book examines the Internet piece by piece to give the reader a holistic perspective and understanding of this communications phenomenon. It is in the spirit of viewing the whole as the sum (and more!) of its parts that this book was written.

Although technical in nature, the material is suitable as an introduction for readers with a beginning to intermediate understanding of communications and the Internet, and as a reference for the advanced reader. Compensation for the time-sensitive nature of the information contained within this book is partially provided by placing the information within its proper context relative to past, present, and future Internet events.

The book is composed of five distinct sections: introduction (Chapter 1), basic technologies (Chapters 2–4), applications and services (Chapters 5–8), security and evolving technologies (Chapter 9), and conclusion. In addition to the technical information provided, the text explains other Internet-related issues, such as other people's perceptions of the Internet, its impact on society, and the reason for its existence.

Several key pedagogical features provide the reader with a consistent set of learning aids with which to successfully absorb the material. The chapter introductions and summaries, for example, guide the reader from one topic to another. Chapter learning objectives, figures, tables, and examples provide the reader with a thorough discussion of the current topic. A comprehensive list of additional Internet-related resources is provided in the appendices.

Acknowledgments

Several individuals and organizations contributed to the successful completion of this book. I would like to express my gratitude to many individuals and organizations:

Charles Stewart (my editor) for the wonderful opportunity to become an author;

Jennifer Stagman, Rachel Besen, Alex Wolf, Carole Horton, and the other individuals at Prentice Hall who aided in the publishing process;

JaNoel Lowe of Custom Editorial Productions and Eileen Kramer, the copy editor;

The Southeastern Library Network (SOLINET);

Southern Polytechnic State University; Georgia State University;

the individuals who contributed quotations to Chapter 1;

Jeff Beasley, New Mexico State University; Shivakant Mishra, University of Wyoming; and Judy Ann Serwatka, Purdue University for their valuable reviews.

I also thank members of my extended family, which includes the Fallons, Russells, Rikes, Talmages, Cordovas, Walls, Walkers, and the Heritage Presbyterian Church. I would like especially to acknowledge my wonderful wife, Lauren, for the million or so hours of proofreading that she devoted to this book.

Any product name mentioned in this book is the trademark or registered trademark of its owner, including but not limited to Connectix QuickCam®; Forté, Inc., Free Agent®; Intervists WorldView®; IpswitchWS.FTP®; Macromedia Director and Authorware®; Microsoft Corporation (Access, ActiveX®, Internet Explorer®, MediaPlayer®, Windows®); Netscape Communications Corporation (JavaScript®, Live3D®, Netscape Navigator® [AOL]); Network Associates Inc., for Networks Associates®, Sniffer®, and Distributed Sniffer System®); Qualcomm Eudora Light; RealNetowkrs RealPlayer®; SGI Cosmo Player®; Sun Miscrosystems Java®; Symantec Corporation Java Console®; Unix®; and WhitePines CUSeeMe®.

All other product names mentioned in this book are all trademarks or registered trademarks of their respective owners.

Thomas J. Fallon

Contents

The Internet Introduced

Chapter Learning Objectives:

- Investigate some popular perceptions of the Internet.
- Understand the Internet's position in the timeline of telecommunications.
- Understand the key components and players of the Internet.
- Gain insight into the impact of the Internet on society.

> *"All the knowledge I possess everyone else can acquire, but my heart is all my own."*
>
> *Goethe,* The Sorrows of Young Werther

Knowledge today is obtained through high-speed digital information systems. The information output of these systems is transported neither by foot, horse-drawn carriage, nor sailing vessel, but by digital transmission over vast communication networks of electrons and photons traveling at relativistic speeds (near and precisely at the speed of light, respectively). This great communications network is affectionately known as the Internet. And so our story begins . . .

1.1 Perceptions of the Internet

It has been said that every story has at least two sides. The story of the Internet, as told in this book, is no exception. The following responses to an Internet survey, by people of different vocational backgrounds, embody the very essence of the Internet. Here is what the respondents had to say:

What is the Internet?

The Internet is the global network of networks, and as some have observed, a unique and wholly new medium of worldwide communications that is challenging the standards and norms of every aspect of our society. As the printing press was to the Renaissance, the Internet will be to the end of the millenium.

"The Internet is the global network of networks, and as some have observed, a unique and wholly new medium of worldwide communications that is challenging the standards and norms of every aspect of our society. As the printing press was to the Renaissance, the Internet will be to the end of the millenium."

Gabe Battista
CEO
Network Solutions, Inc.

"By definition, the Internet is a very large wide area network (WAN). But this definition does not take into account the fact that this WAN is more than a corporate tool and is not controlled by a single entity. This WAN is a community. Inside the Internet are all the facets of community life right at your fingertips. Education, employment, entertainment, crime, terrorism. If you want to know about it, someone on the Internet has posted information about it. The Internet is a worldwide community where anyone with a modem can move right in."

Mike Ameye
Webmaster
Channel Reps, Inc.

"To me, the Internet is a vehicle that allows people to communicate with one another electronically."

William D. Clarida, D.D.S., F.A.G.D.

"The Internet is a combination of web hosts and web sites connected by generally publicly switched access and trunk facilities that use intelligent switches (servers and routers). The Internet was, until 1996, funded at the core by a U.S. agency (DARPA). Its original purpose was for academic research, but that function has long since been overwhelmed by its commercial aspects. It is characterized by access companies and search and content companies. Its primary asset is its flexible and scalable address plan. It delivers quality and reliability on a best-effort basis. It is currently governed by a series of loose committees and address administrators."

Richard K. Snelling
Executive VP Retired
Network Bell South

"From an operator's perspective, the Internet is a means of communicating with other people. It can be more formal than a telephone call because it leaves a written record, more convenient than face-to-face because it doesn't require the other person's physical presence, and more efficient than writing because you

can enclose electronically generated information. It does require that the other person have a system to send (if you're receiving) and receive (if you're sending) the information."

Janice Voss, Ph.D.
NASA Astronaut

"The Internet to me is a worldwide computer network for transporting electronic ideas and information."

Wade McGee
Hair Stylist

What significant changes in the Internet do you foresee within the next five years?

"Mainly an increase in bandwidth for many users via xDSL, and for some to gigabit speeds even, along with the attendant concerns addressed—quality of service for real-time services such as voice and video. I also expect to see much better ways to manage access to digital information and to use the Net to help in design and manufacturing."

Robert Kahn, Ph.D.
Co-creator of TCP/IP

"If the major bandwidth and political issues can be resolved (that is a big if), it will become the most influential 'utility' available to mankind. It will likely be the telephone, radio, TV, and video rental store all in one. In addition, there will be services and product offerings that are on the edge of imagination today. Some such offerings could include fully interconnected and online smart homes, cars, boats, and airplanes, in-home interactive education, real-time virtual workplaces, and physically and sensory realistic cyber games and experiences."

Mike Taylor
Partner
MicroTechnix International, Inc.

"As a public official, I see the Internet over the next five years changing the landscape in the public policy arena dramatically. The quick access to current and useful information will allow public policy makers to be more responsive to the needs of their constituents in the twenty-first century. I look forward to the continued growth in digital communications."

Michael Hightower
Vice Chairman
Fulton County Board of Commissioners, Atlanta, Ga.

"The Internet promises to be significantly faster in the near future. With this increased speed a wide range of applications will be possible. Most visible will

be the proliferation of video information—from movie clips to real-time med-ical imaging. Imagine a physician being able to contact a heart specialist on the other side of the world and have him look at a patient's heart."

Scott J. Tippens
Associate Professor
Southern Polytechnic State University

"I believe the Internet will split into at least two and possibly more components that will accommodate the original academic noncommercial best-efforts net-work and a high quality of service multimedia broadband commercial compo-nent with common carrier or private network access costs fully compensated. The above precursor is possibly Internet II. This new commercial Internet will be broadband, well designed with reliability (paid for) in the historic 99.99% range with 1.5 to 2.0 megabit range common for access, and with trunks typi-cally at the 150-megabit range."

Richard K. Snelling
Executive VP Retired
Network BellSouth

How does the Internet benefit you?

"The Internet has benefited me in many ways in the short time that I have been online. I have used MapQuest to plan travel routes. I use the Internet daily to check the weather forecast. I can use it to read my hometown newspaper. I guess the most interesting thing so far has been that I tracked down an old high school buddy that I had not seen in over twenty years, and it only took me five minutes to locate him. Now we are able to keep in touch with each other."

Frank Ucciferri
Firefighter/EMT

"I can look things up that I want to know or get help with homework."

Michael Marien
Third Grader

"In my role as a legislator, the Internet has helped me to better communicate with my constituents as well as the general American public. One of the first things we implemented in the 104th Congress was the Thomas System. Thomas is the online legislative guide to the activities of Congress. As soon as a bill hits the House Floor, people who have access to the Internet can go online, access the bill, and judge whether it is acceptable. In turn, they can contact their representatives to voice their opinion. This is just one example of how the Internet has helped broaden the lines of communication between individuals and their elected officials."

Newt Gingrich, Ph.D.
Former Speaker of the House

"My job requires communicating with people all over the world. That process has become much faster and more efficient since we've started using the Internet, especially with people many time zones away."

Janice Voss, Ph.D.
NASA Astronaut

"As a librarian, the Internet brings with it tremendous advantages. It greatly enhances our ability to deliver information at a reasonable cost. The services we offer today at no visible cost to the library user were unavailable—or available only for an exorbitant fee—just a few years ago. The "library without walls" is nearly a reality as we have almost immediate access to information that is not in our own library. Our public access catalog is actually a shared resource made possible by the Internet."

Steven Vincent
Librarian
Southern Polytechnic State University

"It allows me to communicate with friends and relatives out of state or country in a very inexpensive manner. Not to mention I can send digital pics to family members very cost-effectively. I also sell and buy a lot of stuff over the Internet, for example, computer equipment, motorcycle parts, car parts, etc."

Wade McGee
Hair Stylist

"Network Solutions has been a pioneer in the development of the Internet for nearly 20 years, and in particular in the past five years providing unique identities to Internet users as the world's leading registrar of domain names. Network Solutions consulting services works with companies worldwide on re-engineering their own networks for intranet, extranet, and Internet uses. As the Internet has grown, so has Network Solutions. On a personal level, I communicate with other professionals and family via e-mail and find convenience and timesaving shopping through web sites for everything from wine to running shoes."

Gabe Battista
CEO
Network Solutions, Inc.

How does the Internet benefit society?

"I believe that society can benefit from this open communication community. Information can be disseminated faster and in graphic format that is easier to understand. Let's take, for example, a missing child. If information about that child were posted to a missing child web site with a picture of the child and

pictures of anyone else involved, that information could be globally available the instant it is posted. Call it a global milk carton."

> *Mike Ameye*
> *Webmaster*
> *Channel Reps, Inc.*

"The answer to this question could fill an entire book. I'll try to narrow it down to a few issues. The most important issue to me is its potential for maintaining a free society. Historically, governments have controlled public opinion and influenced society by removing or controlling access to information. With the Internet these barriers are all but eliminated. Discussion groups abound and a wide diversity of viewpoints can be heard. With the expanded worldwide communication possibilities available via the Internet, maybe the hidden atrocities of the past can be revealed in time to make a difference.

Another important benefit is the capability to link sections of the population that have in the past been in isolation. Specifically, a number of elderly find companionship and advice via newsgroups, e-mail, and the web. Some have even been saved by this electronic connection with society."

> *Scott J. Tippens*
> *Associate Professor*
> *Southern Polytechnic State University*

"The Internet allows access to libraries and museums in different cities, states, and countries. If you have access to the Internet, you have virtual access to the world. In addition to providing a vast medium of communication, it's yet another venue for commerce. It allows small or large businesses to be evaluated by the quality of their products and services, not the physical trappings of the office with a view of the sales staff with the BMWs. It allows for collaboration and discussion on issues by people of different cultures and on different continents. It can even translate your text into another language. Hey, on a more personal and basic level, it even ends phone tag."

> *Col. Mike Bernath (Ret.)*
> *U.S. Army Signal Corp*

"Rapid access to information helps provide more efficiency for individuals, allowing them to do more in less time (or have more free time). Access to information via intranet and extranet helps companies improve internal and external efficiencies. Improved efficiencies result in keeping prices down. Many experts believe that a key factor in the sustained U.S. economic growth is a result of such improved efficiencies. The Internet has certainly contributed in this area."

> *Mike Taylor*
> *Partner*
> *MicroTechnix International, Inc.*

Are there any negative aspects of the Internet?

"The Internet is far from being a 'final product.' It is inevitable that we will continue to encounter problems with the transfer of inappropriate information over the Internet, such as access to adult material by minor users. As advanced as computers and technology have become, the human brain is even more advanced. As long as creative minds continue to develop and experiment with information-age tools such as the Internet, there will be negative aspects including money-making scams, junk e-mail, and security problems. However, the question is not whether there will be negatives but how we handle those negatives. I view the Internet as a positive, innovative tool that can literally set the world at your doorstep, but at the same time its positive value to each of us will be determined by our own imagination, judgment, and personal responsibility. How we use the Internet and how it impacts our lives will, in many ways, be determined by each of us and by the personal decisions we make."

Newt Gingrich, Ph.D.
Former Speaker of the House

"Downsides exist for any new technology because it can be misused as easily, in some cases, as it can be used. Ultimately, it is a matter for society to determine whether the positives sufficiently outweigh the negatives. If, on the balance, the positives win out, then steps will be taken to deal with the negatives, as appropriate. Else the technology will have a hard time establishing itself in society."

Robert Kahn, Ph.D.
Co-creator of TCP/IP

"As far as negative aspects of the Internet are concerned, I understand some unwanted and unsolicited information is available to those who shouldn't have it, especially children."

William D. Clarida, D.D.S., F.A.G.D.

"I hear grousing about the perils of having your children on the Internet. I read about lawsuits, in this country and others, where Internet service providers are being sued because someone objects to the subject matter that can be actively pursued there, or possibly more alarming, have passively delivered to their e-mail inbox. My thoughts are that if you wouldn't leave your children unattended on a busy street corner, then you shouldn't let them surf the Net unsupervised either. Just as you encounter people on a street corner, there are also people on the Net. Some percentage of them are just rubbing their hands, awaiting your arrival. Maybe you'd like to talk to them, maybe you wouldn't. It's your choice."

Col. Mike Bernath (Ret.)
U.S. Army Signal Corp

"We all are aware of the so-called 'porno' and other such sites. If it is something that I object to, I am also free not to look at it."

Frank Ucciferri
Firefighter/EMT

"Some of the negative aspects are essentially the same as the positive ones. Many persons who publish on the web have no credentials to do so, and the content they create is of little value. A lot of press and most of the attention of legislators has been drawn to "inappropriate" information made freely available over the Internet. I think, however, that a larger problem has drawn little notice. The evaluative skills of those who read information from the Internet are not always equal to the task of sifting the wheat from the chaff. We have a lot of work to do in teaching evaluation of Internet information.

Another problem is in the nature of the Internet itself. It provides for rapid transfer of relatively small quantities of current information, but provisions are almost never made to archive information of lasting value. Future generations will have only knowledge that we keep, and we are risking a Dark Age in which vital information is lost because we lacked the foresight to preserve it."

Steven Vincent
Librarian
Southern Polytechnic State University

"Yes. People can e-mail someone and write negative things about them."

Michael Marien
Third Grader

1.2 Timeline of Telecommunications

Whether the entities are human, computer, or extraterrestrial, a common encoding scheme and communication protocol must exist for communications to be established.

Prior to discussing salient points of its chronology, let us define telecommunications. *Telecommunications* is the transmission and reception of encoded information between two or more "intelligent" entities over an appreciable distance using an agreed-upon protocol. Whether the entities are human, computer, or extraterrestrial, a common encoding scheme and communication protocol must exist for communications to be established.

Any existing technology's timeline terminus must be the present. However, the starting point can be chosen arbitrarily. We could set our starting point at circa 3000 B.C., where we find clay tablets bearing ancient Sumerian cuneiform being transported to and from remote cities on the backs of oppressed camels. Perhaps our starting point focuses on the final selfless act of a Greek soldier who relayed a critical military message by running from Marathon to Athens in 490 B.C., or on the battlefields of medieval Europe where semaphore systems of flags were used to guide events from distant hilltops. Although all of these events offer an excellent beginning, they share the absence of one critical present-day element: they are not electronically based.

The morse code phrase .— .... .- - .... .- - .... —. — -.. — -. — ..- —. .... - ("What hath God wrought.") required approximately 5 seconds to be successfully transmitted across the 36 miles from Baltimore, Maryland to Washington, D.C. Each individual character, however, traversed the telegraph wire in only 250 millionths of a second! The date of this first public demonstration of Samuel Morse's telegraph (see Figure 1.1) was May 24, 1844. More than 15 years would pass before the outbreak of the Civil War. In 60 years, mankind would witness the further loosening of gravity's grip as the Wright Flyer took to the air for the first time. It would be precisely 115 years and 58 days later, however, before Neil Armstrong would set foot on the moon and communicate his message of hope to the anxious people of planet Earth some 240,000 miles away. The advent of the telegraph was a giant leap indeed.

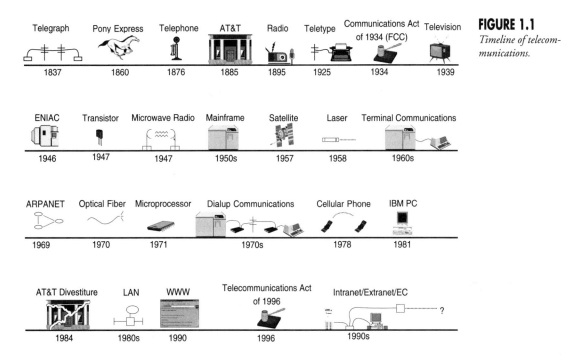

FIGURE 1.1

Timeline of telecommunications.

The overland route stretched approximately 2000 miles from Saint Joseph, Missouri to Sacramento, California. Inaugurated on April 3, 1860, the Pony Express consisted of 100 relay stations, 80 riders (one of whom was Buffalo Bill), and 400 to 500 horses. Its purpose was to ship satchels of mail across the "Wild West" via horseback in 10 days. Previously, such deliveries took the better part of a month. The Pony Express is credited with delivering news of Lincoln's election and the outbreak of the Civil War to the state of California. Although an ambitious entrepreneurial venture, the Pony Express was discontinued in October 1861 upon completion of a telegraph line to San Francisco. The moral of the story is that prudence dictates the necessity of remaining abreast of changing technologies.

It is easy to imagine the process by which information is sent over a telegraph system. A key is depressed, and a tone of given duration is sent across the wire. "Dots" consist of a short duration tone, whereas "dashes" are a long duration tone. This system uses only two states to encode information, long and short tones; therefore, we refer to it as a *binary system.* Since the dots and dashes are of a discrete duration (dots last one-third the length of time of dashes), this further defines the system as being *digital.* Now suppose that using the same system we are able to vary not only the duration of our information but the tone as well. One such rendition of this scenario is the telephone. In fact, while working on an experimental telegraph system that he had designed, Alexander Graham Bell inadvertently conceived the idea of the telephone.

"Mr. Watson, come here; I want you" was the first utterance of a human voice ever to be heard by electronic means. This famous event took place on March 10, 1876, and the fortunate soul who heard the message was Thomas A. Watson, Bell's assistant. Ironically, Bell was calling Watson not out of joy for their success, but because he had spilled acid on his pants. The following year the Bell Telephone Company was established, and, as the saying goes, the rest is history. The telegraph, a *digital system,* actually preceded the telephone, an *analog system.* Yet today we partake in the mass exodus from the world of analog communications to the more sophisticated world of digital.

Several regional telephone companies quickly emerged to establish franchises with the Bell Telephone Company. To interconnect these geographically dispersed companies and their customers, a long-distance infrastructure was needed. In 1885, the American Telephone and Telegraph Company (AT&T) was formed to build and operate the infrastructure. In 1900, AT&T purchased the Bell franchises and therefore gained control of them. In 1911, they were reorganized into 22 regional operating companies known collectively as the Bell System. AT&T continued to gain strength, and to monopolize the telecommunications industry, by purchasing several independent telephone companies that were established after the original Bell patents expired in 1893 and 1894. Competing companies and the courts tried in vain for several years to force a divestiture of the AT&T/Bell System monopoly but were unsuccessful.

Regulation of the telecommunications industry within the United States began with the Post Roads Act of 1866, which granted the Postmaster General the authority to set rates for government-related telegrams. Eleven years later, the federal Interstate Commerce Commission (ICC) was granted authority over the existing modes of communications, telegraphy, and the nascent telephony. In 1910, the ICC would also begin regulation of radio communications. By the early 1930s, the telecommunications infrastructure within the United States had become quite extensive and complex. A new regulatory body with much broader powers was needed to oversee interstate and international telecommunication-related issues, current and future. Therefore, the Communications Act of 1934 was enacted, creating the Federal Communications Commission (FCC).

Interstate and intrastate communications authority would actually be shared by the public utilities commissions (PUCs) of individual states and the FCC. The FCC was not intended to be a legislative body.

In 1946, the year that the United States detonated an atomic bomb at Bikini Atoll in the Marshall Islands and "It's a Wonderful Life" flopped at the box office, the Electronic Numerical Integrator And Computer (ENIAC) was installed at the U.S. Army proving grounds located in Aberdeen, Maryland. It was commissioned to perform mathematical calculations of ballistic trajectories. The ENIAC may not have been the first computer, but it was the first successful all-purpose electronic digital computer.

Weighing in at a mere 30 tons, the ENIAC consisted of 18,000 vacuum tubes and occupied the area of a typical college classroom, and then some. Boasting the ability to perform complex mathematical calculations at the blistering rate of 5,000 per second, it left its ancestral electromechanical computers in the proverbial dust. Optimism over this new behemoth and its manifold potential was very high. In fact, the May issue of *Popular Mechanics* predicted that "computers of the future may have only 1,000 vacuum tubes and perhaps weigh no more than 1 1/2 tons." The dawn of the digital age had arrived.

Vacuum tubes can be used to either amplify signals or act as a simple on-and-off switch. The latter made it the perfect physical device to carry out digital computations electronically. These tubes, however, were bulky, made of fragile glass, and, regarding power consumption, operated like space heaters. Such relative inefficiency helped motivate scientists to invent a device with essentially the opposite physical attributes: small, sturdy, and consuming minimal power.

In late 1947, research scientists William Shockley, John Bardeer, and Walter H. Brattain at Bell Telephone Laboratories in New Jersey invented the transistor. Perhaps inadvertently discounting the tremendous significance of their invention, Shockley invited some of his colleagues to drop by and observe "some effects" they had produced in their lab. Indeed, the world had changed overnight. In less than a decade, every teenager would sport a transistor radio blaring out the tunes of Chuck Berry and Buddy Holly. Transistors would find their way into virtually every corner of modern civilization. Advances in telecommunication switching devices, aircraft avionics, medical and scientific instrumentation, automotive gadgets, household appliances, and even children's toys would use this new technology.

In time, through the process of miniaturization, thousands and even millions of transistors would be incorporated into the design of high-density integrated circuits. Early versions of the Intel Pentium microprocessor, for example, consisted chiefly of an arrangement of 5.5 million transistors packed into an area approximately the size of a fingernail. The required spacing of each individual transistor, for such a circuit, is on the order of 1/2 of one millionth of a meter. In comparison, human viruses are typically 1/4 of one millionth of a meter in length. It is astounding that the entire physical evolutionary track of the modern computer is founded on the successful efforts of three scientists, working in their lab to create the first transistor 50 years ago.

The space race would find its auspicious beginning several years into the Cold War between the United States and the former Soviet Union. The sense of urgency born of the fears created by the escalating arms race between the two super powers escalated as the first artificial satellite, Sputnik I, rocketed into space on October 4, 1957. The implications of this success were crystal clear to the American public. The United States was not as technically superior as it had once thought, and it was, in an instant, vulnerable to nuclear attack from platforms perched in orbit about the earth. Within four months of the launch of Sputnik I, the United States entered the space race, as the satellite Explorer I hurtled toward space atop a Vanguard rocket. This new technology was quickly put to work, creating technological quantum leaps in such areas as telecommunications, military reconnaissance, and astronomical research.

Motivated by the desires of several universities, research institutions, and the federal government to conduct collaborative research, share computer resources over wide geographical areas, and create a highly redundant national communications infrastructure, the Advanced Research Project Agency (ARPA), an agency within the Department of the Defense, created *ARPANET*. The original contract specifying the initial research sites to be connected was won by Bolt, Beranek, and Newman (BBN) in December 1968. The following year, the University of California in Los Angeles and Santa Barbara, the Stanford Research Institute, and the University of Utah were successfully linked together with leased telecommunication lines interconnected by special switches called *Internet Message Processors (IMPs)*. The seed that would sprout to become today's global Internet had been planted.

In the late 60s, two landmark events paved the way for significant advances in the modem (modulator-demodulator), a key telecommunications device that has helped provide connectivity for the masses. In 1968, the Carter Electronics Corporation successfully sued AT&T for the right to attach its Carterfone to the public telephone network. Prior to the Carterfone decision, the U.S. public telephone network was essentially monopolized by AT&T, preventing competing companies from selling products that might use the telephone network as a data transport medium. In 1969, the Electronic Industries Association established a revised serial interface standard, RS-232-C, which eventually became the standard for communications between computers and modems.

Although the Bell Telephone Company leased its own models of modems, the aforementioned events assisted companies like Hayes Microcomputer Products in generating the competition that would eventually change the future direction of modem design. Modems would allow employees to access mainframes from remote locations, thus extending the boundaries of data communications a bit farther. Of course, modems are used today to allow telecommuters access to their employer's local area network and to allow anyone access to the Internet through an *Internet Service Provider (ISP)*.

The first breach in the mighty AT&T monopoly occurred in 1974, when the aspiring communications giant Microwave Communications Incorporated (MCI) and the Department of Justice filed suit against AT&T, claiming violation of the Sherman

Antitrust Act. Eight years later, an agreement on the suit was finally reached. The 1982 Consent Decree defined the manner in which AT&T would be restructured and divested of its 22 Bell Operating Companies (BOCs). Within another two years, on January 1, 1984, the detailed Modified Final Judgement (MFJ) of the Consent Decree was implemented and the restructuring began.

The original 22 BOCs were reorganized into 7 independent Regional Bell Operating Companies (RBOCs): Pacific Telesis (PACTEL), U.S. West Communications, Southwestern Bell Corporation, American Information Technology (AMERITECH), Nynex Corporation, Bell Atlantic, and BellSouth, which would thereafter be referred to as the "Baby Bells." History would deem the implementation of the MFJ as one of the most important events in the evolution of the telecommunications industry.

Signed into law on February 8, 1996, by President Clinton, the Telecommunications Act of 1996 defined many new provisions for the sorely needed overhaul of the Communications Act of 1934. These include the following:

1. Shifting of the authority to interpret and enforce communication policy from the courts and other regulatory bodies to the FCC.

2. Levying fines and/or imprisonment when an information service provider knowingly transmits obscene or indecent material to persons under the age of 18.

3. Termination of the regulation of cable television programming rates on March 31, 1999.

4. Prevention of exclusion of new or existing companies desiring to provide interstate and intrastate telecommunication services.

5. Permission to offer both interregional and intraregional long distance services by RBOCs.

6. Requirement of local telephone companies to resell their services and allow access to rights-of-way to their competition.

7. Termination of the ban on cross-ownership of services between cable and telephony-based companies in rural communities.

A mere two years have passed since the signing of the Telecommunications Act of 1996, yet much new competition and a myriad of new services have already sprung up in response. Only time will tell what the far-reaching consequences of this new law will be. One thing is certain, however; a win-win situation for the consumer and the service provider is likely.

The dawn of a new millenium is imminent. Inundated by a flood of telecommunication buzzwords and concepts, we stand poised to face the future. ISDN, xDSL, cable modems, ATM, vBNS, Internet II, e-commerce, security, extranets, intranets, viruses, streaming technologies, multimedia, and many more terms permeate every corner of both the private and commercial sectors. Everyone from the local grocery store manager to the President of the United States has been and will continue to be affected by the rapid changes in telecommunications. With the Internet as the major impetus, the convergence of the computer and telecommunications industries is rapidly occurring. Might we someday be able to consult with our physician from the comfort of our living room, via the flat screen monitor posing as a picture on the wall? Perhaps, while leaving on vacation, you forget to electronically secure your home. Don't fret. Simply issue the command "secure home for vacation" to your hands-free cellular phone. A voice-recognition-based program authenticates your voice pattern, dials your "intelligent" house, and initiates the necessary steps to secure your home. Where are we going in this Information Age? Where do you want to go?

1.3 Timeline of the Internet

The Internet is the result of the achievement of a certain critical mass, and the individuals and organizations that properly exploited it.

Throughout history, many of humanity's great achievements can be traced to the moment when a critical mass in certain key sociological, cultural, political, and/or technological areas was obtained. Individuals or groups of people who grasped the significance of the moment produced the events or institutions born out of this critical mass. For example, it is difficult, if not impossible, to conjure up tribal names of scattered ancient peoples who lived off the land prior to about 3500 B.C. (the earliest known establishment of human civilizations). Many people, however, would recognize the names of such civilizations as the Sumerians of Mesopotamia or the Maya of Mexico who, having obtained a critical mass in key cultural and technological areas, built great cities, created means of reading and writing, and established sophisticated political and religious systems. The Internet is also the result of the achievement of a certain critical mass, and the individuals and organizations that properly exploited it.

By 1961, the Cold War was in full swing. The newly elected President, John F. Kennedy, exhorted the citizens of the United States to "pay any price, bear any burden, meet any hardship, support any friend, oppose any foe to assure the survival and the success of liberty." A few months later, the former Soviet Union created a wall around West Berlin to prevent skilled and professional workers from emigrating westward to capitalism. Joseph Heller's satirical novel on U.S. military bureaucracy, *Catch 22*, was published; Audrey Hepburn starred as party girl Holly Golightly in Breakfast at Tiffany's; and a young MIT graduate student named Leonard Kleinrock published a paper on the topic of packet switching (see Figure 1.2).

At the beginning of every episode of Star Trek, the voice-over reiterated the mission of the USS Enterprise: "to seek out new life and new civilizations, to boldly go where no man has gone before." Apparently Star Trek and the ARPANET had the same mission. Coincidentally, they also shared the same innocuous beginning in 1966. One a child of the space race, the other a child of the Cold War. It would be several years later, however, before each would mature and begin to boast legions of followers. None other than the great Captain James T. Kirk commanded the Enterprise, whereas the first director of the ARPANET was an MIT research scientist named Larry Roberts.

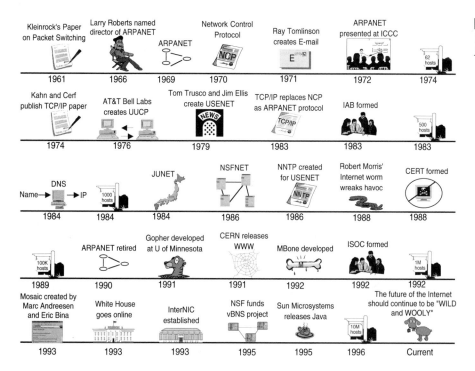

FIGURE 1.2
Timeline of the Internet.

Roberts assembled a talented team of scientists and engineers to begin work on the network. Influenced by Kleinrock's research in packet switching, Roberts had the team draft and issue an RFP (Request for Proposal) for the creation of a packet switch, called Internet Message Processors (IMPs), used to route data packets between the ARPANET sites. In an interview for the October 21, 1997 issue of *Data Communications,* Larry Roberts recalls that "a group of us issued an RFP for switches based on a minicomputer. The only contractor who said it couldn't be done was IBM. We knew they were saying that because they didn't have a computer small enough." The RFP also stipulated the connection of the first four sites (UCLA, UCSB, SRI, and the University of Utah) via IMPs and relatively high-speed telecommunication lines. In January 1969, BBN, the aforementioned contract winner, set out to construct the ARPANET.

BBN installed the first IMP in Leonard Kleinrock's laboratory at UCLA over the Labor Day weekend. In preparation for making the ARPANET a success, Kleinrock assembled an impressive team of individuals. Their initial tasks were to design an interface between their lab computer and the IMP, and to concoct a primitive communications scheme to transmit and receive information between their site and the next ARPANET site to come online, SRI. Among the team members were Jon Postel, Charley Kline, and Vint Cerf, who was one of the principal co-creators of *TCP/IP (Transmission Control Protocol/Internet Protocol),* the language of the Internet.

When contemplating the tremendous impact that the Internet has already had on society and the potential changes that it will inevitably produce, one may be rather surprised to discover the primitive nature of the very first ARPANET communiqué. As recalled by Kleinrock, "One of our programmers, Charley Kline, was to log in to the SRI machine. The procedure was to type 'LOG' and the system at SRI was set up to be clever enough to add 'IN.' Charley and his counterpart at SRI had telephone headsets so they could talk. Charley typed in the 'L' and asked SRI if they received it. 'Got the L' came the voice reply. We typed in the 'O,' and they got it. Charley then typed in the 'G' and the whole thing *crashed!* It was hilarious."

For all of the turmoil of the 1960s, the 70s offered little solace. By the middle of the decade, the country would witness the resignation of a President; approximately 60,000 Americans would never return home from a distant land called Vietnam; and the Mideast oil cartel, OPEC, would hike oil prices by an unprecedented 200 percent. Fortunately, however, there were positives. Soviet gymnast Olga Korbut would dazzle the world with her sterling performance at the 1972 Olympics. Two years later another top performer, the ARPANET, would grow to a size of 62 hosts.

TCP/IP's progenitor, *NCP (Network Control Protocol)* was first implemented on the ARPANET in 1970. Its job was to transport information between the various nodes, or site connections. The initial services offered over the network, via NCP, were file transfer, remote login, and electronic mail (developed by Ray Tomlinson in 1971). In October 1972 at the ICCC (International Computer Communications Conference) in Washington, D.C., Bob Kahn, Vint Cerf, presented the ARPANET and its capabilities to the rest of the world. By 1973, the shortcomings of NCP were readily known, and Kahn and Cerf were already diligently developing a new and greatly improved protocol. In May 1974, they published "A Protocol for Packet Network Intercommunication." In another two years, the protocol would be split into the separate constituents TCP and IP. TCP/IP would not replace NCP, however, for an additional six years.

The second half of the 70s was relatively quiet in terms of ARPANET-related advances. In 1976, AT&T Bell Labs developed a new file transfer program called *UUCP (Unix-to-Unix Copy)*. Three years later, two Duke University graduate students, Tom Truscott and Jim Ellis, created USENET. *USENET,* essentially a system of electronic newsgroups, is still a popular service of the Internet.

One vilified, the other idolized, J. R. Ewing and John Lennon's lives would come to an abrupt end as the new decade began. The 80s would bear witness to the discovery of a hideous new medical enigma known as AIDS (acquired immunodeficiency syndrome), the searing images of the Space Shuttle Challenger explosion, and the toppling of the Berlin Wall by two million East Germans. In the end, the extraordinarily versatile voice of American jazz singer Bobby McFerrin would remind us "Don't Worry, Be Happy," and the Internet would be poised to revolutionize the world.

Version 4 of TCP/IP, an integral part of most modern network operating systems, became a recognized communications protocol standard for use by the ARPANET in 1981. The following year, TCP/IP was officially adopted as the protocol suite to be used on the ARPANET. The protocol's adoption gave rise to the term "Internet," to describe an interconnected set of computer networks. The spirited efforts of Kahn and Cerf finally came to fruition on a truly wide scale on January 1, 1983, when the inadequate ARPANET protocol NCP was finally replaced by TCP/IP. Later that year the Internet Activities Board (IAB) was established to oversee future developments in the TCP/IP protocol and related technologies. As new protocols are ratified, they are published by the IAB, in a document called an *RFC (Request For Comment)*. Five hundred hosts would become part of the exponentially growing network by year's end.

1984 would bestow an indispensable service on the ARPANET, the *Domain Name Service (DNS)*. The primary responsibility of DNS, then and now, is to alleviate the operator's burden of identifying a host's numerical IP address, prior to attempting communications with it. Recognized by all modern Internet surfers, the syntax host.domain.domain-type, for example, ficticious.spsu.edu, is the telltale sign that a DNS server probably lurks somewhere relatively nearby. In 1984, the number of connected hosts increased to 1,000, and Japan went online with the creation of its own JUNET (Japan Unix Network), a network based on UUCP. Other major data communication networks, such as BITNET (Because It's Time Network) and CSNET (Computer Science Network), were already in existence and, like JUNET, were separate from the ARPANET.

A major milestone in the Internet's evolution occurred in 1986 when the NSFNET (National Science Foundation Network) was created. This TCP/IP-based network was designed to support the academic and research communities. Five of the key nodes connected to the 56-Kbps NSFNET backbone were NSF-established supercomputing centers scattered across the country. Within a decade of its inception, NSFNET would be decommissioned, but not before its influence would see the connection of 4,000,000 hosts worldwide. The total number of hosts at the end of 1986, however, was a mere 5,000. USENET received a facelift that year in the form of the new news transport protocol *NNTP (Network News Transfer Protocol)*.

In late 1988, the *worm* was released, infecting a minimum of 6,000 Internet hosts. Its creator, Robert Morris, had accomplished his mission. A viruslike program, the worm seeks to gain unauthorized access and then, if possible, to replicate itself onto the unsuspecting host. When executed by the infected host, the worm may perform any number of malicious acts. Due to the exposure of major vulnerabilities to Internet hosts, in part because of Robert Morris' worm, *CERT (Computer Emergency Response Team)* was established. The primary function of CERT was to generate CERT reports that were used to inform system administrators of potential security breaches within a particular operating system. Unfortunately, the CERT reports are also of a certain value to deviant individuals wreaking havoc on connected hosts.

By 1989, the number of Internet hosts had grown to 100,000 and the NSFNET had increased its backbone bandwidth (data transmission capacity measured in bits per second, bps) by upgrading its major links to T1 circuits, which are capable of transmitting 1.544 Mbps. A consulting software engineer named Tim Berners-Lee wrote a proposal to his boss at CERN (European particle physics lab) for a research project that he called the World Wide Web—he received no response.

The 1990s, the stepping stone of the new millenium, are proving to be as dramatic as any previous twentieth-century decade. Set in motion by the dreams of a tenacious yet apparently timid Mikhail Gorbachev, the Soviet Union finally dissolved in 1992. In another hemisphere, imprisoned for his heroic fight against apartheid, African National Congress leader Nelson Mandela won a landslide victory in the 1994 presidential race of the newly democratic South Africa. People around the world are still pondering the weather phenomenon known as El Niño, and the media is abuzz with the word "Internet."

In 1990, the ARPANET was retired. *Gopher*, a menu-driven card catalog of sorts, was developed in 1991 by two students at the University of Minnesota, and named after their team mascot, the Golden Gophers. One of the best Internet user interfaces available at the time, Gopher was not friendly or attractive enough to garner a great deal of attention. The World Wide Web, however, was developed the same year, and would set the stage for a global migration toward the Internet. Obviously, Berners-Lee had finally received permission to do his research project! By year's end, the number of Internet-connected hosts had climbed to 617,000, and the NSFNET began upgrading its backbone from T1 to T3 (44.736 Mbps) circuits.

A form of videoconferencing, *MBone (Multicast Backbone)* broadcasts first traversed the Internet to multiple destinations in 1992. Hosts capable of being configured for IP multicasting can tune in to a scheduled MBone broadcast and, if appropriate, can interact online. Also that year, the Internet Society (ISOC) was formed, in part, for the financial support of the Internet Engineering Task Force (a component of the IAB) and its ongoing development of Internet standards. One million hosts were finally online!

Prior to being enlivened with graphics and other clever innovations, the World Wide Web went largely unnoticed. A program called *Mosaic,* however, released in early 1993, was about to seriously rattle the status quo. In the October 21, 1997 issue of *Data Communications,* one of its co-inventors, Marc Andreessen, describes the vision he and Eric Bina had for the creation of Mosaic. "From the start, we thought making this interface graphical was the key. We had a disagreement with Tim Berners-Lee, who invented the Web. Tim was looking for a way to connect a bunch of high-energy physicists, and he thought graphics were frivolous, unnecessary, and destructive. We didn't see it that way—we thought the information you see should be the interface." Also in 1993, the White House went online, the President and Vice-President received e-mail addresses, NSF created the *InterNIC (Internet Network Information Center),* and the number of connected hosts climbed to 2,000,000.

In April 1995, the NSF shifted most of its funding of NSFNET, hence decommissioning it, to an experimental project called the *vBNS (Very-High-Speed Backbone Network Service).* The infant Internet had become a toddler. No longer dependent on support from the federal government and lined up squarely in the cross-hairs of the commercial sector, the Internet was poised to take a quantum leap forward. The great race to get online had begun. *Internet Service Providers (ISPs),* the on-ramps to the "information super-highway," began signing up customers in droves. CompuServe, Prodigy, and America Online (AOL) (online service providers more akin to a bulletin board service) provided user-friendly access for the more novice (through expert) Internet surfer. Nascent software technologies such as RealAudio, Java, and CGI (Common Gateway Interface) scripts equipped webmasters with a potent arsenal of design features. In two years, the number of connected hosts would more than double to more than 4,000,000.

Consisting of several different telecommunications technologies, the Internet would inevitably be affected by the 800 pages of legalese contained in the Telecommunications Act of 1996. The most controversial portion of the law holds online service providers liable for the transmission of "indecent" material to minors. IP Telephony, the transmission of voice traffic over a TCP/IP-based network such as the Internet, found an advocate in 1996 with the establishment of the *Voice over IP (VOIP)* forum. With a stellar debut the previous year, IP Telephony startled the telecommunications industry with the prospect of a viable new competitor. Ten million hosts were connected to the Internet community.

At the top of the DNS hierarchy, a catastrophe occurred early one morning in July 1997. The records containing address information for two of the Internet's top-level domains became corrupted, and the InterNIC, administered by Network Solutions, Inc., had a partial meltdown. Many connected hosts were, quite suddenly, rendered unreachable. Yet as if nothing had happened, the clamor of activity beginning to inundate the Internet continued to steadily increase. Today, new services and technologies are vying for the attention of the Internet aficionado and for the most precious Internet resource, bandwidth. Organizations are researching the concept of the *Virtual Private Network (VPN)* to explore the possibility of connecting their various branches via the Net in what is commonly referred to as an *extranet.* Merchants and financial institutions are already collaborating by means of electronic commerce to create virtual storefronts and electronic malls. Colleges and universities are developing distance learning programs using online curriculum and videoconferencing. Three-dimensional multimedia will begin to invade our once-peaceful desktops as the standards governing these technologies, such as VRML (Virtual Reality Modeling Language), solidify. If "the richest nerd in America," Bill Gates, gets his way, the blending of the Internet and the television will take another leap in the near future. This is just the beginning.

1.4 Major Components of the Internet

There are several perspectives from which one may view and study the Internet. So that we might accomplish our goal of weaving the whole Internet story together, we shall start from the ground up. Figure 1.3 and the accompanying set of overlays exemplify three distinct aspects of the Internet: the telecommunications backbone, connectivity options, and typical services. In addition to standard services offered, the latter category includes some of the aspects of security and a typical TCP/IP transmission; each of these topics will be discussed in subsequent sections.

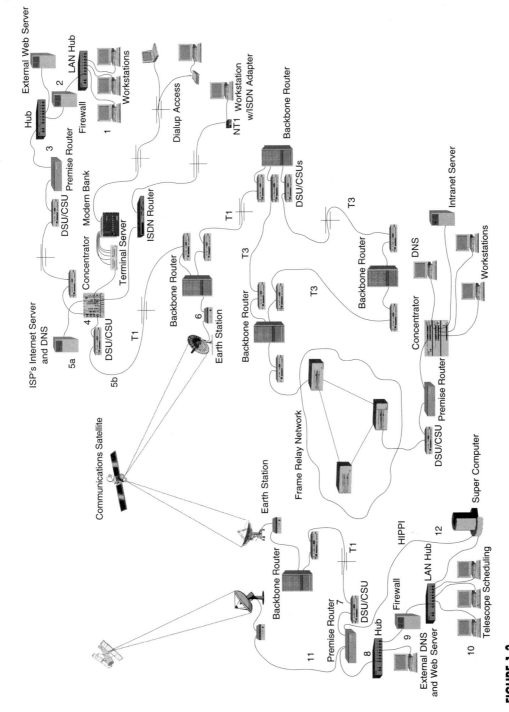

FIGURE 1.3

Major components of the Internet.

Although rapidly evolving, the Internet's main infrastructure, or backbone, consists primarily of several point-to-point and switched telecommunication links. Terrestrial links bearing names such as T1, T3, OC3, and OC12 carry the lion's share of data traffic between the various connection points, or nodes. Other telecommunication solutions, such as Frame Relay, ATM, and satellites, also play an important role. As we shall see, the need for this diverse set of solutions is driven by an equally diverse set of connectivity requirements.

Backbone routers, or *packet switches,* are the devices responsible for determining a data packet's intended destination, and routing them accordingly. An analogy often cited in the clarification of a router's function is the routing of a piece of mail (the data packet) via the U.S. Postal System. Of course, distribution centers are essentially routers, whereas boats, planes, trucks, and their operators represent the various telecommunication technologies used to transport the information between the multitude of nodes. Routers must, therefore, accommodate many disparate types of telecommunications hardware. The connection of a router to a high-speed terrestrial-based link, for example T1, requires the installation and configuration of a high-speed serial interface within the router. Similarly, for a router to participate in a Frame Relay network requires it to have a Frame Relay interface, and so on. A *DSU/CSU (Data Service Unit/Channel Service Unit),* similar in purpose to a modem, completes the connection by linking the router and telecommunications circuit.

A highway system without on and off-ramps serves little purpose. Without means for individuals, organizations, and countries to connect to the backbone, the Internet would not exist. ISPs, online service providers, regional networks, and countries are directly connected to the backbone, providing a connectivity front end for virtually everyone else. In some instances, however, the demarcation between the backbone and other networks, such as a large regional network, is a bit fuzzy.

A *concentrator,* as the name implies, is a device that concentrates several networking technologies into a single chassis. A *router,* equipped with many different types of interfaces, may be considered a concentrator. The concentrator, shown in the upper center of Figure 1.3, might constitute the core of an ISP's network configuration. The bandwidth consumed by the aggregate data traffic flowing into or out of the concentrator on the customer side must not exceed the available bandwidth that the ISP leases on the backbone side.

A site router installed on the customer's premises connects the customer to the ISP via a 56Kb link. This single link consumes 1/24 of the ISP's output bandwidth of approximately 1.5 Mbps (megabits per second), assuming, of course, that the ISP must support the customer's bandwidth needs around the clock. In reality, data traffic, and therefore bandwidth requirements, can be calculated with stochastic modeling. The data traffic generated by a single customer site, for example, will ebb and flow several times throughout the day. Customers accessing the Internet via their ISP's analog (modem) or digital (ISDN adapter card) dialup lines, also contribute copious amounts of data traffic.

Although rapidly evolving, the Internet's main infrastructure, or backbone, is comprised primarily of several point-to-point and switched telecommunication links.

Perhaps the backbone router in the lower left-hand corner of Figure 1.3 connects an entire continent to the greater Internet. The smaller network attached to it represents one of many similar networks scattered throughout the continent. In all likelihood, however, distinct sites would be connected to a larger regional network or an ISP. Evidently, this particular site is a research facility used for gathering and processing significant amounts of data. Research scientists from around the world retrieve their own data over the Internet. Although this specific example might be a better candidate for the vBNS, we choose to use it in the context of the Internet for its rich possibilities as a data transport example.

A research scientist requires confirmation of a unique stellar event that has recently occurred in a neighboring galaxy. She decides that use of the space telescope, controlled by computers at a research facility across the Atlantic Ocean, offers her the most efficient means of retrieving the necessary data. Furthermore, she realizes that the facility's supercomputer can refine the data to produce the information she seeks. She selects the space telescope's web address from her list of bookmarks and clicks the mouse button. Within seconds, a dialog box, requesting an encrypted password, appears on her screen. She enters the appropriate password, clicks the Submit button, and sits back to ponder this electronic marvel with which she is interacting. A few more seconds elapse, and her screen fills with the standard electronic form required for scheduling usage of the space telescope and supercomputer. She fills out the form and once again clicks the Submit button. A smiley face appears on the screen and informs her that her requests have been accepted and that she should expect to receive her processed information within six hours of her scheduled time slot.

Let us follow the data, constituting the research scientist's initial request, on its journey from her desktop to the database of the scheduling computer thousands of miles away. To avoid unnecessary complexity, the following discussion is intentionally devoid of concepts pertaining to the handling of data by local and wide area networking devices, except as they relate to the web browser application and TCP/IP. A more detailed treatment of the handling of data will be presented in subsequent sections.

Referring to the numbers in Figure 1.3, the initial mouse click on the space telescope's bookmark directed the web browser to send the corresponding web address or URL *(Uniform Resource Locator)* to the computer's TCP/IP software (1). This software immediately "realized" that it had to acquire a numerical version of the web address (its IP address) to properly communicate with the scheduling computer. Therefore, it "decided" to send a request to a computer running a program called Domain Name Service, hence referred to as a DNS, to look up the proper IP address associated with the given web address. The packet of binary information sent to the DNS contained, among other things, the DNS lookup request, the web address to be resolved, the source address (IP address of the research scientist's computer), and the destination address (IP address of the DNS).

Having arrived at the network's firewall (2), a transfer agent program swapped the source address, contained in the packet, for that of the firewall, effectively "hiding" the source computer from the outside world. The packet was sent to the site router (3), where it was routed to the ISP's concentrator (4). The concentrator's routing software, in turn, routed, by examination of the destination address, the request packet to the DNS (5a) via the appropriate concentrator interface. Unable to properly resolve the web address, the DNS passed the request to another such system of higher authority that ultimately resolved, perhaps by consulting with the research facility's DNS (9), the web address into an IP address. The IP address was then sent to the source computer. This DNS resolution process occurred in a mere fraction of a second.

Equipped with the proper IP address, the source computer's TCP/IP software constructed a new packet primarily containing the source and destination (research facility web server) addresses and type of service (port) desired of the remote system. The packet, having traversed the same initial path, again arrived at the ISP's concentrator. This time, however, the concentrator routed the packet toward the intended destination via its T1 link (56Kb) to the backbone router (5b). Routed over the satellite link (6) and through two backbone routers, the packet arrived at the research facility's site router for processing (7). It was then routed through the interface configured to support the facility's local area network and external security systems (8), where it was received by the web server. After examining the packet, the web server transmitted the requested web page back to the research scientist's web browser.

With another mouse click, the process repeated. The new packet, requesting access to the telescope's scheduling database, arrived at the web server in essentially the same manner. Once again, the server transmitted a web page back to the browser. This particular page was an electronic form with fields requesting items of information. Once completed, the third mouse click sent the string of information, bundled in a packet of 1s and 0s, to the waiting server. In this interaction, unlike the previous ones, the server relayed the form information to another program that parsed the various fields. Information extracted from the account and password fields was, in turn, relayed to the firewall server for authentication. Once approved, the same program that performed the parsing operation transmitted the proper commands to update the database (10) with the research scientist's account, coordinates, date, and time information. At the scheduled date and time, the proper coordinates of the relevant region in the neighboring galaxy would be transmitted to the space telescope's on-board positioning computer (11). The data would be collected, transmitted to the supercomputer (12) for processing, and finally, delivered to the research scientist's computer.

1.5 Major Players

Several organizations and institutions have played a major role in the evolution of the Internet. MCI, AT&T, the Baby Bells, British Telecommunications (BT), and Nippon Telegraph & Telephone Company (NTT) have been some of the key players responsible for advances in the global telecommunications infrastructure. IBM, Sun Microsystems, Apple Computer, Motorola, and Intel Corporation have been instrumental in bringing the power of the microprocessor to the fingertips of humanity. Cisco Systems, Cabletron Systems, and Bay Networks have lead the way in the development of local area networking technologies, whereas Hayes Microcomputer Products and U.S. Robotics have provided us with dialup access.

Several organizations and institutions have played a major role in the evolution of the Internet.

RSA Data Security and Security Dynamics have been among the small army of corporations creating products to ensure the secure transmission of critical information. MIT, Carnegie Mellon University, and the Georgia Institute of Technology have been constantly in the forefront of the development and implementation of communication technologies. CyberCash, First Virtual, and Verifone, to name a few, have helped to pave the way in the electronic commerce (e-commerce) revolution. Microsoft, Novell, and Netscape Communications have provided us with the operating environments and applications that have made Internet travel considerably more friendly.

Some organizations exist solely for the advancement of the Internet and its standards. ISOC, an internationally recognized, nonprofit organization consisting of industry professionals, was formed primarily for the financial support of other key Internet administrative bodies, such as the IAB and IETF. However, the Society also helps coordinate global Internet development in conjunction with the International Telecommunications Union (ITU) and the World Intellectual Property Organization (WIPO). In 1996, ISOC formed the International Ad Hoc Committee (IHAC) to devise strategies for the future development of the DNS. IHAC has since been reorganized under the name Policy Oversight Committee (POC).

Originally named the Internet Activities Board, the IAB was renamed the Internet Architecture Board in 1992. It is the body responsible for ratifying new Internet standards, advising the ISOC on technical issues related to the Internet's architecture, and governing several task forces. The Internet Research Task Force (ITRF), IETF, and Internet Engineering Steering Group (IESG) constitute the three main task forces. The ITRF is the consolidation of several smaller task forces that are concerned primarily with the ongoing development of nascent networking technologies. The IETF is responsible for the development and review of proposed standards affecting the evolution of the Internet's architecture and protocols. Several distinct working groups were established by the IETF. The directors of these groups are representative members of the IESG.

The Internet Assigned Numbers Authority (IANA) was established by the Federal Networking Council, an 18-member federal government advisory board, and the ISOC; it was charged with the supervision of the allocation of IP numbers. In 1998, the Internet Corporation for Assigned Names and Numbers (ICANN), a 19-member, non-federal government advisory board, began to assume the role, and therefore, the responsibilities of IANA.

Initially, the process of domain name registration was provided by InterNIC (Internet Network Information Center), which was operated solely by NSI since 1993. APNIC (in the Asian-Pacific) and RIPE (Reseaux IP Europeens) perform the same functions as the InterNIC for those regions of the globe. Recently, however, a new system referred to as the *Shared Registry System* (developed by NSI) was implemented to allow multiple registrars to manage the .com, .net, and .org top-level domains (TLD).

Eugene Kashpureff created the AlterNIC to establish an alternate root server capable of creating entirely new TLDs. In 1997 he created a hack that apparently rerouted domain registration requests destined for the InterNIC to the AlterNIC. Although he settled out of court with NSI, which filed a civil action suit against him, he is currently awaiting trial for possible wire-fraud charges brought up by the federal government.

Other Internet-related organizations play an ancillary, yet important, role in the services and philosophies that are so vital to the Internet's character. The World Wide Web Consortium (W3C), directed by Tim Berners-Lee, collaborates with organizations worldwide to develop new standards for the Web, the most popular service on the Internet. The Electronic Frontier Foundation (EFF), a nonprofit civil liberties organization, strives to ensure First Amendment rights for everyone who accesses the Internet. The Center for Democracy and Technology (CDT), similar to the EFF, promotes constitutional civil liberties for Internet travelers filtered, however, through a democratic sieve. The White House Interagency Working Group on Domain Names has devised a plan, known as the Green Paper, that advocates the privatization of the DNS upon the expiration of the NSI contract. Several other organizations, scattered throughout the world, are working diligently to nurture and mold the Internet and its derivatives into a communications medium that will dramatically improve the human condition well into the next millenium.

1.6 Impact on Society

When the onboard attitude control system of the Galaxy 4 satellite, owned by PanAmSat Corporation, failed, its transmit antenna was rendered useless. Instantly, 80 to 90 percent of all pager service for the continental Unites States fell silent. ATM machines and credit card authorization systems were also affected. Hospitals couldn't locate emergency room physicians, drivers couldn't pay for gas at the pump, and National Public Radio had to turn to the Internet for help. A major telecommunications system failed, sending engineers scrambling to discover the cause and, more important, to restore service. How crucial are these new modes (the Internet included) of communication? We have become dependent on them. Humanity would, of course, continue to exist if the Internet were suddenly excised from the face of the planet. As this relatively new technology becomes more integrated with our everyday lives, however, the excision becomes more painful.

As the Niña, Pinta, and Santa Maria skirted the coasts of Hispaniola and Cuba, what might have been the thoughts of Christopher Columbus? What motivated him to undertake such a daring expedition? Valentine Michael Smith was a Martian of human ancestry. Brought back to earth by humans, Smith was indeed a *Stranger in a Strange Land.* What must it be like to be a perfect stranger in a distant exotic land?

Via the Internet, we can choose to "travel" to Cuba and visit the magnificent caves of Cotilla, or perhaps "sit" on a wall of the 16th-century Fort Morro and look out over the Bay of Havana. It wouldn't be worthwhile to search for the Smiths, but we could scan the horizon of the Martian terrain. We might even witness the formation of a cloud. How does the ability to learn of a foreign culture through the medium of cyberspace affect us? The Internet enables us to venture across the same vast stretch of water witnessed by Columbus' expedition in 1492 within a few seconds. It took them five and a half weeks! The ability to instantaneously "visit" and partake of the activities of a distant culture via the Internet allows us to become more familiar with and less of a stranger in other lands.

What impact did the invention of the airplane, the printing press, and money have on the civilized world? The Internet is a blend of all of these concepts and technologies, and much more.

What impact did the invention of the airplane, the printing press, and money have on the civilized world? The Internet is a blend of all of these concepts and technologies, and much more. Has this technological marvel, born of the twentieth century, become just a mere commodity? Perhaps it should. Whether we purchase our shoes in person or "in virtual person" is irrelevant. If we believe our transactions to be secure, inevitably our spending behavior will conform to the new system. Do you have an ATM card? With the advent of e-mail, Internet telephony, and video conferencing, we, as a global society, are beginning to communicate globally. The concierge and ambassador may play a different role in the not-so-distant future.

Summary

There are many different perceptions of the Internet. Vocational backgrounds, philosophical beliefs, age and gender, and technological access influence one's perception of the Internet. The harmony and dissonance of the perceptions of many people struggle against one another, ultimately molding the present and the future of this colossal network.

Telecommunications is the transmission and reception of encoded information between two or more "intelligent" entities over an appreciable distance using an agreed-upon protocol. The first public demonstration of a modern, electronic-based telecommunications system occurred on May 24, 1844, when the message "What hath God wrought" was transmitted over Samuel Morse's telegraph system. A close relative of the telegraph, the telephone was invented on March 10, 1876. "Mr. Watson, come here; I want you," uttered by Alexander Graham Bell, was telephony's analog to the message keyed by Mr. Morse.

In 1885, AT&T was established. Shepherding all of the Bell System franchises under its administrative aegis, it grew to become one of the world's largest corporations and monopolies. Nearly 100 years after its inception, AT&T was divested of its 22 Bell Operating Companies, when in 1984 the Modified Final Judgement of the Consent Decree was implemented. Seven Regional Bell Operating Companies (RBOCs) emerged from the reorganization of the original 22.

The Telecommunications Act of 1996, signed into law by President Bill Clinton, was essentially a legislation overhaul required to modify several provisions of the Communications Act of 1934. It also enacted several new, state-of-the-art provisions. One major immediate outcome of the Act has been the obscuring of traditionally distinct boundaries between various media providers.

The ancestor of the modern Internet, the ARPANET project, started in 1966. Larry Roberts, an MIT research scientist, was named its first director. In 1969, the first four sites (UCLA, UCSB, SRI, and the University of Utah) were connected via high-speed telecommunication links and Internet Message Processors (IMPs). By 1974 this fledgling network boasted 62 hosts connected. "A Protocol for Packet Network Intercommunications" was published in May of the same year. Its authors, Bob Kahn and Vinton Cerf, are considered early pioneers of the Internet. Two years after the publication, their specification for a new protocol suite would be called TCP/IP. Today, TCP/IP is the language of the entire Internet.

In 1986, the NSFNET was created by the interconnection of five supercomputer sites. The NSF played a major role in financing a high-speed network backbone that stretched from coast to coast. This backbone, and NSF funding, had a profound influence on the exponentially growing Internet. In 1986, the Internet consisted of a mere 5,000 hosts. By 1995, when the NSFNET was decommissioned, the Internet had grown to a staggering 4,000,000 hosts.

In 1991, CERN (European particle physics lab) released the World Wide Web, created by Tim Berners-Lee. Communications would never again be the same. The frenzy to utilize this new wonder tool has never before been seen. Literally overnight, the planet shrank.

The Internet's backbone comprises chiefly point-to-point and switched telecommunication links. Other technologies, such as Frame Relay, ATM, and satellites also play a significant role. The primary internetworking device found throughout the Internet is called a router. Similar to the manner in which the U.S.P.S "routes" the mail, a router "routes" a datagram. A modemlike device, called a DSU/CSU, connects a router to the telecommunications link.

ISPs, online service providers, regional networks, and countries are directly connected to the backbone, providing a connectivity front end for virtually everyone else. Concentrators are devices that concentrate several networking technologies, such as Ethernet, Token Ring, and Frame Relay, into a single chassis. DNS is a TCP/IP-based system responsible for the translation of text-based Internet addresses, such as www.acme_planes.com, into an IP address, such as 193.29.16.3. Computers communicate via strings of binary numbers, hence the need for a numerical IP address.

Several organizations and institutions contribute to the ongoing development of the Internet. ISOC, an internationally recognized, nonprofit organization consisiting of industry professionals, was formed primarily for the financial support of other key Internet administrative bodies. The IAB is the body responsible for the ratification of new Internet standards, whereas the IETF develops and reviews proposed standards affecting the evolution of the Internet's architecture and protocols.

The Internet is one of the world's most widely used telecommunications-based services. The failure of the Galaxy 4 communications satellite serves as a prime example of the vulnerabilities imposed by the dependence on such technologies. Although designed with a high degree of redundancy, the Internet still possesses possible single points of failure. Recall the InterNIC "hack" performed by Eugene Kashpureff in 1997. For approximately one week, domain registration requests were intentionally redirected toward his AlterNIC. Other critical security breaches, software maladies (e.g., viruses), and system failures have and will occur throughout the Internet.

●

The world is a considerably smaller place because of the Internet. It is possible to travel virtually to any part of the globe and partake of a foreign culture.

The world is a considerably smaller place because of the Internet. It is possible to travel virtually to any part of the globe and partake of a foreign culture. Telephony, video conferencing, and the purchasing of goods via the Internet have become a reality with the rapid advances in technology. Soon, perhaps, your living room may become the equivalent of a doctor's waiting room—your appointment will occur in cyberspace.

Consider the social implications of e-mail and its derivatives. Corresponding with an acquaintance 10,000 miles away requires very little effort. The message can traverse the expanse in fractions of a second. If all intermediate systems are functioning properly, the intended recipient of the message will be reading your note shortly after the click of your mouse button. We have come a very long way indeed since the days of the telegraph.

The TCP/IP Protocol: The Language of the Internet

Chapter Learning Objectives:

- Understand the elements of a communications protocol.
- Study the layers that constitute the TCP/IP protocol suite.
- Investigate the various fields and address-related information of TCP/IP.
- Discover how DNS is vital to the operation of the Internet.
- Understand how the protocol works and how problems are diagnosed.
- Study some of the derivatives of TCP/IP.

> *"My language? Heavens! I am the best of them that speak this speech, were I but where 'tis spoken."*
>
> *Shakespeare,* The Tempest

Pitfalls can arise in any form of communication. Although two participants in a conversion may be exchanging their messages, they may be using different encoding and decoding schemes. Like humans, computers are capable of "misunderstanding" each other. The proper information may be reliably transmitted and received, but the interacting programs are not deriving the same meaning from that information.

Note: Permission to reproduce screen shots in this chapter from Distributed Sniffer System has been provided by Network Associates, Inc. Network Asssociates, Sniffer, and Distributed Sniffer System are registered trademarks of Network Associates, Inc. and/or its affiliates in the United States and/or other countries.

In computer jargon, a *protocol* may be defined as the "language" that two or more computers use to communicate, and the set of rules and procedures governing the communication. In addition to protocols, the reliability and clarity of the transmission medium must be taken into account.

2.1 A Protocol Primer

When we contemplate the term "protocol," several ideas come to mind. Military officers saluting one another, diplomats following certain rules while conducting the affairs of state, and a document prior to ratification are all considered protocols. In computer jargon, however, a *protocol* may be defined as the "language" that two or more computers use to communicate, and the set of rules and procedures governing the communication. In addition to protocols, the reliability and clarity of the transmission medium must be taken into account.

What communication protocols are required during a conference call involving several people (see Figure 2.1)? Initiated by Kim, the conference call is placed by dialing multiple numbers, first Bob's and then John's. Notice that all parties require two distinct addresses just to establish the call. Kim's congressional office, Bob's home, and John's high-rise office represent the physical addresses to which the patterns of speech signals will be transmitted and from which they will be received. Their phone numbers, on the other hand, represent the logical addresses by which they are located via the telephone system. The physical addresses are more-or-less fixed, whereas phone numbers can be reassigned. In computer networking parlance, physical addresses are referred to as *MAC (Media Access Control)* addresses; they identify the interface between the computer and

FIGURE 2.1

Communication protocols.

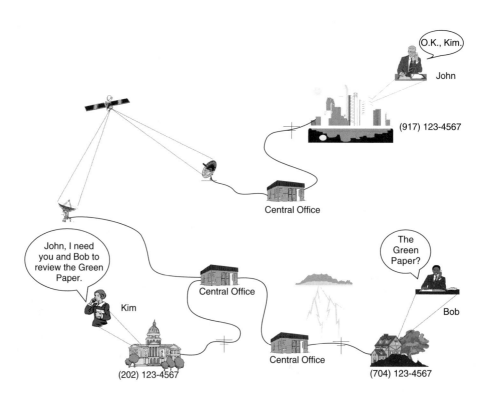

the network to which it is attached. In terms of the Internet, logical addresses are known as *IP addresses.*

The address information represented by the phone numbers deserves further scrutiny. As an example, we dissect Bob's number. The area code 704 informs us, and more importantly the telephone switches, that Bob's residence is located within the regional telephone network that encompasses western North Carolina. The prefix 765 further indicates the specific subnetwork within the regional network, and the extension 4321 identifies the house. As we shall see, the fields that constitute an IP address are strikingly similar.

"John, I need you and Bob to review the Green Paper." This statement contains a wealth of protocol-type information. Our common encoding scheme is, of course, the English language and all of its grammatical rules. Rules of conversation also apply. For example, while Kim is speaking, the other(s) should listen and vice versa. Should the conversational partners not abide by conversational rules, their conference call would quickly dissolve into a session of mere jabberwocky.

To whom is the statement directed? It would appear that John is the intended recipient; however, we know that Bob is also online, and both names were used. Therefore, the message was sent to both of them simultaneously. In the computer world, the names John and Bob are analogous to host names. The phrase "review the Green Paper" represents another piece in the protocol puzzle. The phrase indicates the particular service (review) and ancillary information (the Green Paper) being requested. In addition to physical and logical addresses, services represent yet a third type of address. In the TCP/IP protocol suite, a *port* is a numerical designator, or address, associated with a service that we desire to run on a remote computer.

"O.K., Kim." John's acknowledgment indicates that he successfully received and decoded the message from Kim. However, Bob's statement "The Green Paper?" indicates possible confusion. Either he did not clearly receive the request or perhaps he is not ready to undertake the task. Assuming that he didn't clearly receive the request, we might attribute the garbled transmission to noise somewhere along the communications medium. Perhaps lightning was the culprit. Regardless of the noise's source, Bob's statement indicates to Kim the need to retransmit the message. TCP plays the role of error recovery agent, and other vital services, for the entire protocol suite.

2.2 OSI versus ARPANET: Communication Models

We are all inextricably bound to a plethora of standards, many of which are quite practical. Interpreting the speed limit in different units of distance such as kilometers per hour, for example, might cause us to be late or get fined for excessive speeding. In the communications industry, standards are equally important.

Developed by the International Organization for Standardization (ISO), the Open Systems Interconnection (OSI) model is intended to serve as a reference by which protocol standards can be designed. The model consists of seven hierarchical layers, the aggregate of which constitutes the network functionality of a single computer.

FIGURE 2.2

OSI communications model using a router.

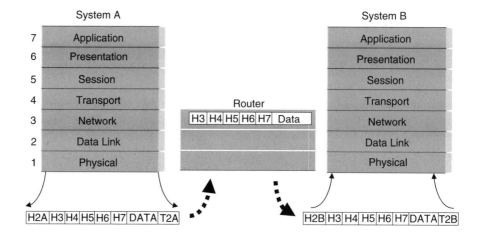

Developed by the International Organization for Standardization (ISO), the Open Systems Interconnection (OSI) model is intended to serve as a reference by which protocol standards can be designed (see Figure 2.2). The model consists of seven hierarchical layers, the aggregate of which constitutes the network functionality of a single computer. Each layer is constructed in a modular fashion functioning independently of the layers immediately above and below it. The purpose of this modular approach is to allow organizations to develop hardware and software products within their area(s) of expertise. For example, a company that produces network adapter cards, which are based primarily on layer 2 (Data Link) protocols, need not necessarily be steeped in the knowledge required to write code for layer 3 (Network). However, the adapter cards that they create must be able to pass information to and from layers 1 (Physical) and 3 (Network).

From the bottom up, the functionality of each layer is described as follows:

1. *Physical:* As the name implies, this layer establishes the electrical and mechanical interface between the computer and local area network (LAN). Whether in the form of light pulses or electrons, the Physical layer transmits and receives a binary bitstream devoid of any encoded information.

2. *Data Link:* Providing the encoding pattern to be supplied to the Physical layer, this layer also aids in the control of the flow of information, recovery from errors, and synchronization of communications between network nodes. Addresses associated with this layer are referred to as MAC (Media Access Control) addresses. Encoded in firmware, MAC addresses are an integral part of network adapter cards. The output produced from this layer is called a *frame*.

3. *Network:* Responsible for the end-to-end delivery of information from one network to another. The Network layer allows for the creation of internets. Protocols associated with this layer bear such names as IP and IPX (Internetwork Packet Exchange). The output produced from this layer is called a *packet*.

4. *Transport:* Capable of providing reliable end-to-end connectivity for the transfer of information, this layer also handles sequencing, flow control, and error recovery services for the information passed to it from higher-level layers. TCP and SPX (Sequenced Packet Exchange) are examples of Transport layer protocols.

5. *Session:* Essentially this layer is tasked with the management of sessions (connections), allowing communications between networked applications.

6. *Presentation:* Deriving its name from its primary function of presenting information to the Application layer in a formatted structure, this layer is also responsible for such functions as data encryption and compression.

7. *Application:* Usually in GUI (Graphical User Interface) format, this layer provides the operator an interface with which to perform a certain task(s). It is simply the programs with which we interact. User data from this layer is bundled with Application layer overhead information and passed to other layers for eventual transmission across a network. World Wide Web browsers are considered network applications.

The OSI model is illustrated in Figure 2.2. Each stack of protocols (layers 1 through 7) represents one of two computers (System A and System B). When an application on one system requires information from the application on the other system, such as a web browser requesting a web page from a web server, it appends overhead information (header) to the beginning of the user data and passes the whole bundle to the next lower protocol. The next lower protocol, in turn, appends its overhead information and continues the process. Eventually the frame of data arrives at the Physical layer of the model, where it is transmitted onto the local network as a highly encoded bitstream of 1s and 0s. The frame is merely a packet passed down from layer 3 that has been framed with a layer 2 header and trailer. The header and trailer provide the information necessary for the frame to traverse the local network.

Ubiquitous to the Internet, the most common type of internetworking device is the *router.* One of its primary functions is the routing of data packets from one type of network technology to another. Routing is accomplished by stripping the frame of the current header and trailer (layer 2), leaving only the packet, and reframing it with a new header and trailer appropriate to the networking technology on which it is being routed. Similar to any other network node, routers communicate with one another via communication protocols. These protocols are referred to as *routing protocols.*

The four hierarchical layers, constituting the TCP/IP architecture, correspond with the seven layers of the OSI model (see Figure 2.3). TCP/IP's Process layer is equivalent to OSI's Application, Presentation, and Session (upper half) layers. Applications and utilities associated with the Process layer include the following:

Telnet: A virtual terminal utility enabling access to remote hosts.

FTP (File Transfer Protocol): A file transfer utility.

SMTP (Simple Mail Transfer Protocol): The predominant protocol responsible for the transmission and distribution of e-mail.

FIGURE 2.3

OSI versus TCP/IP architecture.

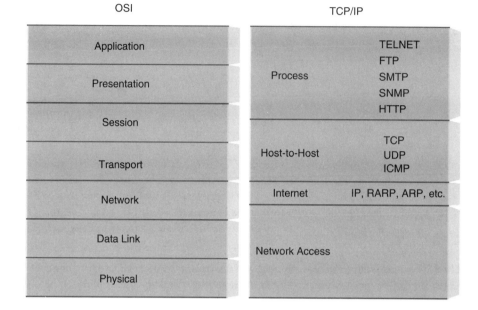

SNMP (Simple Network Management Protocol): The predominant protocol responsible for the transmission of vital network and system statistics and commands.

HTTP (Hypertext Transfer Protocol): The predominant protocol responsible for the transmission of information throughout the World Wide Web.

The Host-to-Host layer is equivalent to OSI's Session (lower half) and Transport layers. It consists chiefly of the protocols TCP, UDP (User Datagram Protocol), and ICMP (Internet Control Message Protocol). Through the use of sequencing, checksums, and acknowledgments, TCP adds reliability to data transmissions using the IP protocol. Deemed a connection-oriented protocol, TCP establishes a virtual connection between two hosts prior to the transmission of data. Upon completion, the connection is dropped. UDP, on the other hand, is deemed a connectionless-oriented protocol. It attempts no connection prior to transmission and therefore lacks the overhead inherent to TCP. ICMP is responsible for providing error and diagnostics feedback to networking nodes. The services provided by ICMP include informing hosts of a system's operational status, the expiration of TTL (time-to-live) values found within IP packets, and routes more suitable for communication with another system.

Many crucial components of the TCP/IP protocol suite lie within the Internet layer. This layer corresponds roughly to the Network layer of the OSI model. Several protocols found within this layer include the following:

IP (Internet Protocol): The predominant protocol of the entire TCP/IP protocol suite responsible primarily for the addressing and segmenting of data packets.

ARP (Address Resolution Protocol): The broadcast protocol responsible for the conversion of IP addresses to MAC addresses.

RARP (Reverse ARP): The broadcast protocol responsible for the conversion of MAC addresses to IP addresses.

RIP (Routing Information Protocol): A lightweight interior router protocol generally used for the dissemination of routing information within an autonomous system (a local area network consisting of routed subnets communicating with similar routing protocols).

OSPF (Open Shortest Path First): An interior router protocol, based on a link state algorithm, used for the dissemination of routing information within an autonomous system.

BGP (Border Gateway Protocol): An exterior router protocol used to exchange routing information between the border routers of autonomous systems.

EGP (Exterior Gateway Protocol): An exterior router protocol used to exchange routing information between autonomous systems.

The Network Access layer corresponds with OSI's Network (lower half), Data Link, and Physical layers. Protocols and technologies within this layer are responsible for the transmission of an encoded bitstream, with some level of error detection, between network nodes. A more formal treatment of issues related to this layer will be given in the next chapter.

2.3 Dissecting IP, TCP, and UDP Headers

The IP protocol lies at the heart of the TCP/IP protocol suite. As illustrated in Figure 2.4, the *IP header* contains several fields of information vital to communications between end nodes. A frame of data is transmitted from our source computer (IP address 192.9.85.200) to our destination computer (IP address 192.9.85.201) via the simple local area network to which they are connected (1). We recall from previous discussions that passing user data from an application down through successive layers of the OSI model to the Data Link layer creates a frame. Each layer is capable of appending its own headers to the growing string of binary information. Layer 3 appends the IP header.

> The IP protocol lies at the heart of the TCP/IP protocol suite.

A device referred to as a *protocol analyzer* "listens" to data traffic traversing the network and captures specific frames that conform to a given set of filtering criteria that were preconfigured by the analyzer's operator. Frame number 42, captured by the analyzer, depicts the field contents of the IP header from an actual transmission between our source and destination computers (2). The analyzer graphic consists of three viewing regions: Summary, Detail, and Hex. The *Summary region* essentially provides the

FIGURE 2.4
The IP header.

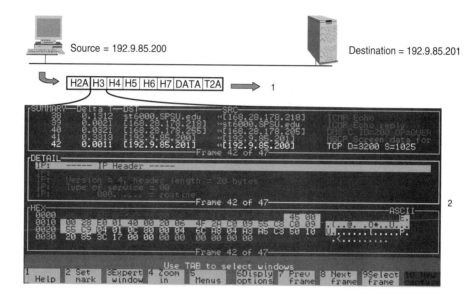

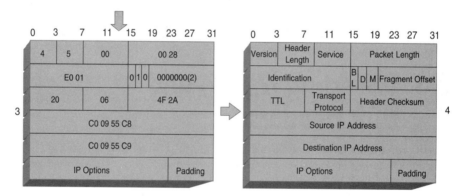

IP addresses and type of transaction utilized by the communicating nodes. The *Detail region* provides the operator with the ability to highlight selected portions of the frame, thus allowing for the dissection of the various frame headers. The *Hex region* contains a hex dump of the field(s) selected in the Detail region. Since this region consists predominantly of hexadecimal numbers, a lightweight treatment of such numbers is given.

Hexadecimal numbers consist of the numbers 0 through 9 and the letters A through F, the latter representing the numbers 10 through 15. Hence, a single hexadecimal number, 0 through F can represent one of 16 possible values. Since 16 is a convenient multiple of the number 2 (2^4 to be precise) hexadecimal numbers can be converted into a binary format consisting of four bits as shown in the following table.

Hexadecimal	Binary
0	0000
1	0001
2	0010
3	0011
4	0100
5	0101
6	0110
7	0111
8	1000
9	1001
A	1010
B	1011
C	1100
D	1101
E	1110
F	1111

From our table of hexadecimal numbers, we deduce that the first number in the IP header of frame 42 must be a $4_{(16)}$. Pondering the stream of communication bits flowing between our nodes, we can visualize this hexadecimal $4_{(16)}$ as merely the binary pattern $0100_{(2)}$. Continuing this line of logic, we determine the second number to be a $5_{(16)}$ and the third to be $00_{(16)}$, and so on. $00_{(16)}$ equals, of course, the byte (eight bits) $00000000_{(2)}$. All of the highlighted values of frame 42 have been replicated, within their proper field locations, onto the monolithic IP header model (3).

A second model juxtaposed with the first serves as a means for relating the captured values to the associated IP header fields (4). Note that the fundamental unit of length, referred to as a *word*, of the header is 32 bits. The fields constituting the IP header are described as follows:

Version: The version of IP being used; 4 is the current version.

Length: The length, in 32-bit words, of the IP header.

Service: Generally set to all 0s, this field indicates to networking nodes that this packet must be processed according to a given set of criteria. Criteria include qualities such as precedence, throughput, and reliability.

Packet Length: The length, in bytes, of the entire packet including the IP header.

Identification: An identifier relating all of the fragments to the particular IP packet from which they were created.

Flags: The three bits that follow the Identification field constitute the flags that control whether an IP packet is fragmented into smaller packets. The first bit is always set to 0. The second bit (Don't Fragment flag), when set, indicates that the current IP packet is not to be fragmented. The third bit (More Fragments), when set, indicates to the receiving host that more fragments of this packet are to be expected.

Upon arrival, the fragments of a given IP packet are recognized, via the Identification field, and reassembled, via the Fragment Offset field. We notice that the value $40\ 00_{(16)}$, in frame 42, corresponds to the flags and the Fragment Offset field. Dissected, $40\ 00_{(16)}$ yields $0100\ 0000\ 0000\ 0000_{(2)}$. In other words, the captured packet is not to be fragmented and therefore requires no fragment offset.

Fragment Offset: The fragment's position relative to the overall packet. End nodes, such as hosts, and interconnecting nodes, such as routers, that are configured to communicate via TCP/IP are capable of utilizing IP's fragmentation process. So why fragment? Different networking technologies are capable of transporting packets of different maximum length. A local area network based on Ethernet, for example, is capable of transporting packets up to, but not exceeding, a length of 1,526 bytes. A particular version of Token Ring, however, transports packets up to, but not exceeding, a length of 4,500 bytes. Clearly a packet being routed from a Token Ring networking environment to that of an Ethernet must be fragmented. It is interesting to note that individual fragments need not follow the same route as the packets preceding or following them.

TTL (Time to Live): The time, in seconds, that a packet is to remain valid. Regardless of whether one second has elapsed, interconnecting nodes must decrement this field by one. Upon reaching zero, the packet must be discarded by the current interconnecting node. This node, in turn, transmits an ICMP message that informs the sender of the packet's fate. Frame 42's TTL field contains the number $20_{(16)}$, which equals $32_{(10)}$. Since it is unlikely that the delay imposed by traversing any given link between interconnecting nodes will exceed one second, the packet can pass through a maximum of 32 of these nodes, where the passage through one node is referred to as a *hop*.

Transport Protocol: The number identifying the transport protocol to which the IP packet must be passed upon reception. Common numbers include 6 (TCP), 17 (UDP), and 1 (ICMP). Viewing the Transport Protocol field, we notice that the transport protocol for frame 42 is indeed TCP.

Header Checksum: A nonrobust error checking value against which the protocol header's accuracy is verified. Meticulous processing in which the determination of the entire packet's accuracy is considered occurs in the checksum fields of higher-layer protocols such as TCP and UDP.

IP Addresses: A 32-bit numerical address by which TCP/IP-configured hosts communicate. Frame 42's Source IP Address field contains $C0\ 09\ 55\ C8_{(16)}$, which equals $192.9.85.200_{(10)}$, whereas its Destination IP Address field contains $C0\ 09\ 55\ C9_{(16)}$, which equals $192.9.85.201_{(10)}$. Notice the source (SRC) and destination (DST) values for frame 42 in the Summary region of Figure 2.4.

Options: A list of optional features that may be appended to the IP header. Such options include:

Source Route: A mechanism whereby a packet is routed through the predetermined path indicated by an appendage to the IP header.

Security: Specifications for handling packets in a secure manner.

No Operation: An option that does literally nothing except pad the options list.

End-of-Option List: A marker indicating the end of the IP options list.

Time Stamp: A mechanism for recording the time associated with a packet's traversal of a given interconnecting node. This information is returned to the sending node.

Record Route: A mechanism for recording the IP address of an interconnecting node through which a packet traverses. This information is returned to the sending node.

Padding: An optional field used, when necessary, to maintain a valid number of 16-bit entries within the IP header by the padding of additional characters.

As we have seen, TCP adds reliability to IP data transmissions. As illustrated in Figure 2.5, the TCP header is appended to the nascent frame at layer 4 of the OSI model and therefore resides deeper within the frame than does the IP header. Routers generally process frames by examining the information contained in the IP header only, hence lending no support in TCP's reliability process. Routers can, however, filter undesired TCP/IP packets by examining the contents of the Port field found in the TCP header. Packets containing undesirable port numbers get discarded. Indeed, the ancestor of today's firewall is merely a router configured with certain access restrictions.

Processing the request of a web browser, our source computer (IP address 168.28.178.218) transmits the appropriate information to the destination computer (IP address 206.246.140.162), Prentice Hall's web server (1). Again we employ the use of a protocol analyzer to dissect the TCP header of our captured packet (2). The header's contents are transcribed from the Hex region of the analyzer graphic onto a monolithic block (3), as before, for the purposes of comparison with the fields within TCP (4). Noting that the standard TCP header word length is also 32 bits, we define the header's fields as follows:

Source and Destination Ports: A number defining the address of a particular service, on the remote host, to be invoked. Generally, the port number assigned to the initiator of the request is referred to as the *client process,* whereas that of the grantor of the request is referred to as the *server process.* In our current example, frame 77, the source port number is $1047_{(10)}$, which equals $04\ 17_{(16)}$, and the destination port number is $80_{(10)}$, which equals $00\ 50_{(16)}$. The source port number is generally not significant. The destination port number 80, however, indicates that that the sender desires to communicate with the server via *HTTP (Hypertext Transport Protocol).* HTTP, of course, is the protocol responsible for exchanging World Wide Web pages. A partial listing of common TCP and UDP port numbers, or services, obtained from the file/etc/services of a Unix server, is as follows:

Service	Port/Transport	Comment
daytime	13/tcp	# date/time
daytime	13/tcp	# date/time
ftp	21/tcp	# file transfer protocol
telnet	23/tcp	#
smtp	25/tcp	# e-mail

FIGURE 2.5

The TCP header.

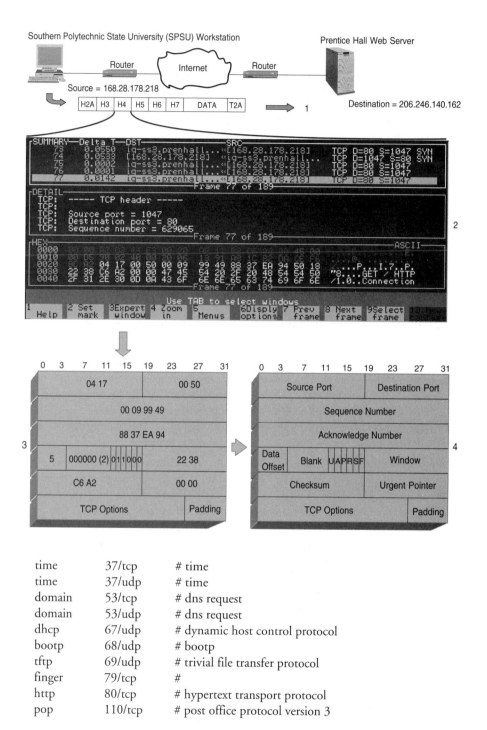

time	37/tcp	# time
time	37/udp	# time
domain	53/tcp	# dns request
domain	53/udp	# dns request
dhcp	67/udp	# dynamic host control protocol
bootp	68/udp	# bootp
tftp	69/udp	# trivial file transfer protocol
finger	79/tcp	#
http	80/tcp	# hypertext transport protocol
pop	110/tcp	# post office protocol version 3

nntp	119/tcp	# network news transfer protocol
snmp	161/udp	# simple network management protocol
talk	517/udp	# ·
rip	520/udp	# routing information protocol

Sequence Number: The number of bytes transmitted to the other end node of a TCP connection. Unique sequence numbers are chosen by each end node, during the establishment phase of the connection, and are incremented as the total number of bytes transmitted increases. Note that the sequence number in the TCP header of frame 77 is $629065_{(10)}$, which equals $00\ 09\ 99\ 49_{(16)}$.

Acknowledge Number: The number of bytes received by the other node in a TCP connection.

Data Offset: The length of the TCP header in 32-bit words. Recall that in the model of the TCP/IP architecture, the Process layer resides immediately above the layer where TCP resides, the Transport layer. Therefore, all information following the TCP header is considered the data that it is attempting to transport.

Flags: Status indicators used to effect a particular TCP action on the recipient's side of the connection. Flags that are set, denoted by the presence of a 1, require the action to occur. Each of the six flags are interpreted as follows:

   U (URG): Urgent Pointer field is valid.
   A (ACK): Acknowledgement Number field is valid.
   P (PSH): Data contained in this packet should be immediately *pushed* to the initiating application. Generally, the remnants of a data file already transmitted to a recipient are bundled into a packet with this flag set.
   R (RST): The TCP connection must be reset due to an invalid transmission.
   S (SYN): A TCP connection request must be acknowledged by the recipient.
   F (FIN): A one-sided connection termination must be acknowledged by the recipient. Since TCP is a bidirectional protocol, both nodes must terminate their respective connection before communication ceases entirely.

Window: A mechanism used to control the flow of data between two communicating nodes. The value transmitted within the Window field informs the other node of the number of bytes that it may transmit. A Window field containing $00\ 00_{(16)}$ would, for example, indicate to the other node that no data may be transmitted for the moment. As soon as the previously transmitted data is processed, however, a window size other than $00\ 00_{(16)}$ would be transmitted to restart the flow of data. TCP is governed by the sliding-window principle, which states that a transmitting node does not have to wait for acknowledgments confirming the successful receipt of previously transmitted data, and that the maximum number of bytes transmitted is equal to the received window size.

Checksum: A robust error-checking mechanism used to verify the accuracy of the TCP header, data, and pseudo header. The *pseudo header* consists of the Source and Destination IP addresses, Transport Protocol, and Packet Length information extracted from the packet's IP header.

Urgent Pointer: A software pointer used in conjunction with the Sequence Number field to indicate to the receiving node the location of an urgent message from the application of the transmitting node.

TCP Options: A list of optional features that may be appended to the TCP header. Such options include the following:

No Operation: An option that does literally nothing except pad the options list.

Maximum Segment Size: An option, transmitted during the establishment of a TCP connection, that informs the other node of the maximum number of received bytes per segment that it will accept. Recall that a segment is merely an individual packet of information that constitutes only a portion of an entire transmission.

End-of-Option List: A marker indicating the end of the TCP options list.

Padding: An optional field used, when necessary, to maintain a valid number of 16-bit entries within the TCP header by the padding of additional characters.

Timing is common to all aspects of communications. In its absence, communication ceases. Several innate timers aid TCP in the maintenance of seamless connections between nodes. Bearing such names as the Retransmission Timeout (RTO), Persistence Timer, and Keep-Alive Timer, *timers* provide TCP with the fail-safe mechanisms required for detecting and remedying anomalous behavior. The RTO, for example, is activated when the maximum time interval between the transmission of a data packet and the reception of its acknowledgment is exceeded. Under these circumstances, the sending node is required to retransmit the lost packet.

The reliability offered by TCP comes at a cost. The overhead information required for establishing and maintaining a TCP connection may not always allow the most efficient interactions. Services provided by SNMP (Simple Network Management Protocol), TFTP (Trivial File Transfer Protocol), and DHCP (Dynamic Host Configuration Protocol) operate in a connectionless mode in which sequence and acknowledgment numbers have no meaning. Such services are not transported by TCP, but rather by UDP, TCP's lightweight cousin.

Recall that routing protocols such as RIP, EGP, and BGP are found within the Network layer of the OSI model. These layer 3 protocols play the critical role of disseminating dynamic routing information to neighboring routers and end nodes, and so should not overly impact a network link's bandwidth or capacity to carry data traffic. EGP and BGP, the predominant routing protocols of the Internet's backbone, rely on TCP for reliable transportation. RIP, a more primitive and lightweight protocol, however, utilizes UDP (see Figure 2.6). RIP-configured routers are capable of periodically broadcasting updated route information to nodes attached to their network segments. The campus router, IP address 168.26.176.1, has broadcast such an update to the campus' broadcast IP address 168.28.255.255 (1). A broadcast address, discussed in the next section, is merely an address shared by all end nodes of a common IP address range, such as 168.28.x.y.

FIGURE 2.6

The UDP header.

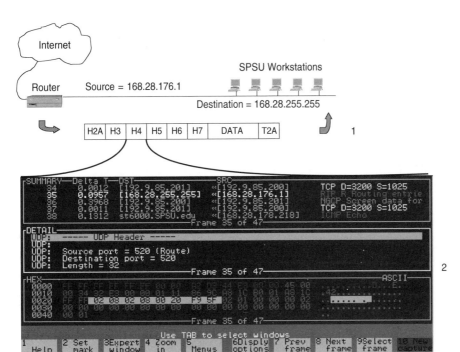

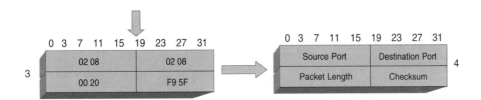

Frame 35, captured by the analyzer, depicts the field contents of the UDP header of the RIP broadcast (2). UDP's lightweight nature is betrayed by its short length, four 16-bit words. In our example, $02\ 08\ 02\ 08\ 00\ 20\ F9\ 5F_{(16)}$, which equals 0000 0010 0000 1000 0000 0010 0000 1000 0000 0000 0010 0000 1111 1001 0101 $1111_{(2)}$, constitutes the entire header (3). The header fields are defined as follows:

Source and Destination Port: Similar in nature to those of TCP. In frame 35, we note that the source and destination port numbers equal $02\ 08_{(16)}$ which equals 520(10), UDP's port number for RIP services.

Packet Length: The length of the UDP header and all higher-layer information.

Checksum: Similar in nature to that used by TCP.

2.4 IP Addresses and Subnet Masks

IP addresses are constructed by the joining of two distinct address fields, Network and Host.

In the previous section, we learned that source and destination IP addresses are 32 bits in length (see Figure 2.4). By scrutinizing frame 42, we were able to show the extracted source IP address C0 09 55 C8$_{(16)}$ to be equivalent to the decimal dot notation 192.9.85.200$_{(10)}$ and the 32-bit number 11000000 00001001 01010101 11001000$_{(2)}$. The latter represents the actual string of numbers transmitted in the IP header, whereas the former, decimal dot notation, represents the format convention used by programmers and network administrators.

IP addresses are constructed by the joining of two distinct address fields, Network and Host (see Figure 2.7). Five classes of IP addresses, A through E, are defined to accommodate varying network sizes (classes A through C), a process known as IP multicasting (class D), and research (class E). Class D IP addresses will be discussed in the subsequent sections related to IP multicasting and the MBone (Multicast Backbone). Class E IP addresses are not depicted in Figure 2.7.

FIGURE 2.7

IP address classes.

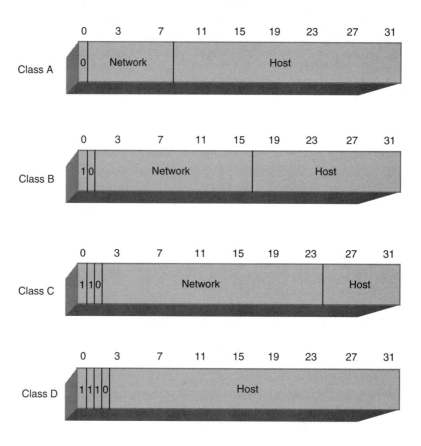

The Network field of a class A address consists of the first 8 bits (also referred to as an *octet*) of the 32-bit address; the most significant bit (left-most bit) is always 0, leaving only seven bits with which to create unique addresses. With seven bits, one can create $128_{(10)}$ network addresses, $0000000_{(2)}$ (0) through $1111111_{(2)}$ ($127_{(10)}$). The IP address 126.x.y.z (where x, y, and z are variables), for example, is recognized as a class A address because the first number falls within the range 0 to $127_{(10)}$. The Host field of a class A address consists of the remaining 24 bits of the 32-bit address. With 24 bits, one can create $16,772,216_{(10)}$ unique IP addresses. Hosts fields containing all 1s or all 0s, however, are used as a broadcast address (all 1s) or a network address (all 0s) and are therefore unavailable for assignment to individual hosts. The total number of hosts per class A address is, therefore, $16,772,214_{(10)}$. Hence, worldwide $128_{(10)}$ class A IP networks exist, each capable of accommodating $16,772,214_{(10)}$ hosts. By similar logic, we derive the following data:

IP Address Class	First Octet	Number of Networks	Number of Hosts Per Network
A	0–127	128	16,772,214
B	128–191	16,384	65,534
C	192–223	2,097,152	254
D	224–239	N/A	N/A

Revisiting IP address $168.28.178.218_{(10)}$ (see Figure 2.5), we identify the network portion of this class B address as $168.28_{(10)}$. For this particular address, the third octet, 178, further specifies the subnetwork, referred to in networking parlance as a *subnet*, to which this host is connected (see Figure 2.8). Depicted are the three subnets, $168.28.174.0_{(10)}$, $168.28.176.0_{(10)}$, and $168.8.178.0_{(10)}$, created from the original network, $168.28.0.0_{(10)}$.

Subnets are created to allow for the practical management of a given range of IP addresses. Referring to the previous data, we note that a network assigned a class B address, for example, is capable of accommodating 65,534 hosts. Such a network, if possible to construct, would be a management nightmare. Data traffic generated from departments within the organization would be indistinguishable, rendering troubleshooting of network-related problems very difficult. Political disputes arising from system resource utilization would fester into a possible impasse, and network configuration changes could disrupt the entire organization's productivity. Subnetting would alleviate these potential problems.

A *subnet mask* is employed by routers and hosts to determine to which subnet a given packet belongs. To illustrate its usage, we track the inbound data, transmitted from some unknown Internet host, to its destination IP address $168.28.178.218_{(10)}$ (a). Once received by the router, the destination IP address field within the packet's layer 3 header is determined and extracted (b). From this IP address is filtered the subnet address, onto which the packet is forwarded. Filtering of the subnet address is accomplished by "anding" the IP address with the subnet mask $255.255.255.0_{(10)}$ (c); the dot is used to

FIGURE 2.8

Subnets and masks.

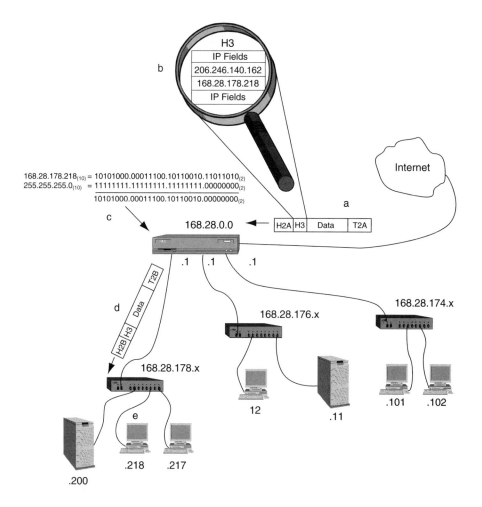

represent the "and" function. Two binary numbers are "anded" together bit by bit. Only the combination of 1 "and" 1 yields a 1. All others, 0 "and" 0, 0 "and" 1, and 1 "and" 0, yield a 0. Our subnet mask, therefore, discards the last octet of the IP address and retains the first three. The resulting subnet address, $168.28.178.0_{(10)}$, is used by the router to determine the port through which the packet will be routed (d). Once on the proper subnet, the packet is received by the intended host (e).

The filching of bits from the original IP address space creates a subnet. In the previous example, the class B address space, $168.28.0.0_{(10)}$, was partitioned into 254 subnets by reassigning the third octet, originally part of the host field, to be used as part of the Network field. Recall that the use of all 1s or all 0s is reserved and therefore cannot be used as subnet addresses. Hence, instead of creating 256 (2^8) subnets, we create 254.

Networks that are not subnetted still employ the use of a subnet mask. However, these "default" subnet masks, shown following, filter only the original Network field of a class A, B, or C address:

Address Class	Default Subnet Mask
A	$255.0.0.0_{(10)}$
B	$255.255.0.0_{(10)}$
C	$255.255.255.0_{(10)}$

Not all subnet masks are as conveniently designed as the one shown in Figure 2.8. If we had procured only four host bits to create the subnet mask $255.255.240_{(10)}$, which equals $11111111.11111111.11110000.00000000_{(2)}$, then only 14 ($2^4 - 2$) subnets could be created from our original class B address space. The subnet address derived from use of such a subnet mask is calculated as follows:

$$168.28.178.218_{(10)} \quad = \quad 10101000.00011100.10110010.11011010_{(2)}$$

$$\underline{255.255.240.0_{(10)}} \quad = \quad \underline{11111111.11111111.11110000.00000000_{(2)}}$$
$$168.28.176.0_{(10)} \quad = \quad 10101000.00011100.10110000.00000000_{(2)}$$

2.5 DNS and DHCP

Generally speaking, it is easier to remember a person's first name than Social Security number. Similarly, a symbolic name for a host, such as www.prenhall.com, is more readily recalled than its numeric IP address, $206.246.140.162_{(10)}$. One manner in which to map symbolic names to IP addresses is by the creation of a local file named *hosts*. A typical example of the file *hosts* is as follows:

```
206.246.140.162      www.prenhall.com
130.207.244.150150    ftp.gatech.edu
198.166.166.10       www.nasa.gov
127.0.0.1            localhost
```

A more practical method for obtaining IP addresses is via a global directory service known as the *Domain Name Service (DNS)*. All protocols contained within the TCP/IP protocol suite, including DNS, are meticulously described in the aforementioned RFC documents. RFCs can be obtained via the following URLs: http://www.ietf.org or ftp://rs.internic.net/rfc/rfcdddd.txt, where dddd represents the desired RFC number. The URL ftp://rs.internic.net/rfc/ displays a directory of the RFCs. In particular, RFCs 1034 and 1035 detail the DNS protocol.

DNS comprises three main elements: the domain name space, name servers, and resolvers. The domain name space can be visualized as a hierarchical tree structure (see Figure 2.9). The base of the structure is referred to as the *root*. Immediately above the root we encounter the top-level domains (TLDs), the tree's branches. Above the TLDs are subdomains, smaller branches, and the leaves, of course, represent end nodes (servers,

A practical method for obtaining IP addresses is via a global directory service known as the *Domain Name Service (DNS)*.

FIGURE 2.9
Domain name space (partial view).

workstations, mail exchangers, etc.). The *domain* of a given institution is formed by following the path originating at the institution's subdomain and terminating at the root. The domain associated with the Georgia Institute of Technology's Electrical and Computer Engineering department, for example, is ece.gatech.edu. Appending a host name to this domain, for example, tesla.ece.gatech.edu, produces an *FQDN (Fully Qualified Domain Name)*. Countries connected to the Internet have their own TLDs that further modify a domain name. For example, ftp.aarnet.edu.au is the FQDN of the host named *ftp*, which is located in Australia.

Name servers are data repositories containing information that describes the structure of the domain name space. These servers are set up as the authority over regions of the domain name space called *zones*, which encompass a particular node, or branch, and all subordinate branches. Subordinate branches, in turn, fall under the auspice of subordinate name servers. Name servers must be capable of proliferating information to other servers, superior and subordinate. In the previous example, the ece.gatech.edu subdomain's name server *ece* is subordinate to *gatech*, which is subordinate to *edu*.

Within a zone, pertinent information about the systems, for example a host's IP address, is contained within the resource records (RR) of the name server. The typical fields of a resource record are as follows:

Field	Description
Owner	Name of domain containing RR.
Type	16-bit encoded value specifying resource type contained in RR. Types include the following:

	A	Host address.
	CNAME	Canonical name of an alias.
	HINFO	CPU and OS used by host.
	MX	Domain's e-mail server.
	NS	Domain's authoritative name server.
	PTR	Pointer to another resource within the domain name space.
	SOA	Start of a zone of authority.

Class	16-bit encoded value that specifies the protocol used. Protocols include the following:

	IN	Internet
	CH	Chaos

TTL	32-bit value containing the time to live, in seconds, of an RR. This value is primarily used to inform resolvers how long a cached RR can be kept. A typical value is 86,400 seconds, which is equal to one day.
RDATA	Actual resource data contained in RR. Data fields include the following:

	A	32-bit IP address for IN class. Domain name and 16-bit octal address for Chaos.
	CNAME	Domain name.
	MX	16-bit value followed by name of e-mail server for domain.
	NS	Host name.
	PTR	Domain name.
	SOA	Fields associated with zone of authority.

A *resolver* is a program that generates queries and interprets replies between user programs, such as a web browser and name servers. Resolvers generally operate on the user system and are capable of caching RR information received from name servers. Cached RRs remain valid for the amount of time specified in their TTL field. The message format for queries and replies consists of a header and four variable-length fields that transport query parameters and reply information. The four variable-length fields are as follows:

Field	Description
Question	Query name and pertinent parameters.
Answer	Requested name server RR(s).
Authority	Alternate authoritative name server(s) that might be able to service the query.
Additional	Optional information such as the alternate authoritative name server's IP address.

If the local name server is unable to provide the requested RR(s), an alternate authoritative name server is contacted. A *recursive query* is one in which the local name server contacts the alternate name server on behalf of the resolver. An *iterative query* is one in which the resolver uses the information provided in the original reply's Authority field to contact the alternate name server directly. Iterative queries are preferred because they are less of a burden on the recipient name server. Figure 2.10 depicts a recursive DNS query from a web browser located on the computer with IP address $168.28.178.218_{(10)}$ to the name server, IP address $168.28.176.11_{(10)}$. DNS queries are transported via UDP, whereas DNS server-to-server transactions require reliable transportation and therefore rely on TCP.

Evidently, the operator, who is using the web browser and the URL www.prenhall.com, is attempting to download web pages from the Prentice Hall web site (a). Prior to successful communications with the intended web server, however, the URL must be resolved into an IP address; recall that end hosts communicate via IP addresses, not symbolic names (b). Unable to directly resolve the IP address using its own RRs, the name server initiates its own query to a name server that can provide the proper information (c). The received information is bundled into a DNS reply (d) and transmitted to the awaiting web browser (e).

dig and *nslookup* are Unix-based software tools available to users for the extraction of DNS information from name servers. *dig*, a command-line tool, is capable of querying name servers and displaying the retrieved information. *nslookup*, an interactive querying tool, is capable of providing the fine details of RRs contained within a name server. The following are several commented examples showing the usage of *nslookup:*

> The nslookup utility is invoked by typing nslookup. Immediately following the command line are the host name and IP address of the default name server. Typing either help or a **?** lists all of the commands and their usage.

```
tfallon [420] nslookup
Default Server:  einstein.sct.edu
Address:  168.28.176.11
```

> The default mode of operation for nslookup is host name to IP address resolution. By typing the desired host name at the prompt, information, including the IP address, is returned. If the

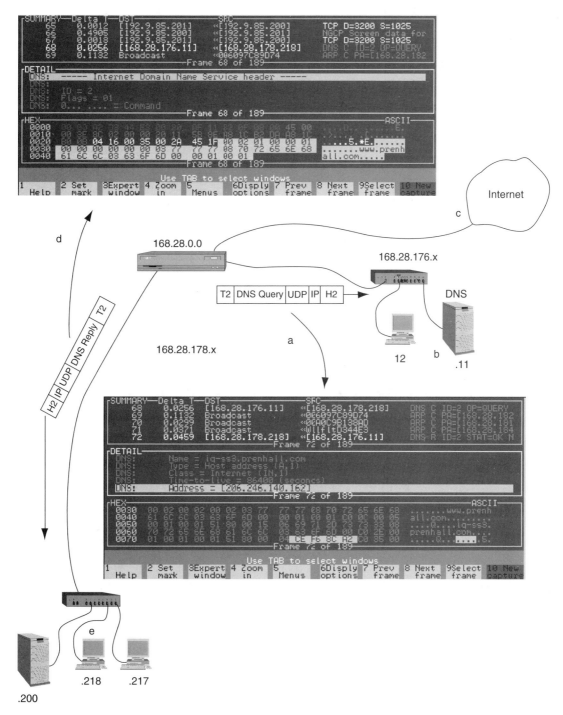

FIGURE 2.10
The DNS protocol.

query is resolved outside of the default name server's subzone, a nonauthoritative answer results.

```
> www.prenhall.com
Server:  einstein.sct.edu
Address:  168.28.176.11

Non-authoritative answer:
Name:    iq-ss3.prenhall.com
Address:  206.246.140.162
Aliases:  www.prenhall.com
```

By setting type equal to ptr (pointer), other regions of the domain name space can be explored. In particular, the domain in-addr.arpa is used for reverse name resolution to discover host names from IP addresses.

```
> set type=ptr
> 162.140.246.206.in-addr.arpa
Server:  einstein.sct.edu
Address:  168.28.176.11

Non-authoritative answer:
162.140.246.206.in-addr.arpa      name = iq-ss3.iquest.net

Authoritative answers can be found from:
140.246.206.in-addr.arpa         nameserver = NS1.iquest.net
140.246.206.in-addr.arpa         nameserver = NS2.iquest.net
NS1.iquest.net   internet address = 198.70.36.70
NS2.iquest.net   internet address = 198.70.36.95
```

By setting type to any, any available RR information is returned. Following this command by a specific domain name yields information for hosts such as name and e-mail servers. The e-mail server for Prentice Hall, for example, appears to be a host named usrlms006.prenhall.com. Similarly, the name server is NS1.prenhall.com.

```
> set type=any
> prenhall.com
Server:  einstein.sct.edu
Address:  168.28.176.11

Non-authoritative answer:
prenhall.com     nameserver = NS1.prenhall.com
prenhall.com     nameserver = AUTH00.NS.UU.NET
prenhall.com     mail exchanger = relay2.UU.NET
prenhall.com     mail exchanger = usrlms006.prenhall.com
prenhall.com     mail exchanger = relay1.UU.NET
```

```
Authoritative answers can be found from:
prenhall.com              nameserver = NS1.prenhall.com
prenhall.com              nameserver = AUTH00.NS.UU.NET
NS1.prenhall.com          internet address = 198.4.159.5
AUTH00.NS.UU.NET          internet address = 198.6.1.65
relay2.UU.NET             internet address = 192.48.96.7
usrlms006.prenhall.com    internet address = 198.4.159.40
relay1.UU.NET             internet address = 192.48.96.5
```

When you set type to mx and specify a domain, then the pertinent e-mail server and other related information is returned. (Note that the e-mail server's subdomain, sct.edu, is apparently incompatible with the one selected, spsu.edu. The former is merely vestigial information of the previous domain name.)

```
> set type=mx
> spsu.edu
Server:  ns1.prenhall.com
Address:  198.4.159.5

spsu.edu                  mail exchanger = st6000.sct.edu
spsu.edu                  nameserver = einstein.sct.edu
spsu.edu                  nameserver = ns.Peach.NET
spsu.edu                  nameserver = ns.PeachNet.edu
spsu.edu                  nameserver = ns2.PeachNet.edu
st6000.sct.edu            internet address = 168.28.176.249
einstein.sct.edu          internet address = 168.28.176.11
ns.Peach.NET              internet address = 198.72.72.10
ns.PeachNet.edu           internet address = 131.144.4.10
ns2.PeachNet.edu          internet address = 131.144.4.9
```

The list command has several possible parameter options. The –a option, for example, lists all available canonical host names and their aliases.

```
> ls -a spsu.edu
[einstein.spsu.edu]
 newton                   st6000.SPSU.edu
 ecet                     ecet_alpha.SPSU.edu
 loopback                 localhost.SPSU.edu
 mail1                    tesla.SPSU.edu
 mail2                    st6000.SPSU.edu
 tmgt_web                 krosner.SPSU.edu
 news                     galileo.SPSU.edu
 www2                     fac_web.SPSU.edu
 www                      st6000.SPSU.edu
```

The server command redirects subsequent queries to the name server specified. The same commands, such as list, can generally be found on these other name servers. The *exit* command is used to exit from nslookup.

```
> server ns1.prenhall.com
Default Server:  ns1.prenhall.com
Address:  198.4.159.5

> ls -a prenhall.com
[ns1.prenhall.com]
 news                           vesta.prenhall.com
 ils                            usrlas010.prenhall.com
 gopher                         iq-ss3.prenhall.com
 emissary                       usrlas015.prenhall.com
 chat                           iq-ss3.prenhall.com
 ssnews                         iq-ss3.prenhall.com
 newsrv                         vesta.prenhall.com
 dev                            chaos.prenhall.com
 www                            iq-ss3.prenhall.com
 webct                          tartarus.prenhall.com
 apps                           oldtas005.prenhall.com
 intranet                       ssweb.prenhall.com
 cpm                            oldtas020.prenhall.com
 ftp                            iq-ss3.prenhall.com

> exit
```

The primary function of the DNS is to resolve host names into IP addresses. How did the host receive an IP address initially? Recall that IP addresses are initially assigned via ICANN (see section 1.5) in conjunction with services provided by the Shared Registration System. Having once acquired an IP address, entities such as businesses, schools, and ISPs allocate the addresses to hosts and other systems distributed throughout the organization. For several possible reasons, the allocation process may be very complex and tedious. For example, each new host connected to the network requires a unique set of configuration information such as an IP, gateway, and domain name server address. Such configurations, if done manually, can take an inordinate amount of time to complete. Additionally, the network may be subnetted and therefore require a unique range of IP addresses and a specific gateway address for each subnet.

Other problems exist as well. Occasionally, for example, systems are inadvertently configured with identical IP addresses, rendering one of them to the temporary and inconvenient state of incommunicado. Systems that are moved from one subnet to another or that require remote access service (see section 2.9) depend on the ability to be dynamically reconfigured. The complexities of allocation and troubleshooting of TCP/IP configurations are, fortunately, mitigated by use of the protocol DHCP (Dynamic Host Control Protocol). DHCP is a client/server-based system whereby client systems receive their configuration via a DHCP server.

DHCP is the progeny of the static allocation protocol BOOTP. Whereas BOOTP supports only configurations that are manually entered into the BOOTP server, DHCP offers three modes of operation, the most primitive of which is manual entry. The other two modes, dynamic and automatic, operate under the principle of a leased configuration. The configuration may be leased for a finite period of time (dynamic) or indefinitely (automatic). IP addresses associated with leased configurations are borrowed from a particular range, or pool, of IP addresses that are managed by the DHCP server.

As set forth in RFC 2131, DHCP client/server transactions use seven distinct message types: dhcpdiscover, dhcpoffer, dhcprequest, dchpdecline, dhcpack, dhcpnak, and dhcprelease. The steps involved in a typical transaction between a DHCP client system seeking TCP/IP configuration information from a DHCP server are as follows:

1. During the boot process, the client system broadcasts a dhcpdiscover message seeking configuration information from any available DHCP server. Along with the dhcpdiscover message is transported the client system's MAC address (e.g., Ethernet or Token Ring address). Ultimately, the DHCP server that leases the configuration information will bind the client's MAC address into its DHCP database, thus associating a client system with a particular lease.

2. DHCP servers capable of providing configuration information to the client system issue a reply in the form of a dhcpoffer message. Included in the message are the potential configuration and the server's IP address. Several servers may have responded to the broadcast.

3. The client system transmits a dhcprequest message to the particular server from which it seeks a configuration lease. Included in the message is the intended server's IP address.

4. The intended server checks the status of the requested configuration and issues a dhcpack message if the information is available. If the configuration information has already been leased to another client system, then the server transmits a dhcpnak message.

5. The client system examines the dhcpack message for potential errors and transmits a dhcpdecline message if one is encountered. If the DHCP server does not receive a dhcpdecline message from the client system, the aforementioned binding process occurs. The duration of the lease and other pertinent information is contained in the dhcpack message.

6. If the client system wants to relinquish the lease, it issues a dhcprelease message to the issuing server. If a lease renewal is desired, the client system will inquire of its server's status halfway through the lease and periodically thereafter. At the end of the lease the request process begins anew.

Several relevant issues arise when using the DHCP protocol. For example, the client system seeking configuration information may be connected to a physically separate subnet from that of the DHCP server. For such a scenario, the router(s) can generally be configured to function as a DHCP relay agent between client and server. An even greater issue, however, is communication between DHCP and DNS servers. Communication of this nature would allow a client system to be fully recognized automatically and to be effortlessly transported throughout the network. Although provisions to develop such a system are defined in RFCs 2136 and 2137, very few currently exist.

2.6 Putting It All Together: An Example

The terms and concepts of the TCP/IP protocol are summarized by an explanation of the events depicted in Figure 2.11. In brief, the individual whose system IP address is $168.28.178.218_{(10)}$ seeks information from the Prentice Hall web site. The following sequence of TCP/IP events (designated by the letters a through j) occurs behind the scenes:

A. Prentice Hall's home page, www.prenhall.com, is requested by a web browser running on our client system; actually the web browser is the client to the web server program running on host $206.246.140.162_{(10)}$. Prior to requesting web pages, however, the remote web server's IP address must be obtained. The client system's resolver program, therefore, prepares a query to be transmitted to SPSU's name server. Utilizing the network's subnet mask $255.255.255.0_{(10)}$ and the name server's IP address $168.28.176.11_{(10)}$, the name server's location is determined to be on subnet $168.28.176.0_{(10)}$.

B. Scanning its routing table, the client system determines that the DNS query must be routed through the router port $168.28.178.1_{(10)}$ (referred to as the *default gateway*) to reach the name server's subnet. Prior to transmission of the frame (see section 2.2) from the client system to the router, the MAC (hardware) address of the specified router port must be retrieved and placed in the frame's destination MAC address field. This task is accomplished by one of two means: 1) The MAC address already exists in the client system's arp cache from a previous communication and is therefore readily extracted. 2) The MAC address is not within the arp cache and must be obtained via an arp broadcast containing the IP address $168.28.178.1_{(10)}$. Responding to the broadcast, the router transmits the appropriate MAC address to the client system.

C. MAC address in hand, the client system transmits the frame containing the DNS query to the router.

D. By use of a subnet mask and the provided destination IP address, the router determines the appropriate subnet, and therefore port, on which to route the query. Using its arp cache or a broadcast, the router determines the name server's MAC address, reframes the query, and transmits it through the port with IP address $168.28.176.1_{(10)}$.

E. The name server receives the query, resolves the provided hostname www.prenhall.com into IP address $206.246.140.162_{(10)}$, and issues a DNS reply to the client system.

F. The client system places the received IP address into the destination IP address field of a new frame. TCP is used as the transport protocol to establish a virtual connection to Prentice Hall's web server, and the SYN flag within the TCP header is set to indicate a requested TCP connection. The same basic methods of events A and B are used to successfully route the TCP/IP packet to the web server.

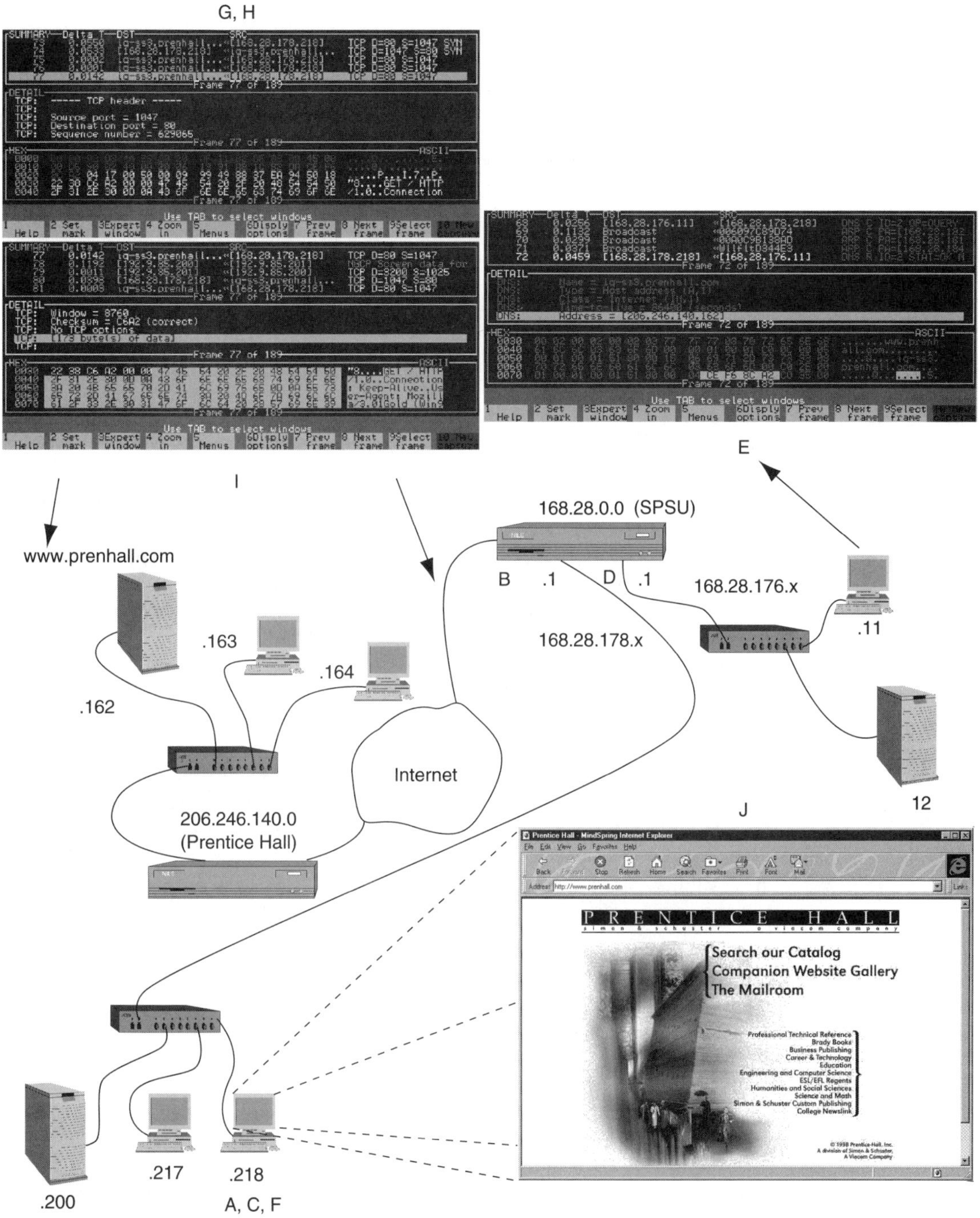

FIGURE 2.11

A typical transmission example.

G., H. The web server and client system establish a TCP connection for the transport of web page content via TCP port 80 (HTTP).

I. The client system requests the web page associated with the provided URL.

J. The content of the requested web page is transmitted from the web server to the client system where it is displayed. After transmission is completed, the TCP connection is released by the exchange of TCP packets with the FIN flag enabled.

2.7 Diagnostic Methods and Tools

There exists a small arsenal of diagnostic and configuration utilities for the administration of TCP/IP-based networks.

There exists a small arsenal of diagnostic and configuration utilities for the administration of TCP/IP-based networks. Operating systems that support the TCP/IP protocol suite generally possess unique subsets of this arsenal. The Unix operating system, in particular, possesses the greatest complement of these utilities, the syntax and usage of which are detailed in the Unix manual pages. The command man traceroute, for example, invokes the manual pages describing the traceroute utility. Several commented key utilities and their usage, inherent to the Unix operating system, are presented below:

Akin to sonar systems in submarines, the ping utility is used to transmit an ICMP echo request to a remote host and wait for a reply. If the host is alive and well, it issues an ICMP echo reply. Ping will merely indicate the remote host's network operational status. It cannot determine whether a particular service on the host, such as a web server, is functioning properly.

Common syntax of the ping utility is ping hostname [data bytes] [iterations]. The ICMP echo request consists of an ICMP header of eight bytes appended to the number of data bytes specified. The command ping localhost 64 5, for example, is used to verify the operational status of the TCP/IP protocol within the local system by issuing 5 echo requests of length 72 bytes each. The hostname localhost is referred to as TCP/IP's loopback driver; its address is always $127.0.0.1_{(10)}$. The default parameters for data bytes and iterations are 56 and continuously, respectively. A summary follows the list of ICMP echo replies.

```
tfallon [389] ping localhost 64 5
PING localhost.sct.edu: (127.0.0.1): 64 data bytes
72 bytes from 127.0.0.1: icmp_seq=0 ttl=255 time=0 ms
72 bytes from 127.0.0.1: icmp_seq=1 ttl=255 time=0 ms
72 bytes from 127.0.0.1: icmp_seq=2 ttl=255 time=0 ms
72 bytes from 127.0.0.1: icmp_seq=3 ttl=255 time=0 ms
72 bytes from 127.0.0.1: icmp_seq=4 ttl=255 time=0 ms

—localhost.sct.edu PING Statistics—
5 packets transmitted, 5 packets received, 0% packet loss
round-trip min/avg/max = 0/0/0 ms
```

By pinging the host www.prenhall.com, we discover that the average round-trip time for the transmission and reception of information between two hosts several hundred miles apart is a mere 42 thousandths of a second!

```
tfallon [391] ping www.prenhall.com 100 5
PING iq-ss3.prenhall.com: (206.246.140.162): 100 data bytes
108 bytes from 206.246.140.162: icmp_seq=0 ttl=241 time=47 ms
108 bytes from 206.246.140.162: icmp_seq=1 ttl=241 time=42 ms
108 bytes from 206.246.140.162: icmp_seq=2 ttl=241 time=41 ms
108 bytes from 206.246.140.162: icmp_seq=3 ttl=241 time=36 ms
108 bytes from 206.246.140.162: icmp_seq=4 ttl=241 time=45 ms

—iq-ss3.prenhall.com PING Statistics—
5 packets transmitted, 5 packets received, 0% packet loss
round-trip min/avg/max = 36/42/47 ms
```

If a remote host is not reachable via ping, the problem may lie within the route connecting the local and remote systems. Such problems are analyzed with the utility traceroute. By transmitting a UDP-transported IP packet, with the TTL field initialized to 1, traceroute causes the first router encountered along the route to decrement the TTL field to 0. Such an action requires the router to discard the expired packet and inform the local host, via an ICMP response, of the packet's demise. By continuously incrementing the TTL field by a value of 1, subsequent routers will discard each new packet and issue appropriate ICMP responses. From the responses received, the local host is able to determine the round-trip time of each successive probe, the address of each router encountered, and the number of hops to the remote host. By default, three separate packets per TTL value are transmitted; thus each traceroute sequence number (hop count) displays three separate delays.

```
tfallon [151] traceroute www.prenhall.com
traceroute to iq-ss3.prenhall.com (206.246.140.162), 30 hops
max, 40 byte packet

 1  168.28.176.1 (168.28.176.1)  2 ms  2 ms  2 ms
 2  131.144.208.37 (131.144.208.37)  6 ms  15 ms  6 ms
 3  GIT2.SPINE-1B.Link.Peach.NET (131.144.100.125)  20 ms  15
    ms  14 ms
 4  GIT1.SPINE-1A.Link.Peach.NET (131.144.100.113)  10 ms  9
    ms  8 ms
 5  Hssi3-1-0.GW2.ATL1.ALTER.NET (157.130.64.25)  10 ms  11 ms
    9 ms
 6  105.ATM2-0-0.XR2.ATL1.ALTER.NET (146.188.232.70)  19 ms
    11 ms  11 ms
 7  100.ATM10-0-0.TR2.ATL1.ALTER.NET (146.188.232.106)  10 ms
    10 ms  10 ms
 8  109.ATM6-0.TR2.CHI4.ALTER.NET (146.188.136.10)  36 ms  24
    ms  23 ms
 9  198.ATM7-0.XR2.CHI4.ALTER.NET (146.188.208.229)  23 ms  26
    ms  26 ms
10  194.ATM9-0-0.GW1.CHI1.ALTER.NET (146.188.208.157)  28 ms
    30 ms  25 ms
11  napnet-gw.customer.ALTER.NET (137.39.130.174)  28 ms  27
    ms  34 ms
12  NChicago1-core0.nap.net (207.112.247.153)  33 ms  26 ms
    27 ms
```

```
13   chi-f0.iquest.net (206.54.225.250)   30 ms   36 ms   32 ms
14   204.180.50.9 (204.180.50.9)   49 ms   38 ms   34 ms
15   iq-ss3.iquest.net (206.246.140.162)   45 ms   *   33 ms
```

The –n option instructs traceroute to print only the IP addresses of the nodes encountered.

```
tfallon [152] traceroute -n www.prenhall.com
traceroute to iq-ss3.prenhall.com (206.246.140.162), 30 hops
max, 40 byte packet
```

```
 1   168.28.176.1   5 ms   7 ms   2 ms
 2   131.144.208.37   9 ms   12 ms   12 ms
 3   131.144.100.125   16 ms   18 ms   20 ms
 4   131.144.100.113   15 ms   12 ms   15 ms
 5   157.130.64.25   18 ms   17 ms   15 ms
 6   146.188.232.70   15 ms   18 ms   17 ms
 7   146.188.232.106   18 ms   21 ms   24 ms
 8   146.188.136.10   30 ms   42 ms   40 ms
 9   146.188.208.229   28 ms   31 ms   40 ms
10   146.188.208.157   31 ms   28 ms   30 ms
11   137.39.130.174   33 ms   32 ms   31 ms
12   207.112.247.153   35 ms   32 ms   33 ms
13   206.54.225.250   35 ms   37 ms   31 ms
14   204.180.50.9   47 ms   42 ms   42 ms
15   206.246.140.162   40 ms   *   36 ms
```

The netstat utility gathers and displays network and interface statistics for the local host. A partial listing of the statistics produced by nestat, operating in default mode, indicates the status of the local host's active protocols, send and receive buffers, and the address of the remote host to which it is communicating.

```
tfallon [375] netstat
```

```
Active Internet connections
Proto    Recv-Q Send-Q  Local Address   Foreign Address
(state)
tcp      0      0        st6000.telnet   CSMIM1.11265          ESTABLISHED
tcp      0      0        st6000.3058     ncd6.SPSU.edu.6000    ESTABLISHED
tcp      0      0        st6000.2496     ncd15.SPSU.edu.6000   ESTABLISHED
tcp      0      0        st6000.2327     aurora.ncat.edu.smtp  ESTABLISHED
tcp      0      0        st6000.1294     199.95.207.73.80      FIN_WAIT_2
udp      0      0        st6000.1053     einstein.domain
```

The –i option instructs netstat to display the status of all operational interfaces. The interface designator, maximum transmission unit (MTU), associated address, and input and output error statistics are displayed.

```
tfallon [376] netstat -i
```

```
Name  Mtu     Network Address       Ipkts    Ierrs   Opkts     Oerrs Coll
lo0   16896                         107999   0       108316    0     0
lo0   16896   127 localhost         107999   0       108316    0     0
en0   1500    2.60.8c.2c.e6.4c      3951321  0       3374253   0     0
en0   1500    168.28.176  st6000    3951321  0       3374253   0     0
```

The –r option instructs netstat to display\ the routing table of the local host. The row with the destination entry default, for example, indicates that the local host's default gateway address is $168.28.176.1_{(10)}$. The interface is currently up and indeed a gateway (UG) is sustaining 50 active connections, it has forwarded 2,920,559 packets, and it is reached via the host's interface en0 (Ethernet adapter 0).

```
tfallon [377] netstat -r

Routing tables
Destination        Gateway            Flags    Refs    Use         Intf

default            168.28.176.1       UG       50      2920559     en0
127                localhost          U        2       4025        lo0
168.28.176         st6000             U        26      557096      en0
Netmasks:
255.0.0
255.255.255
```

The –p option instructs netstat to display statistics about the designated protocol.

```
tfallon [378] netstat -p ip
ip:
    :
        4058117 total packets received
        0 bad header checksums
        0 with size smaller than minimum
        0 with data size < data length
        0 with header length < data size
        0 with data length < header length
        0 with bad options
        0 with incorrect version number
        0 fragments received
        0 fragments dropped (dup or out of space)
        0 fragments dropped after timeout
        0 packets reassembled ok
        3761572 packets for this host
        0 packets for unknown/unsupported protocol
        0 packets forwarded
        296554 packets not forwardable
        0 redirects sent
        3481348 packets sent from this host
        462 packets sent with fabricated ip header
        0 output packets dropped due to no bufs, etc.
        0 output packets discarded due to no route
        0 output datagrams fragmented
        0 fragments created
        0 datagrams that can't be fragmented
        0 IP Multicast packets dropped due to no receiver
        0 ipintrq overflows
```

The ifconfig utility is used primarily to configure the TCP/IP parameters of a host's network interface. The syntax ifconfig interface displays configuration information.

```
tfallon [380] ifconfig en0
en0:
flags=8080863<UP,BROADCAST,NOTRAILERS,RUNNING,SIMPLEX,MULTICAST>
        inet 168.28.176.249 netmask 0xffffff00 broadcast 168.28.176.255
```

The route utility is used to examine and create routing table entries for the local host. Although route is found within the Unix operating system, the following screen capture was obtained using Microsoft's route print command because of the available print option.

```
C:/windows> route print

Active Routes:
```

Network Address	Netmask	Gateway Address	Interface	Metric
0.0.0.0	0.0.0.0	207.69.150.38	207.69.150.38	1
127.0.0.0	255.0.0.0	127.0.0.1	127.0.0.1	1
207.69.150.0	255.255.255.0	207.69.150.38	207.69.150.38	1
207.69.150.38	255.255.255.255	127.0.0.1	127.0.0.1	1
207.69.150.255	255.255.255.255	207.69.150.38	207.69.150.38	1
224.0.0.0	224.0.0.0	207.69.150.38	207.69.150.38	1
255.255.255.255	255.255.255.255	207.69.150.38	207.69.150.38	1

The arp utility is used to manipulate entries in the local host's arp cache. The syntax arp hostname issues an arp request to the designated host. The response contains the designated host's Ethernet address.

```
tfallon [381] arp einstein.spsu.edu
einstein.spsu.edu (168.28.176.11) at 8:0:5a:cd:87:f5 [ethernet]
```

The whois utility is used to search a whois database for specific user or network information. The default database searched resides on the host internic.net. Other whois databases generally service disparate regions of the globe. The syntax whois .lastname,firstname retrieves contact information about specific individuals. Obviously, some individuals are more famous than others!

```
tfallon [382] whois .fallon,tom

Fallon, Tom (TF2456)    janswowbow@PRODIGY.NET      516-254-6064
Fallon, Tom (TF2355)    tfallon@BRIGHTLINES.COM     724-457-0717
```

```
tfallon [383] whois .gates,bill

Gates, Bill (BG2028)    billg40@TIAC.NET       954-489-3981
Gates, Bill (BG4278)    i@WINSERVER.COM        +85-4512365
Gates, Bill (BG1341)    billg@CARROLL.COM      201-440-2558
Gates, Bill (BG2529)    ez@INAME.COM           03-6658-5541
Gates, Bill (BG3779)    billgates@MICROSOFT.COM 123-4567
```

The syntax whois *domain displays pertinent domain contact information.

```
tfallon [384] whois *spsu.edu

Registrant:
Southern Polytechnic State University (SPSU-DOM)
   1100 South Marietta Parkway
   Marietta, GA 30060-2896

   Domain Name: SPSU.EDU

   Administrative Contact:
      Murphy, Mike  (MM14189)  mmurphy@SPSU.EDU
      770-528-3440 (FAX) 770-528-3442
   Technical Contact, Zone Contact:
      Skopitz, Ron  (RS2098)  rskopitz@SCT.EDU
      770-528-7346
   Billing Contact:
      Thursby, Randall A  (RT870)
Randall_Thursby@OIT.PEACHNET.EDU
      (404) 656-6174 (FAX) (404) 657-6673

   Record last updated on 28-May-98.
   Record created on 13-Sep-96.
   Database last updated on 21-Jul-98 05:18:29 EDT.

   Domain servers in listed order:

   EINSTEIN.SCT.EDU        168.28.176.11
   NS.PEACH.NET            198.72.72.10
```

The finger utility is used to display login and other information pertaining to a specific individual or individuals associated with a specific host. The most common syntax used is finger account_name@FQDN, where FQDN is the fully qualified domain name.

```
tfallon [385] finger fallon@chara.gsu.edu
[chara.gsu.edu]

Thomas Fallon (fallon) is not presently logged in.
Last seen at hujer.chara.gsu.edu on Tue Jul 21 21:50:07 1998
```

```
tfallon [386] finger tfallon@st6000.sct.edu
[st6000.sct.edu]

Login name: tfallon                     In real life: Tom Fallon
Directory: /u/b/tfallon                     Shell: /bin/ksh
On since Jul 21 23:44:48 on pts/0
    from user-37kb5h6.dia
No Plan.
```

The syntax finger @FQDN displays current login information.

```
tfallon [387] finger @st6000.sct.edu
[st6000.sct.edu]
Login        Name               TTY Idle   When         Site
tfallon   Tom Fallon           p0          Tue 23:44
jware     Joshua Ware          p1          Tue 23:46
clee2     ChunTou Lee          p2   1      Tue 23:47
jwen      Jing Wen             p3          Tue 23:32
abamidel  Adebunmi Bamidele    p4   58     Tue 22:53
lbush     Lucien Bush          p5          Tue 23:31
cphan     Chinh Phan           p6          Tue 23:50
msapale   Mayur Sapale         p7          Tue 23:23
pgao      Pingze Gao          *p8   3      Tue 23:26
hedwards  Howard Edwards       p9          Tue 23:51
bbilz     Brian Bilz           p10         Tue 22:19
bpayton   B. Kelly Payton      p11  13     Tue 23:01
jlicata   Jon Licata           p13         Tue 22:26
tfallon [388] logout
```

2.8 Tracking a Packet through the Internet

Using the traceroute utility, we scrutinize the route that a packet might traverse from our local host to the host ftp.aarnet.edu.au located in Australia. Figure 2.12 depicts the addresses and approximate locations of key nodes (designated by the letters A through D) along the route, extracted from the following traceroute information:

A. Originating from the client system st6000.sct.edu, the successive probe packets reveal the route traversed within the Atlanta area. The first router encountered, $168.28.176.1_{(10)}$ (SPSU's default gateway port), connects the campus network to the greater Internet (see traceroute sequence number 1). Sequence number 2 defines the route segment from SPSU, via a high-speed telecommunications link (referred to as a *T1*) administered by the State of Georgia's Board of Regents regional network Peachnet, to the Georgia Institute of Technology (Georgia Tech). Located on the campus of Georgia Tech, two key routers (sequence

FIGURE 2.12

Tracking a packet through the Internet.

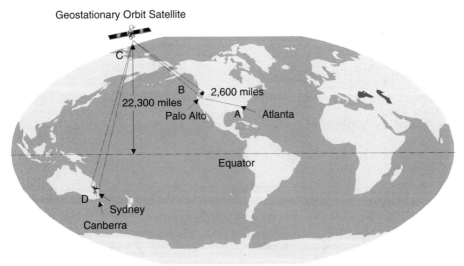

numbers 3 and 4) provide connectivity for Peachnet and Georgia Tech to BBN Planet, their ISP. It is interesting to note that the company Bolt, Beranek and Newman (the original ARPANET contractor) created the national ISP BBN Planet (currently GTE Internetworking).

B. The route segment represented by sequence numbers 5 through 11 consists of routers located within BBN Planet's Atlanta and Palo Alto (California) POPs (Point-of-Presence major connectivity sites) and the high-speed telecommunications link joining them. Examining the average delay of 110 ms from the client system to the farthest BBN Planet router (sequence number 11), one might reasonably assume that the link between the POPs probably consists of an optical fiber-based network technology (such as a T3). Satellite-based technologies generally impose a greater delay (for example, .250 for GEOs) and most long-haul networks within the U.S. use optical fiber-based technology.

C. Beginning with sequence number 12, the average delay increases dramatically. Although technically not between nodes, the marked increase can probably be attributed to the 250 ms delay incurred by communication via a geostationary satellite. Sequence number 13 reveals that the Australian ISP Telstra provides the route segment to the destination host, ftp.aarnet.edu.au.

D. Sequence numbers 13 through 18 define the elements constituting the final route segment. Traversing such network technologies as Fast Ethernet (13), a High-Speed Serial Interface (14), and a Fiber-Distributed Data Interface network (15), the UDP probe packets finally reach their destination, nico.telstra.net (18). ftp.aarnet.edu.au is, apparently, an alias for nico.telstra.net.

```
tfallon [169] traceroute ftp.aarnet.edu.au
traceroute to nico.telstra.net (139.130.204.16), 30 hops max,
40 byte packets

 1   168.28.176.1 (168.28.176.1)   2 ms   3 ms   3 ms
 2   131.144.208.37 (131.144.208.37)   6 ms   6 ms   6 ms
 3   GIT2.SPINE-1B.Link.Peach.NET (131.144.100.125)   7 ms   7 ms
     22 ms
 4   SURA.SURA-GIT.Link.Peach.NET (131.144.134.1)   22 ms   11 ms
     23 ms
 5   f1-0.atlanta2-br2.bbnplanet.net (4.0.2.90)   22 ms   42 ms
     16 ms
 6   h8-0-0.atlanta1-br1.bbnplanet.net (4.0.1.149)   19 ms   12
     ms   19 ms
 7   p1-0-0.atlanta1-br2.bbnplanet.net (4.0.1.170)   306 ms   274
     ms   210 ms
 8   h10-1-0.paloalto-br2.bbnplanet.net (4.0.1.197)   73 ms   77
     ms   *
 9   p2-0.paloalto-nbr2.bbnplanet.net (4.0.2.197)   115 ms   75
     ms   85 ms
10   p0-0-0.paloalto-cr18.bbnplanet.net (4.0.3.86)   75 ms   79
     ms   88 ms
11   h1-0.atteasylink.bbnplanet.net (131.119.26.126)   148 ms
     91 ms   92 ms
12   205.174.74.186 (205.174.74.186)   384 ms   627 ms   419 ms
13   FastEthernet0-0-0.pad-core3.Sydney.telstra.net
     (139.130.249.238)   400 ms   388 ms   400 ms
14   Hssi6-0-0.civ-core1.Canberra.telstra.net (139.130.249.34)
     403 ms   386 ms   388 ms
15   Fddi0-0.civ2.Canberra.telstra.net (139.130.235.227)   392
     ms   389 ms   413 ms
16   Serial2.dickson.Canberra.telstra.net (139.130.235.2)   492
     ms   388ms   417 ms
17   games1.telstra.net (139.130.204.242)   391 ms   396 ms   401
     ms
18   nico.telstra.net (139.130.204.16)   389 ms   396 ms   419 ms
```

2.9 SLIP versus PPP

Implemented by Rick Adams in 1984, SLIP (Serial Line IP) provided the first quasi-standard means for transporting IP packets over a serial line; SLIP was never drafted as an official Internet standard but is described in RFC 1055. SLIP is a lightweight framing protocol that is devoid of the traditional layer 2 fields such as packet type identification, error detection and correction, and addressing. Unlike other serial line protocols, SLIP offers no means of compression. Its function is merely to frame an IP packet (layers 3 through 7) for transmission across a point-to-point link.

The SLIP framing characters, ESC ($DB_{(16)}$) and END ($C0_{(16)}$), are appended to the beginning and end of the packet, respectively, thus enabling the receiver to distinguish one packet from another. Additional characters are appended to ESC and END in the event that the values $DB_{(16)}$ or $C0_{(16)}$ occur as data within the packet. By convention, the commonly accepted maximum packet size associated with SLIP is $1006_{(10)}$ bytes. SLIP provided the necessary host-to-host, host-to-router, and router-to-router connectivity via dedicated serial lines and analog dialup lines at a time when telecommunication solutions and bandwidth were in short supply. Today a veritable plethora of telecommunication solutions sporting considerably more bandwidth and more advanced layer 2 protocols have made SLIP obsolete.

Ubiquitous to Internet dialup services, PPP (Point-to-Point Protocol) has superseded SLIP. PPP, described in RFC 1661, was designed to transport multi-protocol packets over various types of point-to-point links. Three essential elements constitute PPP: multi-protocol encapsulation capabilities, a Link Control Protocol (LCP) automaton, and Network Control Protocols.

PPP encapsulation allows for the multiplexing of disparate network protocols such as IP, IPX, and Appletalk. Encapsulated (framed) packets consist of the following three fields:

Protocol: A one- or two-byte field identifying the protocol used within the packet.

Information: A field of dynamic length in which the transmitted packet resides. The maximum length of this field is 1,500 bytes.

Padding: A field of dynamic length used to pad the Information field with nondata, thus creating a packet of a certain minimal, but acceptable, length.

The LCP automaton is a program that reacts to events and initiates various actions. LCP's primary responsibilities include the establishment, configuration, maintenance, and termination of the link. The lifecycle of a typical PPP link consists of the following distinct phases:

Link Dead: No link is currently established or a previous link has been successfully terminated.

Link Establishment: The exchange of link configuration packets occurs to establish a connection across the point-to-point link.

Authentication: A nonmandatory phase that, when enabled, has provisions to authenticate the identity of the system seeking a connection.

Network Protocol: During this phase, NCPs are used to configure each individual network protocol. The successful execution of this phase allows for the transmission

SLIP provided the necessary host-to-host, host-to-router, and router-to-router connectivity via dedicated serial lines and analog dialup lines at a time when telecommunication solutions and bandwidth were in short supply.

and reception of PPP (LCP and NCP) and network protocol (for example IP) packets to begin.

Link Termination: Events such as loss of carrier, failed authentication, and administrative intervention trigger the LCP to terminate packets and close the link.

NCPs manage the configuration and support issues associated with their respective network protocols. Although capable of terminating the flow of packets associated with a particular network protocol, NCPs are not responsible for terminating a PPP link.

Summary

For successful communication to occur, several distinct addresses describing locations and services must be exchanged between the two or more communicating partners.

A protocol is the language that two or more computers use to communicate, and the set of rules and procedures governing the communication. In addition to protocols, the reliability and clarity of the transmission medium must be taken into account. For successful communication to occur, several distinct addresses describing locations and services must be exchanged between the two or more communicating partners. In our telephony-based scenario, we identified four distinct addresses: physical location, phone number, recipient, and topic or service. We discovered that the TCP/IP protocol suite also utilizes four distinct addresses: MAC (physical address), Network (IP) address, transport protocol, and port.

The OSI model is a seven-layer hierarchical model often used to depict the process flow between communicating nodes in a computer network. A dissection of the TCP/IP protocol suite reveals that several subprotocols within the suite are associated with layers 3 (Network layer) and 4 (Transport layer) of this model. TCP/IP applications such as FTP and Telnet are associated with layer 7 (Application layer).

Each subprotocol within the suite consists of several fields of unique information. We discovered that IP addresses, for example, are carried within two 32-bit fields, Source and Destination, of an IP header. Dissection of actual field values yielded the network address and host identifier information for both Source and Destination nodes.

DNS (Domain Name Service) is a global directory service that resolves symbolic host names into numerical IP addresses. Generally, a program associated with a client system, called a resolver, is responsible for issuing DNS queries on behalf of a client program. The client program, such as a web browser, utilizes the retrieved IP address to initiate communication with a server program on a host capable of providing the requested service. DHCP (Dynamic Host Control Protocol) is a subprotocol that leases IP addresses, generally for a fixed duration, to requesting hosts. DHCP servers bind the host's MAC address to the leased IP address in a database for record keeping and address management.

Several TCP/IP-based diagnostic and configuration utilities exist in operating systems that support TCP/IP. Traceroute, for example, provides the system operator with a means of analyzing the probable route traversed by IP packets transmitted from the local host. Whois is used to glean information pertaining to specific individuals or domains found throughout the Internet.

SLIP (Serial Line IP) and PPP (Point-to-Point Protocol) are protocols capable of delivering IP packets over point-to-point serial links and analog dialup circuits. Both protocols encapsulate the IP packets within layer 2 headers and trailers designed to transport information across serial links and analog dialup circuits.

Internet Connectivity: Fundamental Issues

Chapter Learning Objectives:

- Understand the basic elements of computer networking.
- Gain insight into the hierarchical structure of the Internet.
- Study file types and their impact on network performance.

Does the human brain possess some of the qualities of a modern personal computer or an entire network of computers? The answer is perhaps both; perhaps neither. We might be tempted to correlate the approximately $100,000,000,000_{(10)}$ nerve cells, or neurons, of the brain to a personal computer endowed with approximately $12,000,000,000_{(10)}$ bytes ($100,000,000,000$ bits) of RAM (Random Access Memory). We would be incorrect, however, because this correlation equates the fundamental cell of the brain, the neuron, to the fundamental cell of RAM, the bit.

The bit is a static entity containing either a 1 or a 0; it has no direct influence over other bits; and it is lifeless. By contrast, the neuron is a multi-state entity that directly influences other neurons, and is, of course, alive. The human brain network consists chiefly of neurons and the connections (synapses) between them. It is likely that as many as 10^{14} (100 trillion) synapses exist within the brain's three-pound mass. Within the synapse, complex electrical and chemical processes regulate the flow of information among neurons. The key to understanding the higher-order processes of the human brain (intelligence, memory, emotions, etc.) is presumed to lie within the understanding of the synaptic junction. The synaptic junction of the human brain is akin to the internetworking devices found in a modern computer network.

3.1 A Network Primer

A computer
network is the
infrastructure
necessary for the
transportation of
information
between two or
more computer
systems.

A *computer network* is the infrastructure necessary for the transportation of information between two or more computer systems. Typically, a system is physically connected to a network via a device generically called an *adapter card* (see Figure 3.1). The adapter interfaces the system's data bus, or internal communications pathway, to a communications network. Adapter cards, in turn, communicate with specific system software components (communication protocols and operating system) via a program known as a *driver*. A driver is analogous to the chain of a bicycle. In its absence the energy exerted by the rider moving the pedals is not translated to the gears that drive the tires, and hence the bicycle. Without the proper driver, a system cannot utilize the functions provided by the adapter card.

FIGURE 3.1

A conceptual view of computer networking.

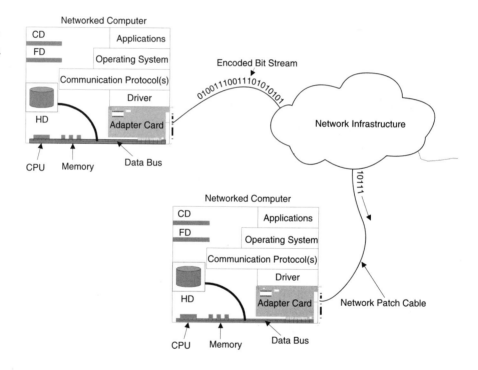

Communication protocols, such as TCP/IP, are associated with drivers of various adapter card technologies via a process known as *binding*. Information received by the communications protocol from a network application, such as a web browser, is transmitted to an adapter card's driver. Conversely, information received from the network by the adapter card is passed to the communication protocol via the driver. Operating systems play a vital role in the successful transmission and reception of information among networked computer systems. They are responsible for the management of system resources allocated to various input/output (I/O) devices (such as adapter cards and disk drives) and the usage of these devices and their drivers by applications dependent on them.

In Figure 2.2 we saw that the OSI model depicts, in a hierarchical manner, the various components required for communications among networked systems. We were predominantly concerned with layers 3 and 4 and their association with TCP/IP. How do IP packets traverse the multitude of disparate network technologies that constitute the Internet? For example, consider an e-mail message transmitted from one part of the globe to another several thousand miles away. The technologies used to transport the message are not entirely the same from source to destination. The different layers of the OSI model are capable of exchanging information with each other, while remaining functionally independent. Put another way, IP packets could traverse a network consisting of tin cans and string, provided the network accepts the format of information contained within the IP packet.

LAN, MAN, and WAN

Networking technologies are associated with layers 1, 2, and 3 of the OSI model. In terms of speed, they cover a spectrum ranging from relatively slow dialup connections to ultra high-speed optical fiber-based systems. Networks consisting of these technologies span geographic areas as small as a few feet, as large as the globe, and everything in between. These networks are generally categorized as either *LAN* (Local Area Network), *MAN* (Metropolitan Area Network), or *WAN* (Wide Area Network). LANs are generally small in geographic coverage, for example, a building or a campus, are owned by a single entity, and possess great amounts of bandwidth. Typical LAN technologies include Ethernet, Token Ring, and FDDI (Fiber-Distributed Data Interface). MANs are generally designed to span either part or all of a metropolitan area, are owned by a public utility, and possess a moderate to great amount of bandwidth. Typical MAN technologies include SONET/SDH (Synchronous Optical Network/Synchronous Digital Hierarchy) and ATM (Asynchronous Transfer Mode). WANs are used in the interconnection of LANs, MANs, regional networks, countries, and continents; are owned by communication carriers; and possess a moderate to great amount of bandwidth. Typical WAN technologies include Frame Relay, dedicated point-to-point links (such as T1 or T3), and VSAT (Very Small Aperture Terminal) satellite services.

A/D and PCM

Several additional terms and concepts crucial to the understanding of computer networking include analog-to-digital conversion (A/D), pulse code modulation (PCM), synchronous versus asynchronous transmission, multiplexing, compression, network topologies, virtual circuit versus circuit switched versus datagram, internetworking devices, and client/server versus peer-to-peer technologies. In the sections that follow we will investigate these concepts in detail.

In this Digital Age all manner of sensory input is digitized. Whether a high-resolution image of a butterfly, a concert recording of Elton John, or the tactile pressure exerted on the flight controls by a fighter pilot, real-world *(analog)* signals must first be digitized before they can be manipulated and transported within a computer and over a network. This process is referred to as *analog-to-digital conversion* (A/D).

A/D is carried out via the following steps (see Figure 3.2):

1. The desired analog signal is recorded with the appropriate sensor (for example, a microphone, camera, or pressure sensor).

2. The amplitude (height) of the recorded signal is sampled at a predetermined rate called the *sampling rate,* T_s. This *sampling* process can be envisioned by multiplying the recorded signal by an impulse train (infinite series of pulses). Each impulse of the train has a height of 1 and a width of 0, theoretically. When an individual impulse is multiplied with its corresponding temporal slice of the signal, a new impulse possessing the slice's amplitude is generated. By multiplying the entire impulse train by the recorded signal, we obtain a new impulse train (sampled analog signal) akin to the original signal. Pertaining to sampling, the *Nyquist Theorem* tells us that the sampling rate, T_s, must be at least twice that of the highest frequency component of our analog signal. For example, if our signal possesses a 1 kHz component, then to fully capture the information contained within the signal, we must sample it 2,000 times per second.

3. Via the process known as *quantization,* the height of each impulse of the sampled analog signal is assigned to a discrete level (quanta). The resolution (accuracy) of

FIGURE 3.2

Analog-to-digital conversion and PCM.

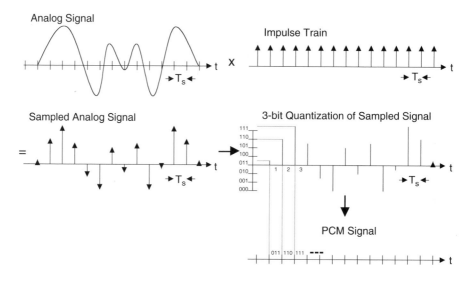

each assignment depends on the number of available levels. For example, if all of the impulse heights were measured against a scale with only 4 (2-bit resolution ~ 2^2) tick marks, the resolution of our measurement would be only half that of one taken with a scale possessing 8 (3-bit resolution ~ 2^3) tick marks. Figure 3.2 shows the first three impulses quantized.

4. Note the degradation in resolution resulting from the quantization of the first and third impulses. The first impulse, for example, is *encoded* as the binary value $011_{(2)}$. Its height, however, is slightly greater than this value. The entire process of sampling, quantization, and encoding is a special form of A/D known as *PCM* pulse code modulation). The resulting PCM bitstream is suitable for use within a computer or over a network. A device that creates a PCM bitstream from an analog signal and vice versa is known as a *CODEC* (coder and decoder).

Synchronous versus Asynchronous

Whether related to the pulsing of the human heart or the reception of signals from a remote space probe, virtually all aspects of nature depend upon timing. In computer networking jargon, we categorize timing as either *asynchronous* or *synchronous* (see Figure 3.3). In asynchronous communications, timing information is not transported with the data. Such systems rely on the use of start and stop bits to indicate to the destination system where the block of data begins and where it ends. Blocks in an asynchronous system are generally characters transmitted via a common encoding scheme such as ASCII (American Standard Code for Information Interchange). Dialup connections using modems, for example, operate in an asynchronous mode. As bursts of information traverse the phone line between your home and the remote system to which you are communicating, the receiving modem waits until it "hears" the start bit indicating the arrival of the new block of data. The receiving modem extracts data from the block by examining the rate at which bits within the block change from one state to another, synchronizing its circuitry to this rate, and sampling the incoming bitstream.

In synchronous communications, synchronization between source and destination systems is achieved by providing clocking within the bitstream, synchronization characters (or flags) that surround the block of data, or a synchronization bit that continuously separates blocks of data. Real-world examples of each method follow. Manchester (Ethernet) and Differential Manchester encoding (Token Ring) employ the use of level changes (high to low or vice versa) in the middle of each transmitted bit to provide clocking information to the receiver of the destination system. HDLC (High-level Data Link Control) and DDCMP (Digital Data Communications Message Protocol) employ the use of synchronization characters to enable the receiver of the destination system to "sync-lock" with the incoming bitstream. A T1 carrier employs the use of a synchronization bit to separate blocks, or frames, that are 192 bits in length. Within this 192-bit block, data occupies one of 24 possible positions known as *time slots*.

FIGURE 3.3

Synchronous versus asynchronous.

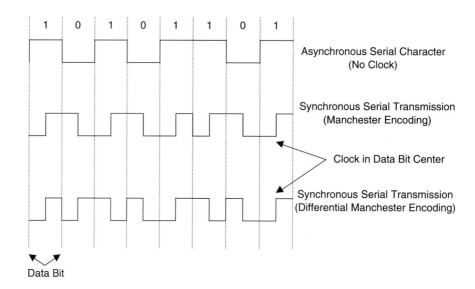

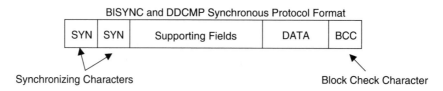

BISYNC and DDCMP Synchronous Protocol Format

| SYN | SYN | Supporting Fields | DATA | BCC |

Synchronizing Characters   Block Check Character

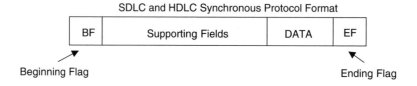

SDLC and HDLC Synchronous Protocol Format

| BF | Supporting Fields | DATA | EF |

Beginning Flag   Ending Flag

Multiplexing

Multiplexing is the process of selectively combining the input from several different source systems onto a single communications channel. The various multiplexing schemes are defined as follows. Of these, TDM and FDM are referred to in subsequent sections and are, therefore, depicted in Figure 3.4. Table 3.1 lists several of the U.S. multiplexing standards that are based predominant on wired pair and fiber-optic media.

   TDM (Time Division Multiplexing): A multiplexing scheme that temporally segregates data traffic originating from distinct sources by using time slots. Information from source 1 is inserted into time slot 1 upon transmission and is extracted from

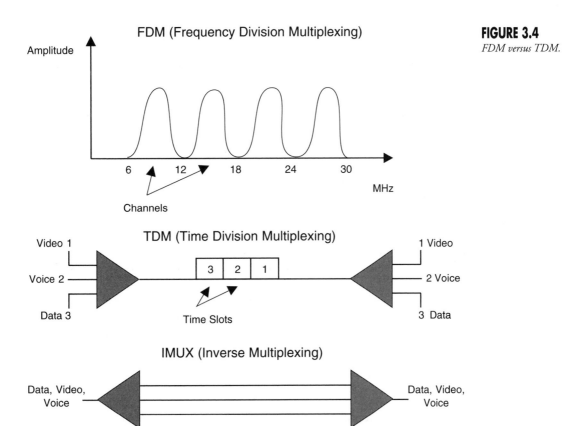

FIGURE 3.4

FDM versus TDM.

Table 3.1 U.S. Multiplexing Standards

Digital Signal	Voice Circuits	bps
DS0	1	64K
FT1	N	64K–768K
DS1 (T1)	24	1.544M
DS2	96	6.312M
DS3 (T3)	672	44.736M
DS4	4,032	274.176M

Optical Carrier	Optical Circuits	bps
OC1	1	51.84M
OC3	3	155.52M
OC12	12	622.08M
OC48	48	2.488G

time slot 1 upon reception. Information from all other sources is transported in the same manner according to its respective time slot. The term *clear channel* is used to describe data traffic originating from a single source, such as a LAN, that occupies all of the available time slots.

A T1 carrier is an example of a technology that uses TDM for the transportation of information. Such systems multiplex the input from twenty-four 8-bit PCM-encoded signals (24 time slots). The transmission frame comprising the 24 time slots is, therefore, $8 \times 24 = 192$ bits in length. A synchronization bit is added to the end of each frame, bringing the total number of bits to 193. Each of the 24 time slots is capable of carrying digitized voice (or data) and therefore, per the Nyquist Theorem, requires the predefined sampling rate of 8,000 samples per second. In other words, a T1 carrier has a capacity of $8,000 \times 193 = 1.544$ Mbps. In Europe, the standard is the E1, which has a capacity of 2.048 Mbps.

STM (Statistical Multiplexing): Akin to TDM, STM also temporally segregates data traffic originating from distinct sources by using time slots. However, data is not sampled from each source in the same round-robin fashion used by TDM. Sources that provide data to the multiplexor more rapidly, such as a video feed, are allocated more time slots. This system, in effect, provides high-speed sources with more band-width than low-speed sources. By exploiting the dynamic, and therefore highly sta-tistical, nature of data traffic, STM is capable of multiplexing an aggregate input bandwidth that exceeds the bandwidth of the single output channel.

FDM (Frequency Division Multiplexing): A multiplexing scheme that spectrally segre-gates data traffic originating from distinct sources by using separate frequency chan-nels. Information from source 1 is modulated onto channel 1 upon transmission and is demodulated from channel 1 upon reception. Information from all other sources is transported in the same manner according to its respective channel. Unlike TDM time slots, FDM channels propagate and are therefore received simultaneously at the destination. CATV (cable television), for example, uses FDM for the transport of information. Recipients of CATV services extract information from the system by tuning their television receiver to the proper channel. FDM can also be used to transport digital data via a device known as a *cable modem.*

WDM (Wavelength Division Multiplexing): Akin to FDM, WDM is a fiberoptic-based multiplexing scheme that spectrally segregates data traffic originating from distinct sources by using separate wavelengths of light. Information from source 1 is modulated onto wavelength 1 upon transmission and is demodulated from wave-length 1 upon reception. Information from all other sources is transported in the same manner according to its assigned wavelength.

SDM (Space Division Multiplexing): A multiplexing scheme that physically segregates data traffic originating from distinct sources by using separate physical channels. An underground telephone trunk cable, for example, is used to transport data across several distinct physical channels that are contained within a common sheath.

Compression

Similar to rush-hour traffic on a highway system, excessive data traffic traversing a communication system causes undesirable delays in transmission and reception times between end nodes. *Compression* is a common means by which such delays can be alleviated. Data is compressed upon transmission to minimize its bandwidth requirements and expanded upon reception to its original state. The ratio of the size, in bytes, of the data to be transmitted before and after compression is referred to as the *compression ratio*. For example, a file that is originally 1,000,000 bytes in size that is compressed to 250,000 bytes exhibits a 1,000,000/250,000 = 4/1, or 4:1, compression ratio. Compression techniques are associated with the A/D process, data storage/retrieval (on local computer systems), and data transportation.

Certain analog signals, such as speech, exhibit nonlinear behavior. The amplitude of a particular signal may, for example, possess a large dynamic range. As a consequence, the amplitude of certain portions of the signal may fall within the quantization range of the A/D converter, whereas others may not. If we compress the signal, prior to quantization, in a nonlinear manner that mimics the inverse of the original signal (that is, small amplitudes are amplified and large ones are attenuated), then all portions of the compressed signal fall within the quantization range of the A/D converter. The process of using such nonlinear schemes to compress and expand signals is known as *companding*. Examples of companding include *A-Law* and *µ–Law*.

Several compression schemes have been designed for the more efficient storage/retrieval and transportation of data. The algorithms on which these schemes are based either eliminate types of data not required to fully reproduce the original information, replace recurrent strings of data or individual characters with special codes (tokens), or combine the two in some hybrid fashion. The *JPEG* (Joint Photographic Experts Group) file format, for example, uses a compression scheme that eliminates visual information from static graphical files that would otherwise be imperceptible by the human eye. In the transportation of data, however, practical compression schemes replace recurrent strings of data, within the bitstream, with tokens.

One popular compression algorithm used in computer networking is called the *Lempel-Ziv algorithm*. It uses the aforementioned method of tokens. A dictionary of the known tokens is stored within the source and destination systems. The source system uses the token dictionary to compress the data prior to transmission, and the destination system uses a synchronized copy of the dictionary to expand the data upon reception. For example, a dictionary used with the phrase "the dog on the log was lost in the fog" might contain the entries: "the" = 1, "og" = 2, etc. Of course, the phrase and dictionary would exist in a binary format. Another such popular, yet older, compression algorithm is called *Huffman encoding*. Unlike the Lempel-Ziv algorithm, Huffman encoding exploits the statistical independence of characters within a language, such as English, to create a token dictionary that is consists of variable-length entries. For example, the letter "e" occurs more frequently than the letter "z" and would therefore be assigned a token containing fewer bits.

Network Topologies

A computer network's *topology* describes the logical manner in which its systems are linked together. Data traffic flows between end nodes in accordance with the topological layout of the network. The five popular network topologies—bus, ring, star, tree, and mesh—are defined as follows (see Figure 3.5).

Bus: A topology based on a shared medium in which all end nodes simultaneously receive transmitted information. Access to the medium is governed by a stochastic process that requires that only one end node may transmit at a time. Simultaneous transmission by multiple end nodes results in an error condition referred to as a *collision.* Ethernet technology is based on a bus topology.

Ring: A topology based on a system of repeaters, the interconnection of which forms a closed loop. Access to the system is governed by a deterministic process that requires that only one end node may transmit and receive at a time. Information within the system flows from one node to the next as it traverses the loop. Nodes are said to have upstream and downstream neighbors. Token Ring technology is based on a ring topology.

FIGURE 3.5

Network topologies.

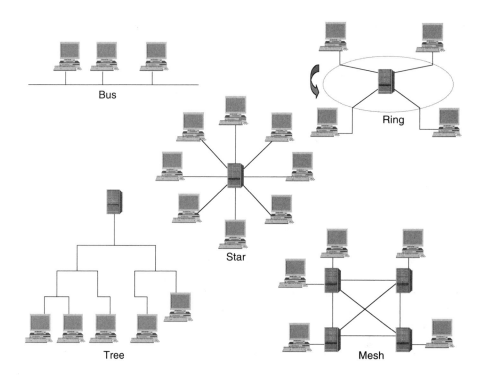

Star: A topology based on a system of repeaters, the interconnection of which forms a star. Repeaters are said to be either active or passive. Communication between end nodes within the system is controlled through a central active repeater. Passive repeaters allow for the interconnection of additional nodes. Arcnet technology is based on a star topology.

Tree: A topology similar in nature to the bus topology that consists of a trunk and several branches. The length of the trunk is extended, and all branches are interconnected to the trunk via repeaters. The *root* of the tree is referred to as the *headend.* CATV technology is based on a tree topology that can be modified to support digital data.

Mesh: A topology based on a system of switches that are interconnected via point-to-point links. Switches are said to route data from one point to the next. The route traversed by data may change as conditions warrant. Frame Relay is based upon a mesh topology.

Switching

Historically, wide area networks have used switching techniques to route data from source to destination. The telephone system, for example, is based on a technique known as *circuit switching.* To accommodate nonvoice types of data, a technique known as *packet switching* was developed. Recently, switching techniques have pervaded the realms of metropolitan and local area networks. Packet switching techniques are categorized as either datagram or virtual circuit. Two additional switching techniques are matrix and multi-rate circuit switching. Matrix switching is a form of SDM based on inputs arranged in a matrix fashion, whereas multi-rate circuit switching is essentially a TDM version of circuit switching. A detailed description of each technique follows.

Circuit Switching: A data switching technique that employs the use of a dedicated communication pathway between end nodes. Three phases are involved in the transmission and reception of data across a circuit switched network: connection establishment, data transfer, and connection termination. Prior to transmission, a dedicated pathway is established between the two communicating nodes via a process known as *signaling.* Once the connection is established, data flows freely between the nodes. When the exchange of data is complete, the two nodes again use signaling to terminate the connection. Data traverses a circuit switched network with a constant bit rate.

Packet Switching: A data switching technique in which information, carried within the header of the data packet, is used by the switching node for routing purposes (see Figure 3.6). Because each switching node encountered en route to the destination node must process this header information, a small storage and processing latency is introduced per node. In the datagram method of packet switching, each packet traverses the network independent of all preceding or subsequent packets and therefore may be routed along different paths between the source and destination nodes. These independent packets are referred to as *datagrams,* and this method of

FIGURE 3.6

Packet switching.

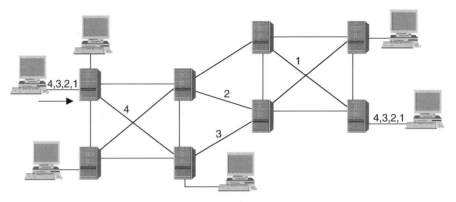

Packet Switching—Datagram

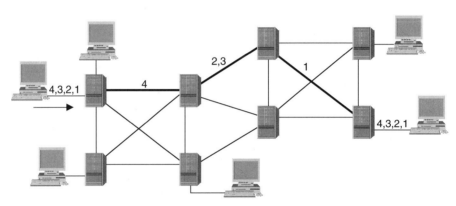

Packet Switching—Virtual Circuit

switching is known as *connectionless.* In the virtual circuit method of packet switching, each related packet traverses the network via the same path. Because the path must be established for the transmission of data, signaling packets must be used to establish and terminate the virtual circuit. Path identification information is included in the header of each packet to be transmitted. This method of packet switching is known as *connection-oriented.* Data traverses a packet switched network with a variable bit rate. The Internet is predominantly a packet switching-based network.

Matrix Switching: A data switching technique in which information is switched between end nodes via physically separate channels. Source and destination ports are connected as the rows and columns of a matrix. Data is switched to a specific port by examining MAC address (OSI model layer 2) information contained within the header of the data frame. Nonparticipating ports will not "hear" the data conveyed between the source and destination nodes. An Etherswitch is based on matrix switching.

Multi-rate Circuit Switching: Akin to circuit switching, multi-rate circuit switching multiplexes different circuit switched channels into one high-capacity channel. Individual channels can be used for simultaneous communication with distinct destination nodes, or channels can be joined together to provide greater bandwidth, hence multi-rate, for specific communication requirements. ISDN is based on multi-rate circuit switching.

Internetworking Devices

Technologies that interconnect similar and/or disparate networking technologies include *repeaters*, *bridges*, *routers*, and *gateways*. The first three are depicted in Figure 3.7. Each of these internetworking technologies provides its own particular type of service, but is often used in conjunction with other internetworking technologies in the implementation of network infrastructures. A *concentrator* is a device that allows for the concentration of several different network technologies within a common chassis. A *hub* generally describes a chassis populated with several ports of one particular network technology. Descriptions of each device follow.

Repeater: An internetworking device used to extend the span of a LAN by interconnecting multiple segments. Data received via any port connected to a particular segment is regenerated and repeated to every other port, and hence, segment. Repeaters are associated with layer 1 of the OSI model and therefore are capable of

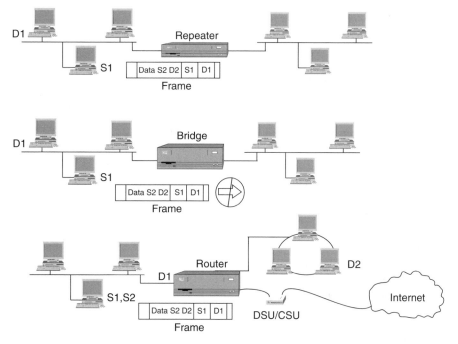

FIGURE 3.7

Internetworking devices.

interconnecting different types of media, such as coaxial and twisted pair cables. They cannot, however, interconnect disparate networking technologies, such as Ethernet and Token Ring. Recall that networking technologies are primarily associated with layer 2 of the OSI model. In Figure 3.7 we see that the repeater interconnects two network segments of a bus topology based network (depicted with horizontal lines). Computer S1 (source MAC address) transmits a frame to computer D1 (destination MAC address). Although computers attached to the right-hand segment are not involved in the communication between S1 and D1, they do nonetheless "hear" the repeated frame. In other words, data traffic from the left-hand segment utilizes available bandwidth of the right-hand segment and vice versa.

Bridge: An internetworking device used to extend the span of a LAN and segregate data traffic between its segments. Data received via any port connected to a particular segment is examined to determine the frame's destination MAC address. If the address indicates that the frame is destined for a computer associated with another port, then the frame is regenerated and transmitted accordingly. If, however, the frame is intended for a computer residing on the same segment as the source computer, the bridge discards the frame. Bridges are associated with layer 2 of the OSI model and therefore cannot interconnect disparate networking technologies. They are, however, more "intelligent" than repeaters. In Figure 3.7 we see that the bridge also interconnects two network segments of a bus topology-based network. Unlike the scenario with the repeater, however, the right-hand segment does not "hear" the transmitted frame.

Router: An internetworking device used to extend the span of a network (LAN, MAN, or WAN), segregate data traffic between segments, interconnect disparate networking technologies, create a hierarchy of subnetworks (subnets), and provide some measure of security. Data received via any port connected to a particular segment is examined to determine the packet's destination network address. Recall that the process of internetworking is associated with layer 3 of the OSI model and that data output from this layer is called a packet. If the address indicates that packet is destined for a computer associated with another network or subnet, then the packet is regenerated and routed accordingly. Therefore, routers are more "intelligent" than bridges.

In Figure 3.7 we see that the router interconnects bus and ring topology-based networks and a high-speed TDM-based T1 link to the Internet. In this scenario, the computer S1, S2 (MAC, network address) is transmitting data to computer D2 (destination network address). The framing headers for the bus topology-based network, however, are incompatible with those of the ring topology-based network. Therefore, router port D1 (MAC address) represents the furthest point on the bus topology-based network, with similar framing headers, that the transmitted frame can traverse en route to the destination computer D2. The frame is, therefore, sent to router port D1. The router receives the frame, strips off the framing header (S1, D1), examines the network header (S2, D2) to determine the destination network address, reframes the packet with a framing header appropriate to the ring network, and routes the new frame through the router ring network port.

Gateway: A computer customized to provide protocol translation for any and all layers of the OSI model. For example, a gateway can simultaneously connect to disparate media types through multiple network adapters (layer 1), translate between different network protocols (layer 3) such as TCP/IP and IPX/SPX, and translate between different e-mail programs (layer 7). Gateway is not a clear term. Earlier routers were called gateways. In fact, routing protocols used throughout the Internet are often named, in part, with the term "gateway." The router port through which LAN data traffic passes en route to the Internet is also called the gateway.

3.2 Understanding Bandwidth and Capacity

The *bandwidth* of a communications system is the width of the band of frequencies assigned to the system. For example, standard voice-grade telephone lines pass frequencies in the range of 300 Hz to 3,400 Hz. The corresponding bandwidth for these circuits is, therefore, 3,400 Hz – 300 Hz = 3,100 Hz. Unlike bandwidth, *capacity* is the true measure of a system's ability to transport data. Capacity is measured in bits per second, or bps. The two terms, bandwidth and capacity, are often incorrectly substituted for one another. The capacity of a communication system can be calculated using the following formula known as *Shannon's Channel Capacity Theorem*:

$$C = B \log_2(1 + S/N)$$

The formula states that the capacity, C (in bps), of a communication channel is equal to the channel's bandwidth, B, times the log base 2 of 1 plus the channel's *signal-to-noise ratio,* S/N. All communication systems possess some form of noise. When the power of the transmitted signal is very weak and therefore close to the "noise floor" of the channel, the signal-to-noise ratio is said to be very low. S/N can be calculated as follows:

$$S/N = 10 \log_{10}(\text{signal power/noise power})$$

The formula states that the S/N, measured in decibels (dB), of a communication channel is equal to 10 times the log base 10 of the ratio of signal-to-noise power. For example, a standard voice-grade telephone line has an S/N equal to 24 dB. Inserting 24 dB into the left-hand side of the equation and working backwards, we calculate the ratio of signal-to-noise power as being equal to 251. In other words, the power of the signal is 251 times greater than the power of the noise. The capacity of this line is C = 3,100 $\log_2$(1 + 251) = 24,738 bps.

The effect of a channel's capacity on data transmission time, service time, is illustrated in Figure 3.8. The service time for several different forms of media is calculated using the capacity of a standard TDM-based DS0. The first entry, for example, shows the service time for a 25-KB text file. By dividing the file size, in bits, by the channel capacity, in bps, we arrive at a service time of 3.125 seconds. The sixth entry, however, has considerably more bits to transmit. One second of uncompressed, color, full-motion video at 15

The *bandwidth* of a communications system is the width of the band of frequencies assigned to the system.

Unlike bandwidth, *capacity* is the true measure of a system's ability to transport data.

FIGURE 3.8

Channel capacity (DS0) versus service time.

- 25 KB Text File = 200,000 bits/64,000 bps = 3.125 seconds
- 3 MB Application = 24,000,00 bits/64,000 bps = 375 seconds
- 1 second of Digital Voice = 64,000 bits/64,000 bps = 1 second
- 1 second of Uncompressed CD Quality Sound = 352,800 bits/64,000 bps = 5.5725 seconds
- Uncompressed 200x200x24 Color Image = 960,000 bits/64,000 bps = 15 seconds
- 1 second of Uncompressed 200x200x24 Color Full-Motion Video at 15 fps = 14,400,000 bits/64,000 bps = 225 seconds
- 1 second of Uncompressed Multimedia = Full-Motion Video + CD-Quality Sound = 230.513 seconds

* Information is uncompressed
**1KB = 1024 bytes, 1MB = (1024)^2 bytes

frames per second, fps, contains 200 pixels (picture elements) $\times$ 200 pixels $\times$ 24 color bits per pixel $\times$15 fps equals approximately 14,400,000 bits and requires a service time of 225 seconds.

Queuing theory enables us to determine if the capacity of a communications channel is sufficient for a given network design. As our model we choose a standard TDM-based T1 telecommunication link that connects, via routers, two bus-type networks (see Figure 3.9). The average frame size, in bytes, that traverses this particular link will be 1,000 bytes, therefore, the average service time is equal to 8,000 bits (1,000 bytes/frame $\times$ 8 bits/byte) divided by 1,536,000 bits per second = .0052 seconds per frame. Note the data-carrying capacity of a T1 is equal to the total 1,544,000 bps – 8,000 bps for timing. The average rate at which either router can service these frames is equal to the reciprocal of the average service time = 1/.0052 = 192 frames per second. Both sides of the link, however, do not experience the average service time. Data transmitted from the left-hand network (typically greater capacity) onto the link (typically less capacity), via the router, experiences a decrease in channel capacity and therefore may be delayed in a queue.

Assuming that an average of 50 frames per second is received by the left-hand router, average arrival rate, the percent utilization of the router, P_{util}, can be calculated as P_{util} = average arrival rate/average service rate = 50/192 = .26 = 26 percent. In other words, the router is idle 74 percent of the time, which indicates that the T1 link is more than sufficient to handle the average capacity requirements for our model network. Using protocol analyzers, RMON (remote monitoring) devices, and statistics logged by routers, actual channel capacity assessments can be calculated.

It is expected that the amount of data traffic traversing the links of the Internet will increase several thousand-fold, and perhaps much more, over the next decade. The capacities of these links will, therefore, also have to increase dramatically. Competition among the telecommunication giants to create more bandwidth is already increasing and should

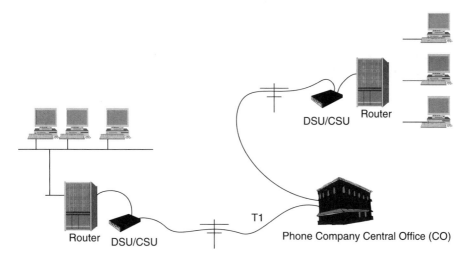

FIGURE 3.9
Queuing theory model.

continue to increase. A great deal of emphasis, however, is being placed on so-called *backbone technologies* as opposed to *access technologies*. Although nascent access technologies, such as xDSL (Digital Subscriber Loop) and cable modems, promise to provide the user with considerably higher access rates, a quantum leap in access will not be realized, perhaps, until optical fibers replace, or augment, the copper running to our homes.

3.3 Understanding File Types

It is important to understand the basic characteristics of certain types of files that might be received via the Internet. Hierarchically, text files consume the least amount of bandwidth, whereas video files consume the most. Audio files fall somewhere in the middle. Other characteristics are also important. Real-time audio and video, for example, should be transmitted and received at a constant bit rate in order to be presented smoothly to the recipient. The Internet, however, is based predominantly on variable bit-rate technologies and therefore exacerbates the burden of queuing and processing of this information on the receiving computer.

Some files are a combination of different media, multimedia, and therefore, may require the installation of a special viewer or player application on the receiving computer. The type of file can generally be identified by its file extension. Modern applications use this extension to look up the file's *MIME* (Multipurpose Internet Mail Extension) type, which, in turn, indicates the proper viewer or player to be used. MIME (RFCs 1521 and 1522) evolved from the need to exchange multimedia information using standard e-mail protocols. Such protocols transport messages in the 7-bit ASCII format. Multimedia files, however, are not ASCII encoded and therefore require a separate encoding and identification scheme. MIME classifies files in types and subtypes. For example, the

Some files are a combination of different media, multimedia, and therefore, may require the installation of a special viewer or player application on the receiving computer.

MIME type for a web page is text/html. Several popular file and MIME types that one might encounter via the Internet are described below.

HTML (Hypertext Markup Language uses text/html): A content-based markup language derived from SGML (Standard Generalized Markup Language) that allows the author to apply special tags to a text document in order for it to be properly rendered by a web browser (see Chapter 5). HTML documents are referred to as *web pages.* The content of a web page can include several different elements such as text, graphics, audio, motion video, hyperlinks, Java applets, and Javascripts.

GIF (Graphics Interchange Format uses image/GIF): A bitmapped file format developed and copyrighted by Compuserve used widely throughout the World Wide Web. The color resolution of a GIF image is 8 bits per pixel, $2^8 = 256$. In other words, each pixel constituting a GIF image can be one of 256 different colors. A special type of GIF file, GIF89a, allows images to be transparent (relative to their background) and animated.

PNG (Portable Network Graphics uses image/PNG): A highly efficient bitmapped file format developed in response to copyright issues related to Compuserve's GIF file format. It is expected that PNG will grow in popularity on the web.

JPEG (Joint Photographic Experts Group uses image/JPEG): A bitmapped file format used widely throughout the World Wide Web. The color resolution of a GIF image is 24 bits per pixel, $2^{24} = 16,777,216$. In other words, each pixel constituting a GIF image can be one of 16,777,216 different colors. The algorithm on which JPEG is based uses a compression technique that excludes visual information that is imperceptible to the human eye.

TIFF (Tagged Image File Format uses image/TIFF): A desktop publishing and scanner file format developed by Microsoft and Aldus. Web browsers do not currently support this format, although many external viewers do.

PDF (Portable Document Format uses application/PDF): An Adobe Acrobat document format that contains all of the actual elements that constitute the document. Web browsers do not currently support this format, but files can be viewed with the Acrobat Reader.

PostScript (PostScript uses application/postscript): A literal markup language that precisely defines the content, layout, font, spacing, style, and position of all elements that constitute the document. PostScript files are generally large and complex. Web browsers do not currently support this format, but some external viewers do.

AU (Audio uses audio/au): An audio file format based on μ–Law companding and developed by Sun Microsystems and NeXT. Players for these files are included with the Unix operating systems associated with the computers developed by these companies.

WAV (Wave Audio File Format uses audio/wav): An audio file format based on μ–Law companding and developed by Microsoft and IBM. Web browsers generally support this format with the aid of an external player.

QuickTime (QuickTime uses video/quicktime): A motion video file format developed by Apple Computer that consists primarily of integrated audio and video compression techniques. QuickTime includes a user-friendly interface for controlling recording, playback, and compression of files. Web browsers generally support this format with the aid of an external player.

MPEG (Motion Picture Experts Group uses video/mpeg): A motion video file format developed by the Motion Picture Experts Group that consists primarily of integrated audio and video compression techniques. MPEG uses the same lossy algorithms incorporated into the JPEG file format and is considered the de facto standard for motion video via the World Wide Web. Web browsers generally support this format with the aid of an external player.

AVI (Audio Video Interleaved uses video/avi): The extension of a file created using Video for Windows (VFW), a motion video file format that is similar to QuickTime and developed by Microsoft. The format consists primarily of integrated audio and video compression techniques. Web browsers generally support this format with the aid of an external player.

3.4 Understanding Data Traffic Characteristics

The nature of the data traffic that traverses the various links of a network may have a profound influence on its operation (see Table 3.2). In a LAN environment, for example, the exchange of typical text-based messages via e-mail contributes very little to the network's overall data traffic. Video conferencing applications, however, can create a copious amount of data traffic and therefore congestion. Congestion is generally manifested to the user as sluggish network performance. In Table 3.2 the traffic characteristics of several different categories of data are compared. The four columns of the table are as follows:

Data Type: The general file or application type.

Relative Required Capacity: The amount of capacity required, relative to the other table entries, for acceptable transmission and reception of such data. A TDM-based DS0, for example, is generally acceptable for text-based transmissions, but would be severely deficient for video conferencing.

Bit Rate: The preferred bit-level behavior, relative to the other table entries, of data traffic. The transfer rate of an application via the Internet, for example, may be high at one particular instance and low at another. Such erratic transfer rates for video and audio feeds require that the receiving computer buffer portions or the entire file prior to playing.

Immediacy: The user's reception time. Information transferred over the Internet via FTP, for example, will arrive as soon as possible, whereas information transferred via a dedicated video conferencing system will arrive virtually "real-time." E-mail exemplifies delayed urgency. A message may arrive at the recipient's e-mail server the instant after being transmitted; however, the recipient may not read the message for another three days.

The nature of the data traffic that traverses the various links of a network may have a profound influence on its operation.

Table 3.2 Network Traffic Characteristics

Traffic Type	Rel. Req. Capacity	Bit Rate	Immediacy
Text File Xfer	Low	Variable	ASAP
App. File Xfer	Low to Moderate	Variable	ASAP
E-mail	Low	Variable	Delayed
Remote Printing	Low to Moderate	Variable	Delayed
Remote Login	Low	Variable	Delayed
DDE	Low to Moderate	Variable	Quasi-RT
Digital Audio	Low to Moderate	C/V	RT/ASAP
Full-Motion Video	High	Constant	RT/ASAP
Distance Learning	High	C/V	RT/ASAP
Video Conferencing	High	C/V	RT
Static Image	Moderate	Variable	ASAP
Multimedia	High	C/V	Quasi-RT
CAD/CAM	Moderate to High	Variable	ASAP
Database Transaction	Low to Moderate	Variable	ASAP

Customers of an *online service provider*, such as America Online (AOL), obtain access to the Internet indirectly via the provider's computers that operate essentially as a bulletin board service (BBS).

Customers of an *Internet Service Provider* (ISP), such as Telstra Big Pond Direct or BellSouth.net, obtain access to the Internet directly via the provider's network.

3.5 Online Service Provider versus ISP (Internet Service Provider)

As the World Wide Web and other Internet-related services gained public attention, organizations generically referred to as *service providers* began offering Internet dialup access. There are two categories of services providers: online and Internet. Customers of an *online service provider*, such as America Online (AOL), obtain access to the Internet indirectly via the provider's computers that operate essentially as a bulletin board service (BBS). A proprietary user interface provides the customer with all the standard Internet services including e-mail, World Wide Web (including a location for personal home pages), USENET, and IRC (Internet Relay Chat). Other services such as community and/or business forums, online travel services, and stock quotes may also be available through the user interface.

Customers of an *Internet Service Provider* (ISP), such as Telstra Big Pond Direct or BellSouth.net, obtain access to the Internet directly via the provider's network. By using standard Internet protocols, the customer's computer becomes a remote node of the provider's network, which, in turn, is essentially a remote node to the greater Internet. Customers are assigned either static or dynamic, DHCP, IP addresses by the provider. These addresses, in part, enable the customer to use primitive TCP/IP applications (e.g., FTP and Telnet) and diagnostic utilities (for example, ping and traceroute) that are found in modern operating systems. In addition to the Internet services offered by online service providers, ISPs provide customers with the option of a Unix-based shell account on one of their systems. This type of account provides the customer access to the feature-rich environment of the Unix operating system.

An ISP composed of several different services, systems, and access technologies (see Figure 3.10). Sporting a wide range of connectivity options, such as dialup access, ISDN (Integrated Services Digital Network), and Frame Relay (discussed in the following chapters), customers can choose a financially and operationally prudent means of access. The switches that connect customers to ISPs are generally located in the central office

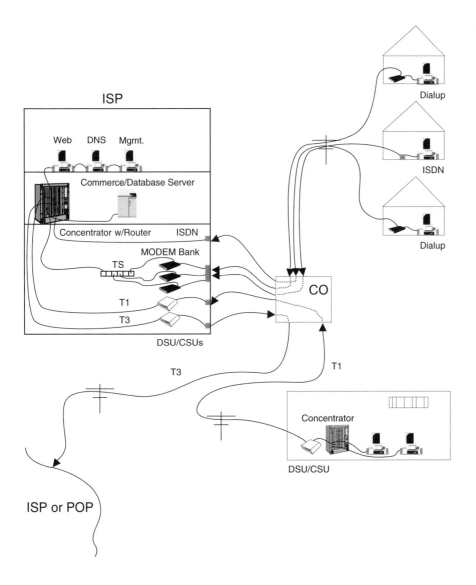

FIGURE 3.10

ISP example.

(CO) of the local carrier. ISPs must have an appropriate number of physical connections, per the various connectivity options, to support the peak bandwidth demand, determined by statistical means, generated by its customers. An ISP's output bandwidth, for example, one or more TDM-based T3s, must exceed its aggregate input bandwidth. Outbound data traffic is generally routed to a major Internet connectivity site referred to as a *POP* (Point-of-Presence). In this sense, ISPs are essentially an Internet frontend to their customers.

DNS, web servers, and management workstations are some of the systems located on the premises of an ISP. E-commerce and database servers, possibly residing on the same system as that used by the web server, may also be present to provide the customer with a wide variety of modern Internet services. For example, a company's virtual storefront may actually be implemented on a system physically located at the ISP. Concentrator(s) are generally used to consolidate the network technologies that constitute the ISP's network backbone and customer access.

Summary

In a physical sense, computer systems communicate by extending their internal data bus, via a network adapter card, to other systems within the network. Communication protocols, such as TCP/IP, transmit and receive information to/from the network adapter card via a program known as a driver. The user interface, or application, is managed by the computer's operating system and interacts with network resources via communication protocols.

●
Computer
networks are
geographically
classified as LAN,
MAN, or WAN.

Computer networks are geographically classified as LAN, MAN, or WAN. Prior to design and implementation, several characteristics of a network technology and the data traffic that it will support should be considered. Access schemes, compression, authentication, encryption, topology, and file types are only a few of these considerations. Several additional terms and concepts crucial to the understanding of computer networking include analog-to-digital conversion (A/D), pulse code modulation (PCM), synchronous versus asynchronous transmission, multiplexing, compression, network topologies, virtual circuit versus circuit switched versus datagram, internetworking devices, and client/server versus peer-to-peer technologies.

Internet Connectivity: Network Technologies

Chapter Learning Objectives:

- Understand several key backbone technologies.
- Understand several key access technologies.
- Discuss infrastructure-related concepts.

"Is it a fact—or have I dreamt it—that, by means of electricity, the world of matter has become a great nerve, vibrating thousands of miles in a breathless point of time?"

Nathaniel Hawthorne, The House of the Seven Gables

4.1 Backbone Technologies

As the term implies, the *backbone* constitutes the core infrastructure of a computer network. Connecting media, hubs, concentrators, and internetworking devices are included within the backbone. Backbone technologies, old and new, span the realms of the LAN, MAN, and WAN. Advances in software technologies, such as multimedia, video conferencing, and intranet applications, coupled with the converging technologies that have traditionally supported data, voice (telephony), and video (television and related media) demand advances in the technologies tasked with the transportation of the data traffic generated by these applications.

Advances in software technologies, coupled with the converging technologies that have traditionally supported data, demand advances in the technologies tasked with the transportation of the data traffic generated by these applications.

Traditional, or legacy, technologies are ill equipped to handle the emerging transportation requirements. Recent and nascent contenders of backbone technologies are "intelligent" enough to detect patterns in data traffic, referred to as *flows,* and/or the type of traffic in order to adjust the quality of service *(QoS)* required for the proper handling of such traffic. The QoS associated with a stream, or flow, of video information, for example, would require the allocation of a fixed amount of bandwidth, whereas the QoS for critical data would require high-priority transportation.

The progeny of some traditional technologies, such as Gigabit Ethernet, circumvent the need for QoS by employing the use of massive amounts of bandwidth. Such technologies, however, are incapable of providing other new services, such as Virtual Private Networking *(VPN)* or in-band service reconfiguration. Improvements in existing protocols, such as TCP/IP, and the creation of new protocols, such as RSVP, promise to augment these progeny with QoS, VPN, and other new services. As we shall see, different backbone technologies are appropriate for different circumstances. In the sections that follow, we examine Ethernet, Token Ring, wireless and satellite, leased circuits, Frame Relay, and ATM technologies. Descriptions of other technologies, such as POTS (Plain Old Telephone System) and SONET (Synchronous Optical Network), are generally excluded because they represent the extreme ends, in terms of capacity and cost, of available backbone technologies.

Ethernet

Ethernet, the most popular LAN backbone technology, is based on a bus topology. A bus topology is considered a shared medium; therefore, systems attached to the medium must contend for available bandwidth. Contention between the systems is managed via an algorithm known as *CSMA/CD* (Carrier Sense Multiple Access/ with Collision Detect). Prior to transmission, a system "listens" to the communications channel to determine if it is busy or idle (Carrier Sense). If the channel is idle, then the system transmits a frame of data. If two or more systems transmit simultaneously, a collision occurs. The contending systems detect the collision (Collision Detect), transmit a jamming signal to alert all other stations of the collision, and retransmit after a random period of time.

The header and trailer associated with the more ubiquitous version of Ethernet, IEEE (Institute of Electrical and Electronics Engineers) 802.3, encapsulate a packet of data (layers 3–7) to form a *frame* (see Figure 4.1). The fields within the header and trailer are described as follows:

Preamble: A 7-byte square wave used for synchronization by the receiving system.

Starting Delimiter (SD): The bit pattern $10101011_{(2)}$ used to indicate the beginning of the frame.

Destination MAC Address (DMA): The MAC address (usually 6 bytes in length) of the recipient system.

Source MAC Address (SMA): The MAC address (usually 6 bytes in length) of the transmitting system.

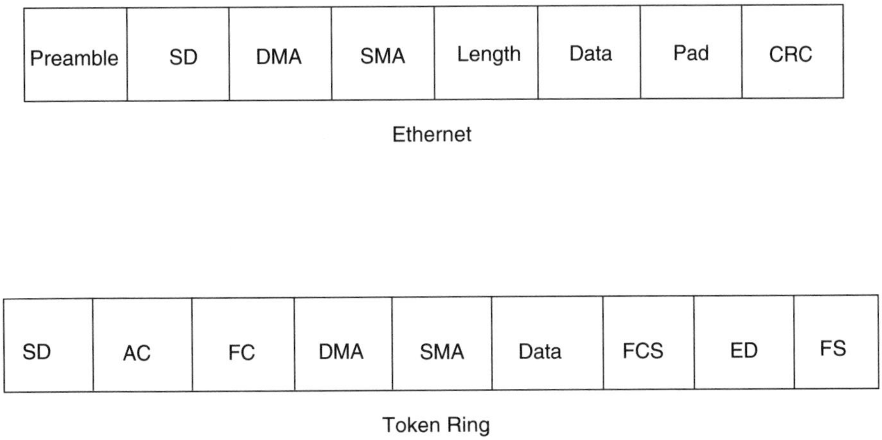

Preamble	SD	DMA	SMA	Length	Data	Pad	CRC

Ethernet

SD	AC	FC	DMA	SMA	Data	FCS	ED	FS

Token Ring

FIGURE 4.1

Ethernet and Token Ring frames.

Length: A 2-byte field used to indicate the length of the packet being transported.

Data: A variable-length field containing the data (layers 3–7) being transported.

Pad: A variable-length field used to ensure that the frame meets the minimal length requirement of 64 bytes. Frames generated with a deficient length are referred to as *runts*. Frames exceeding the maximum length requirement, 1,518 bytes, are referred to as *giants*. Both types of malformed frames are discarded upon reception.

Cyclic Redundancy Check (CRC): A 4-byte field used to establish the validity of a transmitted frame.

Several derivatives of Ethernet exist. Legacy Ethernet systems, for example, operate at a capacity of 10 Mbps, whereas Gigabit Ethernet systems operate at 1 Gbps (1,000,000,000bps). The following table describes the salient features of most of these derivatives.

Derivative	Medium	Segment Length (Maximum)	Capacity
10Base2	Coaxial Cable	185 meters with daisy-chained nodes	10 Mbps
10Base5	Coaxial Cable	500 meters with parallel nodes	10 Mbps
10BaseT	Twisted Pair	100 meters with distinct node cables	10 Mbps
10BaseF	Optical Fiber	500 meters with distinct node fibers	10 Mbps
100BaseT	Twisted Pair	100 meters with distinct node cables	100 Mbps
Gigabit	Optical Fiber	500 meters with distinct node fibers	1,000 Mbps

An *Etherswitch* is a device that employs matrix switching to eliminate contention among attached systems. A 10-port Etherswitch, for example, consists of 10 distinct Ethernet ports, each of which provide 10 Mbps of capacity to attached system(s). The aggregate capacity of the entire switch, therefore, is 10 × 10 Mbps = 100 Mbps. By examining incoming destination MAC address fields, the Etherswitch "switches" frames between appropriate ports, and hence systems. In this manner, nonparticipating ports will not "hear" the transmission between source and destination systems.

Token Ring

Token Ring, a LAN backbone technology, is based upon a ring topology. Unlike Ethernet, systems in a Token Ring network do not contend for available capacity; instead, they "wait their turn." Data is received from a system's "upstream" neighbor and transmitted to its "downstream" neighbor. When the ring is idle, a 3-byte token circulates. When a system is ready to communicate with another system, it captures the token, modifies a bit within the token to indicate that it is "busy," appends additional fields (including addressing) and the packet of data (layers 3–7), and transmits the new frame "downstream." As the frame circulates, each system checks the destination MAC address field to determine if it is the intended recipient. If it is, the transported packet of data is copied to a buffer, appropriate frame status bits are modified, and the frame is once again transmitted "downstream." Once the frame is received by the system from which it was initially transmitted, frame status bits are examined to verify that it was properly received by the intended recipient, and a new 3-byte token is generated and transmitted onto the ring to start the process anew.

The header and trailer associated with a particular version of Token Ring, IEEE 802.5, encapsulate a packet of data (layers 3–7) to form a frame (see Figure 4.1). The fields within the header and trailer are described as follows:

Starting Delimiter (SD): The bit pattern $JK0JK000_{(2)}$ used to indicate the beginning of the frame. "J" and "K" are referred to as coding violations and are intentionally generated as unique characters to aid in the identification of the frame's starting and ending delimiter fields. A "J" is akin to a malformed 1, whereas a "K" is akin to a malformed 0. The Starting Delimiter field constitutes the first byte of the original 3-byte token.

Access Control (AC): A 1-byte field that is used to control access to the ring and frame prioritization. One particular bit, the token bit, is set to indicate that the token is busy transporting a frame. The Access Control field constitutes the second byte of the original 3-byte token.

Frame Control (FC): A 1-byte field used to indicate whether the frame is transporting either user or ring maintenance data.

Destination MAC Address (DMA): The MAC address (usually 6 bytes in length) of the recipient system.

Source MAC Address (SMA): The MAC address (usually 6 bytes in length) of the transmitting system.

Data: A variable-length field containing the data (layers 3–7) being transported.

Frame Check Sequence (FCS): A 4-byte field used to establish the validity of a transmitted frame.

Ending Delimiter (ED): The bit pattern $JK1JK1IE_{(2)}$ used to indicate the end of the frame. "J" and "K" are referred to as coding violations and are intentionally generated as unique characters to aid in the identification of the frame's starting and ending delimiter fields. The "I" bit (intermediate frame bit) is set by the source system to indicate to the destination system that additional, consecutive frames will be transmitted. The "E" bit (error detected) is set by any system in the ring that detects an error in the frame. When set, the destination system will not accept the received data. The Ending Delimiter field constitutes the third byte of the original 3-byte token.

Frame Status (FS): A 1-byte field used to indicate to the source system the status of the transmitted frame. Certain bits within the field, the "A" and "C" bits, when set, indicate that the destination system recognized its address and successfully copied the transmitted data into its buffers.

Several derivatives of Token Ring exist. The most common possess a capacity of 4, 16, or 100 Mbps. The hub of a legacy Token Ring system (4, 16 Mbps derivatives) is referred to as a *MAU* (Multi-station Access Unit). Systems, or stations, attach to the MAU by using a similar type of twisted pair cable as that used in some of the Ethernet derivatives. By using the RI (Ring In) and RO (Ring Out) ports, MAUs can be connected together to form a larger ring. The typical number of ports per MAU is 8, whereas the maximum number of systems that can be networked is 260. The maximum frame lengths for these two derivatives are 4,500 (4 Mbps) and 18,000 (16 Mbps) bytes.

FDDI (Fiber-Distributed Data Interface) is a Token Ring derivative that has a capacity of 100 Mbps. The FDDI equivalent of a MAU is generally an FDDI module within a router or an FDDI concentrator. Although versions of FDDI based on twisted pair cable exist, the standard connectivity medium is optical fiber that can span 2 Km per segment. The ring is constructed of two pairs of fiber. During normal operation, data circulates in a specific direction on a specific pair of optical fibers. A fault in this primary pair of optical fibers causes the data traffic to be shifted onto the secondary pair of optical fibers and counter-rotated in the opposite direction. A more severe fault, such as the severing of both pairs of optical fibers or the failure of an FDDI interface, causes data traffic to be wrapped from one pair onto the other at both interfaces "upstream" and downstream" from the fault. Such a condition forces the ring to be dynamically reconfigured in a C shape.

Although similar in many respects to its IEEE 802.5 counterpart, such as possessing a maximum frame length of 4,500 bytes and nearly identical header and trailer fields, FDDI has a few key differences:

1. FDDI encodes signals using a scheme known as 4B/5B, whereas IEEE 802.5 uses Differential Manchester encoding.

2. FDDI can dynamically allocate capacity to attached systems in order to support both synchronous and asynchronous data traffic, whereas IEEE 802.5 cannot.

3. FDDI systems can attach to either a single pair of optical fibers (SAS–Single Attachment Station) or both pairs (DAS–Dual Attachment Station). IEEE 802.5 systems attach to a single pair of copper wires within the cable.

Wireless Communications

In January 1997, the FCC held an auction, which, in effect, sold a portion of the electromagnetic spectrum for $7.7 billion. Licenses were issued (to the highest bidder) that allow the exclusive usage of a particular band of frequencies within a specific region of the United States or its territories. The bidders were providers of Personal Communications Services (PCS). It may seem odd that the American government has the authority to sell what is essentially a piece of nature. However, we are an integral part of nature and our existence depends on our ability to interact with it. Indeed, every moment of every day we are inundated with the often silent harmonies and cacophonies of electromagnetic waves, both natural and synthetic, that permeate our world. *Wireless* communications, as the name implies, is that portion of the synthetic contribution that enables us to communicate without copper wire, coaxial cable, or optical fiber-based media.

In May 1997, the PanAMSat Corporation satellite, Galaxy 4, became disoriented due to a malfunction in the on-board attitude control system. Although the problem was remedied within a few days by the relocation of another satellite, paging and other critical services for millions of people were disrupted nationwide. Wireless communications have become an indispensable part of our lives. The gamut of wireless applications enables us to connect geographically remote facilities, provide greater mobility to the global workforce, and turn the wheels of a child's remote control car. Communication solutions for environments incapable of supporting the installation of wire-line communication systems, such as the asbestos-laden infrastructure of an older building or the vast expanse between the surfaces of Mars and Earth, are also found in wireless.

In the following sections, we examine several popular wireless services including wireless LANs (WLAN), satellite, cellular (analog and digital), and PCS. These services are employed in both Internet and non-Internet-related applications to augment, create, or access a network backbone and generally occupy different portions of the electromagnetic spectrum (see Table 4.1). They are typically based on one or more of the following access schemes:

TDMA (Time Division Multiple Access): A TDM-based access scheme whereby multiple sources transmit information across a common channel, or carrier, within a unique, predetermined time slot. TDMA-based systems are frequency independent.

FDMA (Frequency Division Multiple Access): An FDM-type access scheme whereby multiple sources transmit information across multiple channels, or carriers, as needed. FDMA-based systems are time independent.

FHSS (Frequency Hopping Spread-Spectrum): A Spread-Spectrum access scheme whereby the signal to be transmitted is spread across a relatively broad band of spectrum by "hopping" from one channel, within the band, to another. One portion of the signal is transmitted on a particular channel, and an instant later another portion is transmitted on a different channel. Both the transmitter and receiver use a digital pseudo-random code (PSR) to code and decode the channel hop sequence. FHSS is time and frequency independent and offers both superior security and noise immunity compared to other non-Spread-Spectrum techniques.

Table 4.1 Electromagnetic Spectrum (Partial)

Service	Spectrum Allocation (MHz)
AMPS (Advanced Mobile Phone System) transmit—N.A. analog cellular	825–845
NAMPS (Narrowband AMPS) transmit—N.A. analog cellular	825–845
NADC (North American Digital Cellular)	825–845
AMPS (Advanced Mobile Phone System) receive—N.A. analog cellular	870–890
NAMPS (Narrowband AMPS) receive—N.A. analog cellular	870–890
NADC (North American Digital Cellular)	870–890
ETACS (Extended Total Access Communications System) receive—U.K. analog cellular	872–905
GSM (Global System for Mobile) transmit—U.S., Europe digital cellular	890–915
ISM (Industrial, Scientific, and Medical) industrial band—WLAN Spread Spectrum	902–928
ETACS (Extended Total Access Communications System) transmit—U.K. analog cellular	917–950
PCS (Personal Communications Services)	920–928
GSM (Global System for Mobile) receive—Europe,U.S. digital cellular	935–960
PCS (Personal Communications Services)	1,800–2,200
PCS (Personal Communications Services)— 1997 FCC auctions	1,850–1,990
ISM (Industrial, Scientific, and Medical) scientific band—WLAN Spread Spectrum	2,400–2,483
C-band—satellite downlink	3,700-4,200
ISM (Industrial, Scientific, and Medical) medical band—WLAN Spread Spectrum	5,725-5,850
C-band—satellite uplink	5,900-6,400
Ku-band—satellite downlink	11,700–12,200
Ku-band—satellite uplink	14,000–14,500
Ka-band—satellite downlink	20,000
Ka-band—satellite uplink	30,000
IR (Infrared)—WLAN	333,000,000–375,000,000

DSSS (Direct Sequence Spread Spectrum): A Spread-Spectrum access scheme whereby the signal to be transmitted is spread across a relatively broad band of spectrum. The data source is first modulated onto a particular channel, or carrier. This modulated-data signal is then multiplied with a wide-band, digital, pseudo-random code (PSR). In other words, the DSSS signal created by multiplying the modulated-data signal with the PSR possesses the same spectral width as the PSR. The bits, 1s and 0s, that constitute the PSR are called *chips.* The chips used by the transmitter must precisely match those used by the receiver for proper encoding and decoding to occur. DSSS is time and frequency independent and offers both superior security and noise immunity compared to other non-Spread-Spectrum techniques.

CDMA (Code Division Multiple Access): A Spread-Spectrum access scheme whereby the signal to be transmitted is spread across a relatively broad band of spectrum. CDMA is similar to DSSS. In CDMA, however, the data source is multiplied with a wide-band, digital, pseudo-random code (PSR) prior to being modulated onto a particular channel, or carrier. In this manner, CDMA signals can occupy several distinct channels or the same channel. If multiple CDMA signals originating from multiple data sources are to occupy the same transmission channel, then each unique CDMA transmitter must possess a unique PSR. These unique PSRs are said to be *orthogonal,* or statistically unrelated. In other words, for a CDMA receiver to extract data (from the received, composite CDMA signal) from a particular source, it must possess an identical copy of the PSR used by the source. CDMA is time and frequency independent and offers both superior security and noise immunity compared to other non-Spread-Spectrum techniques.

FAMA (Fixed Assigned Multiple Access): An access technique whereby the channel capacity assigned to a particular system remains constant. FAMA is based upon an FDMA, TDMA, or CDMA access scheme and is typically employed in satellite-based systems.

DAMA (Demand Assigned Multiple Access): An access technique whereby the channel capacity assigned to a particular system is adjusted as warranted by changing data traffic conditions. DAMA is based upon an FDMA, TDMA, or CDMA access scheme and is typically employed in satellite-based systems.

WLAN

In June 1997, the IEEE approved a new standard, IEEE 802.11, for wireless LANs *(WLAN).* Wireless products based on this standard generally support conventional Token Ring and Ethernet devices, such as repeaters, MAUs, bridges, routers, adapter cards, and printers (see Figure 4.2). Access to the medium at the MAC sublayer (OSI model layer 2) is managed by the access scheme *CSMA/CA (Carrier Sense Multiple Access/with Collision Avoidance).* Similar to the access scheme used in Ethernet, CSMA/CD, CSMA/CA also employs a carrier sense mechanism. Systems deployed throughout a wireless LAN, however, may not be able to "hear" every other system. Therefore, prior to the transmission of data, a *Request to Send (RTS)* frame is sent to the destination

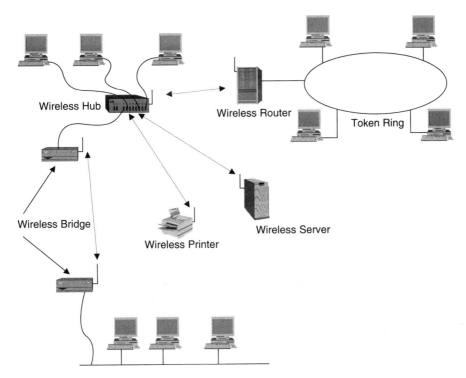

FIGURE 4.2
*Wireless LAN
(WLAN).*

system. If the medium is available, the destination system will reply with a *Clear to Send
(CTS)* frame. This process is, in essence, a virtual carrier sense mechanism. After the
successful exchange of RTS and CTS frames, a data frame is transmitted to the destination system. If the received frame is error-free, an acknowledgment is transmitted to the
source system. The fields of the RTS and CTS frames are described as follows:

Frame Control (FC): A 2-byte field used to indicate the frame type.

Duration (D): A 2-byte field indicating the total time in microseconds required for
the source system to transmit the next frame, receive an acknowledgment packet
from the destination system, and pause for three predefined intervals. The value
found in the duration field indicates the amount of time that the medium will be
busy and therefore is used to provide a means of collision avoidance (CA). Duration
is not typically found in wire-line MAC protocols.

Destination MAC Address (DMA): The 6-byte MAC address of the destination
system.

Source MAC Address (SMA): The 6-byte MAC address of the source system. This
field is only contained in the RTS packet.

Frame Check Sequence (FCS): A 4-byte field used to establish the validity of a transmitted frame.

To ensure secure data transmission, the 802.11 standard specifies a Wired Equivalent Privacy *(WEP)* mechanism as part of the MAC sublayer. WEP uses authentication and encryption techniques between the source and destination systems. The standard also specifies a mechanism whereby end systems may "roam," or be physically transported, about the wireless LAN. When an end system is relocated within a different section of the LAN, it immediately begins to scan for a new wireless access point (AP), an interconnecting device such as a wireless hub. Once detected, the end system transmits a Reassociation Request packet to the AP. If accepted, the AP replies to the end system and updates its system table.

The 802.11 standard has provisions for three different physical (OSI model layer 1) access schemes: FHSS, DSSS, and IR (Infrared). The first two schemes operate within the ISM (Industrial, Scientific, and Medical) band of the electromagnetic spectrum. Products based on these schemes generally operate at a data rate of either 1 or 2 Mbps. Solutions do exist, however, with greater capacities. IR is based on optical wavelengths and therefore operates within a considerably higher band of the electromagnetic spectrum. IR wireless LAN products generally support data rates compatible with legacy Token Ring and Ethernet LANs and are categorized as either diffused or direct IR. Diffused IR systems employ scattering and/or reflecting techniques to "illuminate" the area of coverage. Walls, ceilings, and floors may be used to convey the signal. Direct IR systems transmit a high-power, line-of-site beam between two systems. They may be used in the interconnection of two or more buildings and are mounted externally to the buildings. The performance of direct IR systems is susceptible to poor weather conditions.

Satellite

A *satellite* can be defined as any celestial body that orbits a larger celestial body. Our planet has only one significant natural satellite, the Moon, but we have many artificial satellites. Most of the latter constitute space debris. The Internet, PCS, global navigation, remote sensing, telephony, and television all depend on the services provided by communications satellites. Satellite systems consist of *Earth stations, uplinks, downlinks,* and, of course, satellites. Earth stations are located within a satellite's terrestrial area of coverage, referred to as a *footprint,* transmit information to the satellite via a communications channel referred to as the uplink, and, similarly, receive information via the downlink. The corresponding transmitter/receiver aboard the satellite is referred to as the *transponder.* Information received on a particular transponder channel is "down converted" to a separate channel, prior to retransmission. The use of distinct uplink and downlink channels enables two-way, simultaneous communications between two or more Earth stations and prevents feedback from the satellite's transmitter to its receiver. Earth stations and satellites generally use FAMA and DAMA access schemes to communicate.

Historically, satellites have operated as repeaters, whereby transmissions are relayed from point A to point B. Satellites currently being deployed operate like routers because they utilize intersatellite communication links to route information. Networks based on these "intelligent" satellites, referred to as *constellations,* are far more flexible, in terms of topology, efficiency, and practicality, than previous generation satellite systems. Satellites are generally classified according to their orbital altitude: GEO, MEO, or LEO.

GEO (Geostationary-Earth-Orbit): The traditional workhorse of the satellite industry. Perched at an altitude of 22,300 miles (36,000 Km) above the equator, the orbital period of a GEO precisely matches the rotational period of the Earth. In other words, it remains stationary above a particular equatorial location. The orbit of a GEO is located on a meridian line with a typical intersatellite spacing of 2°. Galaxy 4, for example, is/was located at 0° North by 99° West and is flanked by Telstar 401 at 0° North by 97° West and Spacenet 4 at 0° North by 101° West.

The extreme altitude of a GEO requires a more powerful Earth-station transmitter and receiver than its LEO and MEO counterparts. Also, a 250 ms delay is imposed on all transmissions, thus rendering GEOs highly suitable for broadcast transmissions, such as television, and less desirable for real-time transmissions, such as video conferencing. Additionally, only three GEOs, spaced 120° apart, are required to provide coverage to the entire globe, less the Polar Regions. GEOs operate in the C-band, 2° intersatellite spacing, and Ku-band, 3° intersatellite spacing, of the electromagnetic spectrum.

MEO (Medium-Earth-Orbit): Located at an average altitude of approximately 6,000 miles (10,000 Km), a MEO satellite does not remain fixed relative to a position on the ground. Such a condition requires either the use of Earth stations equipped with tracking antennas or the deployment of a satellite constellation to provide continuous coverage. Odyssey, for example, is a 12-satellite, MEO-based constellation that is being developed by TRW and Teleglobe to support global satellite phone service and PCS.

As a MEO satellite approaches an Earth station, the carrier frequency, channel, is shifted slightly higher; it possess a Doppler shift. The same carrier frequency is shifted slightly lower as the satellite recedes. The transmitters and receivers of MEO-based systems must be designed to compensate for this shift. A MEO satellite's relatively low altitude translates into a lower power requirement for the proper operation of the Earth station's transmitter and receiver. Therefore, a battery-operated, miniature "Earth station," such as a hand-held phone, can be used to communicate with a MEO satellite. The delay between the transmission and reception of a signal from one Earth station to another is only 1/16 of a second; therefore, MEO-based systems are better suited for the transmission of data and voice than GEO-based systems.

LEO (Low-Earth-Orbit): Located with the range of altitudes between 450 miles (750 Km) and 900 miles (1500 Km), a LEO satellite does not remain fixed relative to a position on the ground. Such a condition requires either the use of Earth stations equipped with tracking antennas or the deployment of a satellite constellation to provide continuous coverage. The Teledesic Network, for example, is a 288-satellite, LEO-based constellation that is being funded primarily by communication industry magnates Bill Gates and Craig McCaw. The network was designed to support relatively high-speed (155 Mbps) data, voice, and video and should have a significant impact on the burgeoning Internet.

Signals transmitted to, and received from, LEO satellites experience a Doppler shift. Transmitters and receivers of LEO satellites must be designed to compensate for this shift. A LEO satellite's low altitude translates into a lower power requirement for the Earth station's transmitter and receiver. Therefore, a battery-operated, miniature "Earth station," such as a hand-held phone, can be used to communicate with a LEO satellite. The footprint of a LEO satellite is considerably smaller than its GEO and MEO counterparts; therefore, a larger number of satellites are required to provide adequate service coverage.

VSAT (Very Small Aperture Terminal) is a satellite-based set of communication services and technologies. As the name implies, the parabolic dish, or antenna, of a VSAT Earth station is very small—typically meter in diameter. Online credit-card approval, database transactions, e-mail, and surfing the web constitute the types of data traffic transported via VSAT networks. VSAT supports standard channel capacities ranging from 64 Kbps to T1 and E1 (European standard uses 2.048 Mbps) and standard backbone and access technologies such as ISDN, point-to-point connectivity, Frame Relay, and ATM.

Historically, VSAT networks were based solely upon a star topology that consisted of one centralized processing facility and several remote, transaction-based facilities. To accommodate the distributed, client/server architectures of today, VSAT networks are configured as either a star or mesh topology. Such configurations are ideal for broadcast and multicast data traffic. PBS (Public Broadcast System), for example, uses VSAT technology to broadcast educational programs directly to public schools. VSAT technology operates in the Ku-band of the electromagnetic spectrum and typically uses TDMA/DAMA for access.

Cellular (Analog and Digital) versus PCS

Cellular telephony is the wireless cousin of POTS. The technology derives its name from the fundamental area of coverage, the cell. A cellular telephone system essentially consists of cell sites, an *MTSO* (Mobile Telephone Switching Office), and cellular phones (see Figure 4.3). Each cell site has an antenna and a base station and is approximately hexagonal in shape. These hexagons, or cells, are created using three corner reflector antennae, the radiation pattern of each being 120° and covering an area of only a few square miles. Because of the small size of the cell, power requirements for communication within the cell are relatively low; cellular phones can operate on rechargeable batteries, and channel frequencies used within the cell can be reused in adjacent cells.

The MTSO controls communication for a region containing several adjacent cells. When a cellular subscriber dials a phone number, the MTSO verifies that the number exists. If it does, then the MTSO assigns a channel to the subscriber's phone and dials the phone number. As the subscriber travels from one cell to the next, the MTSO reassigns a different channel to the subscriber's phone. This process is referred to as a *handoff*. Calls between cellular regions are handled MTSO-to-MTSO, whereas calls between cellular regions and wire-line numbers are handled MTSO-to-CO (Central Office). *Roaming* means that the cellular subscriber is calling from outside of his or her home cellular region.

FIGURE 4.3
*Cellular telephone
system.*

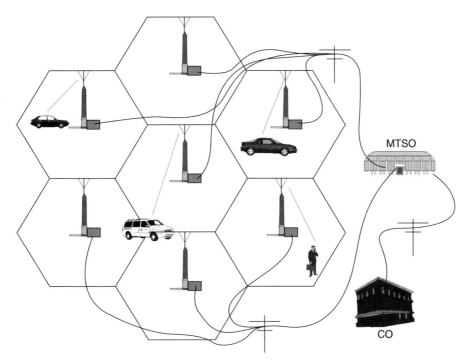

Many standards exist for analog and digital cellular telephony. In the United States, for example, AMPS (Advanced Mobile Phone Service) is the standard for analog cellular, whereas ETACS (Extended Total Access Communication System) is the standard in the United Kingdom. The following are several such standards and their access schemes:

Standard	Region	Format	Access
AMPS (Advanced Mobile Phone Service)	N. America	Analog	FDMA
NAMPS (Narrowband AMPS)	N. America	Analog	FDMA
NADC (North American Digital Cellular)	N. America	Digital	TDMA, CDMA
ETACS (Extended Total Access Comm.)	UK	Analog	FDMA
GSM (Global System for Mobile)	Europe, US	Digital	TDMA, FDMA

CDPD (Cellular Digital Packet Data) is a cellular communications protocol and overlay network that enables packet switching techniques to be used via analog cellular systems. The overlay network employs common WAN technologies, such as Frame Relay, to interconnect cell sites. The cell site's base station, in turn, connects to the WAN via a router. At some point, the WAN connects to the Internet. In this respect, a CDPD network is, in essence, a wireless ISP for cellular subscribers. Although CDPD supports TCP/IP, slow data rates (typically 19.2 Kbps) may render some applications, such as Web browsing, impractical and cost prohibitive. CDPD uses idle channel capacity to transmit information and employs authentication and encryption techniques to secure it.

PCS (Personal Communications Services) is a system of technologies and services combined to provide the subscriber with a complete communications solution. Among the services offered by PCS are paging, facsimile, voice mail, e-mail, telephony, and web browsing. Hand-held units such as PDAs (Personal Digital Assistants), palmtop computers, and PCS phones are lightweight and battery operated. Pundits of PCS envision a single, universal identification number that is associated with the subscriber's hand-held unit, not location. The access standards used by hand-held units and the other components of a PCS system are GSM (which is based on TDMA) in Europe and TDMA, CDMA, and GSM in the United States.

Similar to its main competitor, digital cellular, PCS is based on cells. A PCS cell spans only hundreds of yards and is therefore referred to as a *micro-cell.* Micro-cell technology and PCS hand-held units require very little power. An MTA (Major Trading Area) is a contiguous area of coverage that may include, for example, an area as large as Washington, D.C., Maryland, and parts of Virginia. Satellite technologies such as Motorola's 66-satellite, LEO-based constellation, Iridium, promise to make PCS a worldwide communications service.

Point-to-Point Connectivity (Leased Lines)

For many years, dedicated leased lines have been used to provide wide area connectivity for businesses, educational institutions, and governmental agencies. In fact, the backbone of the Internet has relied heavily on the use of these lines to provide point-to-point connectivity between POPs. Leased lines are, in essence, digital information conduits that collect input from point A and deliver it to point B. They are based on a TDM access scheme with standard data rates consistent with the North American Multiplexing Standards (see Table 3.1). Leased lines are generally used to connect two or more customer premises, a customer to an ISP, or a customer to another network technology, such as Frame Relay.

Originally designed to carry multiplexed, PCM-encoded voice signals, leased lines carry all manner of data traffic. Analog voice circuits interface to the leased line via a device known as a *digital channel bank.* The channel bank performs the sampling and encoding of the input voice signal to produce a PCM bitstream. This bitstream, in turn, is multiplexed into an available time slot to be carried over the line. LANs typically interface to the leased line via a router and a DSU/CSU (see Figure 4.4). One port of the router interfaces to the LAN backbone, and another port interfaces to the DSU/CSU. The latter is usually a high-speed serial port. The DSU/CSU, of course, completes the connection to the leased line.

The demarcation is the location within the customer premises where the telecommunications carrier terminates the leased line. The device used to terminate the circuit is an "intelligent" phone-type jack that can be remotely programmed for purposes of troubleshooting. When communication errors occur, the customer informs the carrier of the suspected problem. If necessary, the carrier can remotely instruct the "intelligent" jack to

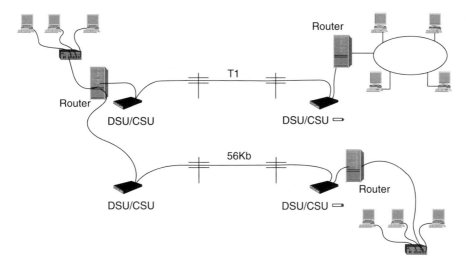

FIGURE 4.4

Point-to-point connectivity (leased line).

loop-back any information sent to it. Once in loop-back mode, various digital patterns can be transmitted up to and back through the jack. A bit-error-rate test, *B.E.R.T*, is performed on the returned data to determine the cause of the problem. The customer can also perform router-to-router loop-back tests.

Wide area networks based solely on leased lines may encounter problems of scalability and complexity. In order to implement a full-mesh design (every site is capable of communicating directly with every other site), for example, the number of additional, leased lines required increases linearly by one for every site added. In other words, a two-site network requires one leased line, a three-site network requires three leased lines, a four-site network requires six leased lines, etc. In order to minimize the cost and complexity of a multi-site network, network engineers might be tempted to utilize leased lines arranged in a star topology. Although such a strategy would limit the number of required leased lines to the number of connected sites, potentially serious problems would be introduced into the design. Internetworking devices at the star's central site represent a single point of failure and a major congestion point. More advanced technologies, such as Frame Relay, were designed to alleviate such problems and provide features such as QoS to the network backbone.

Frame Relay

A streamlined version of an older protocol known as X.25, *Frame Relay* is a packet switching protocol that supports traffic types such as voice, Internet, video conferencing, and corporate data. A Frame Relay network consists physically of switches, Frame Relay Access Devices *(FRAD)* and/or routers with Frame Relay ports, and leased lines (see Figure 4.5). A FRAD is merely a customized router that connects LAN technologies, such as Ethernet or Token Ring, to a Frame Relay network. The FRAD and/or router constitute the Customer Premise Equipment *(CPE)*. Frame Relay networks are generally

FIGURE 4.5

Frame relay.

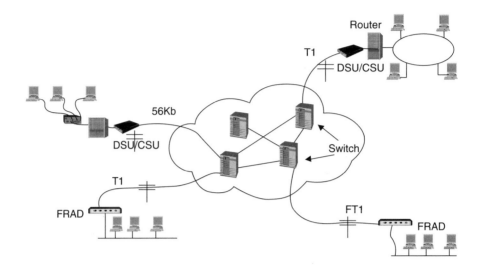

owned by public communication carriers and are, therefore, referred to as Public Data Networks *(PDN)*. Network engineers represent these networks schematically by enclosing the system of switches within a *cloud*. Inter-switch connections are referred to as the Network-to-Network Interface *(NNI)*, whereas connections between switches within the cloud and the CPE are referred to as the User-to-Network Interface *(UNI)*.

The range of capacities for a typical UNI leased line is 64 Kbps (DS0) to 1.544 Mbps (T1)/ 2.048 Mbps (E1). The minimal guaranteed capacity, or Committed Information Rate *(CIR)*, provided to the customer is, however, less than the capacity of the leased line. Although a customer may transmit information at a rate that exceeds the CIR, the network may discard customer frames during periods of high congestion. Frame Relay possesses minimal QoS functionality. By flagging certain types of frames as Discard Eligible *(DE)*, traffic prioritization can be accomplished. Frame Relay is an efficient technology. Of the maximum 4,096 bytes that constitute a frame, only eight represent overhead. Descriptions of the fields within the header and trailer of a frame follow.

Opening Flag: An 8-bit field used to indicate the beginning of a frame.

Data Link Connection Identifier (DLCI): A 6-bit field used to indicate the upper 6 bits of the DLCI, a communication endpoint originating at the CPE.

Command/Response (CR): A 1-bit field used to indicate the nature of the frame.

Address Extension (AE): This bit is set to 0.

Data Link Connection Identifier (DLCI): A 4-bit field used to indicate the lower 4 bits of the DLCI, a communication endpoint originating at the CPE.

Forward Explicit Congestion Notification (FECN): A 1-bit field used to notify the CPE of congestion in the forward direction of the frame. A set FECN indicates that the CPE must idle back to the CIR.

Backward Explicit Congestion Notification (BECN): A 1-bit field used to notify the CPE of congestion in the backward direction of the frame. A set BECN indicates that the CPE must idle back to the CIR.

Discard Eligibility (DE): A 1-bit field used to indicate to recipient switches or CPE that the present frame may be discarded during times of high congestion.

Address Extension (AE): This bit is set to 1.

Data: A variable-length field containing the data (layers 3–7) being transported.

Frame Check Sequence (FCS): A 16-bit field used to establish the validity of a transmitted frame.

Closing Flag: An 8-bit field used to indicate the end of a frame.

Information is transported between sites via pathways known as *virtual circuits.* As the name implies, a virtual circuit is a circuit that is not based on a physical connection between communication end points. Rather, it is a software-configured pathway that is established between the switches en route to each site. Virtual circuits are categorized as permanent *(PVC)* or switched *(SVC).* PVCs are configured by the carrier and remain intact until otherwise requested by the customer. SVCs are established and discontinued automatically by the CPE. A Virtual Private Network *(VPN)* between two or more sites can be established over a public Frame Relay network by employing the use of PVCs.

ATM (Asynchronous Transmission Mode)

The infrastructure of a traditional digital, telephony-based WAN is based on a TDM access scheme and, for the most part, copper wire circuits. Due to the time-sensitive nature of digital voice, the TDM access scheme provides optimal communication performance, and the copper wire circuits provide sufficient network capacity. As the need to transport information possessing different characteristics, such as digital data, became more prevalent, traditional WAN technologies were found to be less than optimal. In order to remedy this performance mismatch, the ITU and other standards bodies conducted research during the 1980s to develop a set of standards and services that could optimally transport all manner of information. The efforts of this research produced the specifications for a new fiber-based network environment known as *B-ISDN* (Broadband Integrated Services Digital Network). The cornerstone technologies chosen for B-ISDN were SONET/SDH and ATM.

In a typical B-ISDN model, the backbone consists of a SONET network with access provided via ATM switches. *SONET* networks consist physically of repeaters, multiplexors, and optical fiber. Such networks are usually configured in ring topologies and support data rates ranging from 51.84 Mbps (*STS*-1, Synchronous Transport Signal 1) to 2.488 Gbps (STS-48, Synchronous Transport Signal 48); STS-n is identical to OCn (for example, STS-1 equals OC1). Information is multiplexed into frames and transported over the network. *ATM* networks consist physically of switches, multiplexors, ATM-enabled concentrators and computers, and optical fiber generally configured in a mesh topology (see Figure 4.6). ATM supports the same data rates as SONET;

FIGURE 4.6

ATM Network.

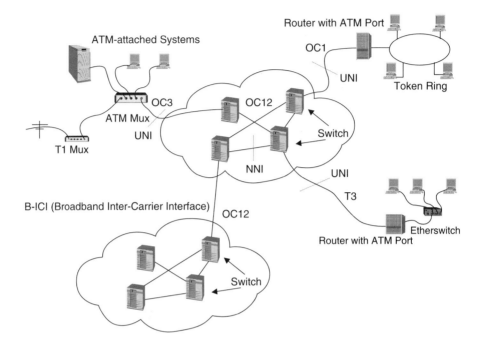

however, the typical inter-switch (referred to as *NNI*, network-to-network interface) data rate is OC12 (622 Mbps) and the typical CPE-switch (referred to as *UNI*, user-to-network interface) data rate is OC3 (155 Mbps). Although SONET may be the primary backbone technology for B-ISDN, ATM may be deemed a backbone technology in its own right.

Contemporary information exists in a multitude of formats. *HDTV* (High-Definition Television), animation, medical imaging, video conferencing, collaborative research, e-commerce transactions, web-based Push technologies, audio streaming, and plain old e-mail represent a few of these formats. The relatively high-bandwidth requirements of most of these formats combined with the Internet's ever-increasing popularity has motivated several organizations and individuals to design and implement separate, high-speed network infrastructures, such as the *vBNS* (Very High-Speed Backbone Network Services) and Internet2. In addition to the increased capacity, services such as format-dependent QoS, bandwidth-on-demand, and traffic management provisions were also sought. The backbone technology chosen for the job was ATM.

ATM is well suited for the LAN, MAN, and WAN environments. In fact, it eliminates the boundary between these various environments. Individual computers and entire networks can interface to an ATM switch, and switches, in turn, can interface to other switches over great distances. ATM has provisions to emulate legacy LAN-type environments, such as Ethernet and Token Ring. End systems within these legacy environments can communicate with end systems attached to the ATM network, as if part of the same LAN. Although related to packet switching technologies, such as Frame Relay, the packets used by ATM are of a fixed, 53-byte length and are known as cells. Each *cell* consists of a 5-byte header and a 48-byte information field. The 5-byte header is associated with the MAC sublayer of layer 2 of the OSI model, and in ATM parlance is referred to as the *ATM layer*. Several bytes within the 48-byte information field are associated with the LLC (Logical Link Control) sublayer of layer 2 of the OSI model. In ATM parlance these bytes are collectively referred to as the ATM Adaptation Layer (*AAL*). The ATM cell format is depicted in Figure 4.7, and the fields within the cell are described as follows:

Generic Flow Control (GFC): A 4-bit field used to control the flow of cells across the UNI. NNI-based cells are used for interswitch communication and are virtually identical in format to UNI-based cells. They do not, however, possess the GFC field.

Virtual Path Identifier (VPI): An 8-bit (UNI) or 12-bit (NNI) field used to route cells through the network via one or more virtual paths.

Virtual Channel Identifier (VCI): A 16-bit field used to route cells through the network via one or more virtual channels.

Payload Type (PT): A 3-bit field used to indicate the type of information (either user or network management) transported within the information field. Congestion is indicated with the user payload type.

Cell Loss Priority (CLP): A 1-bit field used to indicate to recipient switches that the present cell could be discarded during times of high congestion.

Header Error Control (HEC): An 8-bit field used in the detection of errors within the 5-byte header.

Information Field: A 48-byte field used to transport user information.

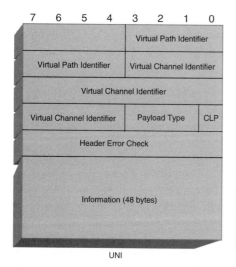 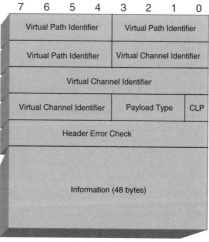

FIGURE 4.7
ATM cell format.

Information, such as an interactive videoconference or a file transfer, traverses an ATM network via a previously established path known as a Virtual Channel Connection *(VCC)*. During the establishment phase of a VCC, traffic QoS and characteristics are negotiated via the UNI on each side of the network and among all NNI. If the CPE and all participating switches agree upon the negotiated parameters, then a VCC is established and cells begin to flow. The VCC generally consists of several linked channel segments, each identified by a unique VCI. For reasons of increased performance and efficiency, several of these segments may be bundled into a Virtual Path, each also identified by a unique VPI. VCCs that are established "on-demand" are referred to as a *Switched Virtual Channel (SVC),* whereas VCCs that are permanent in nature are referred to as a *Permanent Virtual Channel (PVC).* The latter can be used to create a VPN between designated customer sites.

AAL provides for the segmentation and reassembly *(SAR)* of frames inserted into and extracted from the cell's information field. Such a service is required to create 53-byte cells from variable length frames. AAL also defines four distinct QoS types that determine information handling:

AAL1: Constant Bit Rate (CBR). This service supports constant bit-rate, connection-oriented traffic where the timing between communication end points is critical. An example is a constant-bit-rate video source such as video playback.

AAL2: Variable Bit Rate (VBR) Timing Critical. This service supports variable bit-rate, connection-oriented traffic where the timing between communication end points is critical. An example is a variable-bit-rate video source such as interactive video conferencing.

AAL3/4: Connection-Oriented and Connectionless-Oriented VBR. An example of a type 3 connection-oriented service is the transfer of a file via FTP. An example of a type 4 connectionless-oriented service is a database query.

AAL5: Simple and Efficient Adaptation Layer (SEAL). A version of AAL3/4 optimized for high-speed LAN and WAN traffic.

4.2 Access Technologies

As the population of domestic web surfers and the virtual workforce (telecommuters, mobile workers, and remote administrators) increases, the quantity and quality of access services must grow proportionally.

As the population of domestic web surfers and the virtual workforce (telecommuters, mobile workers, and remote administrators) increases, the quantity and quality of access services must grow proportionally. *Access technologies* are those categories of devices, protocols, and policies that provide access to the network backbone and hence the desired service(s). Laptops, desktop computers, and PCS devices equipped with the appropriate modem constitute user access devices, whereas dialup, xDSL, ISDN, PCS, cable modem, and VPN constitute the access schemes, and associated protocols, used by these devices. The policies that are applied to these access schemes generally include items such as tariffs, access procedures, audit trails, and authentication and encryption techniques.

Dialup Access

Perhaps the most prevalent scheme, *dialup access* requires the use of a standard modem, such as the 56Kbps variety, and an analog phone line. The three categories of dialup access include terminal emulation, remote control, and remote node. As implied by the name, *terminal emulation* requires that the end user's computer behave like a terminal. In other words, commands are transmitted to a remote host where the desired process, pending access approval, is executed. Screen updates are transmitted from the remote host back to the end user's terminal. Terminal emulation is essentially a parasitic means by which the end user can execute applications on remote systems. The TCP/IP application Telnet, for example, is used for terminal emulation.

Remote control technologies enable the end user's computer to possess a remote host. Such remote hosts are usually connected to the LAN associated with the user's place of employment. In a typical remote control scenario, the end user would start the remote control host program on his or her office computer prior to leaving work. Once at home, the end user would dial up a modem directly attached to the serial port of the office computer using a remote control client program. After some initial negotiation between the systems, the screen information of the office computer would appear on the screen of the home computer. Commands typed on the home computer's keyboard would be transmitted to the office computer and executed. WinFrame by Citrix Systems, for example, is a remote control technology used with Microsoft Windows products.

The most ubiquitous dialup access technology is *remote node.* During a remote node session, the home computer participates fully in the LAN environment to which it is attached; that is, the communication protocols that traverse the LAN, such as TCP/IP, also flow back and forth over the end user's phone line. Effectively, the LAN has been "stretched" to the user's home or current residence. Either a terminal server or a remote access server (RAS) is used to manage remote node connections on the LAN side. A *terminal server* is a device that is usually consists of several serial ports and one LAN port. Each serial port connects to a unique port of a modem pool, or a standalone modem, and, therefore, supports one unique dialup phone number, or extension. Data arriving from the remote user is essentially multiplexed onto the LAN via the LAN port.

A *RAS* is a computer equipped with multiple serial ports and a LAN adapter card that behaves similarly to a terminal server. A RAS is generally more adaptable and thus feature rich than a terminal server. For example, RAS can be outfitted with an ISDN adapter(s) to support users who have an ISDN line installed at home. They are also usually configured as an Authentication, Authorization, and Accounting (AAA) server, and, therefore, behave as the LAN's sentry for remote access. A RAS typically supports features such as user callback, compression, the RADIUS (Remote Authentication Dial-In User Service) authentication protocol, the DES (Data Encryption Scheme) or Triple-DES private key encryption protocol, and the RSA (developed by RSA Data Security) public key encryption protocol. Most remote node access schemes employ the PPP protocol to transport protocols such as TCP/IP or IPX/SPX.

xDSL (Digital Subscriber Loop Services)

The telephone circuit between the customer's premises and the carrier's CO is often referred to as the *last mile*, or *subscriber line*. These circuits are in analog format and are apparently limited in bandwidth, and thus capacity, to 3,100 Hz (4,000 Hz with guard band) for a standard voice circuit. Or are they? In fact, most of these copper-based circuits possess a bandwidth of approximately 1 MHz. Filtering devices (referred to as *load coils*) and repeaters limit these circuits to a bandwidth of 4 KHz. Such circuits can be conditioned to support higher bandwidths. A relatively new set of access technologies referred to collectively as *xDSL* (where x represents a variable such as A or S) are designed to exploit the unused bandwidth (4 KHz–1 MHz) of these circuits and to operate simultaneously with regular phone calls, or POTS.

Although POTS and xDSL services occupy the same physical medium, they have virtually no other similarities. xDSL are TDM-based, digital access technologies that require no dial tone, are never "busy," and support both *symmetrical* (same upstream and downstream capacities) and *asymmetrical* (different upstream and downstream capacities) data traffic. Asymmetrical versions of xDSL provide greater capacities for data traveling toward the user (downstream) and lesser capacities for data traveling away from the user (upstream). The web is an example of an application that is well suited for asymmetrical xDSL, whereas interactive video conferencing is well suited for symmetrical xDSL.

A typical xDSL configuration consists of an xDSL modem, located at the customer's premises, connected to an xDSL modem, located within the carrier's CO or in a communications box within the customer's neighborhood, via the subscriber line. The output of the carrier's xDSL modem connects to the input of a DSL Access Multiplexer *(DSLAM)*, which, in turn, connects to the carrier's backbone, which, in turn, connects to the customer's place of business and/or the Internet.

The two communicating xDSL modems divide the unused bandwidth of the subscriber line into multiple-frequency channels via FDM. Modulation of information into these frequency-divided channels is accomplished via one of two modulation schemes: Carrierless Amplitude/Phase Modulation *(CAP)* or Discrete Multi-Tone *(DMT)*. Each channel is typically allocated a bandwidth of 4 KHz and functions similarly to a standard analog modem channel. Distinct channels are subdivided into either low-speed or high-speed time slots via TDM. The following table describes the various types of xDSL, their maximum service distance, and maximum upstream and downstream capacities at this distance:

xDSL Type	Distance (feet)	Upstream (bps)	Downstream (bps)
ADSL (Asymmetrical DSL)	18,000	64,000	1,544,000
ADSL Lite	18,000	100,000	500,000
RADSL (Rate-adaptive DSL)	18,000	128,000	1,000,000

SDSL (Symmetric DSL)	10,000	1,100,000	1,100,000
UDSL (Universal DSL)	18,000	1,000,000	1,000,000
IDSL (ISDN-like DSL)	18,000	128,000	128,000
VDSL (Very-high-speed DSL)	4,500	1,800,000	12,980,000
HDSL (High-bit-rate DSL)	12,000	1,544,000	1,544,000
HDSL 2	12,000	1,544,000	1,544,000

ISDN (Integrated Systems Digital Network)

The precursor to xDSL, *ISDN* was developed in the 1970s and formerly standardized by the ITU in 1984. Unlike xDSL, however, ISDN is a high-speed, circuit-switched technology; that is, ISDN connections are set up in milliseconds. A typical ISDN connection physically consists of CPE (such as fax machines, ISDN and non-ISDN-equipped computers and phones), ISDN routers, ISDN switches (located at the CO), and ISDN subscriber lines (see Figure 4.8). ISDN routers are capable of supporting data, voice, audio, and video input in both analog and digital formats. They are used for user-to-LAN, LAN-to-LAN, user-to-ISP, and LAN-to-ISP scenarios. The following four distinct ISDN reference points (U, T, S, and R) are used to describe the various router interfaces, both internal and external:

U: An external interface between the ISDN router and the subscriber line. The ISDN router interfacing circuitry is referred to as an *NT1* (Network Termination 1).

T: An internal interface between the NT1 and CPE router interface, referred to as an *NT2* (Network Termination 2).

S: An external interface between the NT2 and ISDN equipment (TE1, Terminal Equipment Type 1), or an internal interface between the NT2 and the terminal adapter (TA) circuit that enables the router to support non-ISDN equipment (TE2, Terminal Equipment 2).

R: An external interface between the TA and TE2.

Information is transported over ISDN via TDM-based channels designated as *D* (Delta), *B* (Bearer), or *H* (High-Speed). The D channel has a capacity of either 16 or 64 Kbps and is used primarily for signaling. When not used for signaling, however, the D channel can be used to transport data. The B channel has a capacity of 64 Kbps and is used to bear the subscriber's information. There are several versions of the H channel, all of which have a capacity that is a multiple of the B channel and provide high-speed access. *BRI* (Basic Rate Interface) and *PRI* (Primary Rate Interface), the two standard classes of ISDN services, consist of two 64-Kbps B channels plus one 16-Kbps D channel (2B+D) and 23 64-Kbps B channels plus one 64-Kbps D channel (23B+D), respectively. Both

FIGURE 4.8

ISDN (Integrated Services Digital Network).

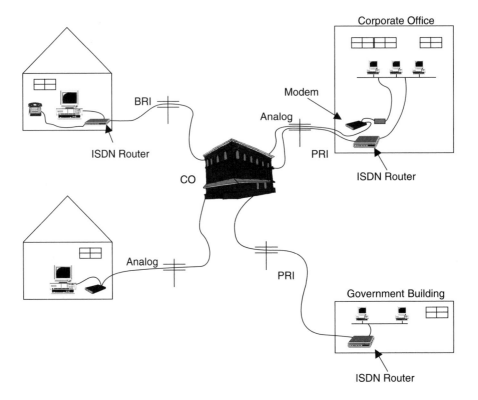

services allow for simultaneous dialing of multiple numbers or the linking of all B channels to form a high-capacity connection. The B channels of BRI, for example, can be used to simultaneously call two ISDN numbers, such as the subscriber's place of employment and ISP, or joined to form a single 128-Kbps connection (144 Kbps when the D channel is used).

Cable Modem

xDSL is to POTS as the cable modem is to CATV. As the name implies, a *cable modem* is a device that enables a CATV subscriber to transmit and receive digital information via the standard coaxial cable installed at home or work. Similar to some versions of xDSL, cable modem technology is always present, can be used concurrently with CATV services, and is asymmetric. Historically, CATV systems have been designed and implemented in a subsplit configuration, whereby the available downstream (towards subscriber) bandwidth has always greatly exceeded the upstream. Such a configuration is ideal for the one-way broadcast of television signals and the asymmetrical transmission and reception of digital information. In fact, the typical downstream capacity for cable modem technology is 27 Mbps, whereas the typical upstream capacity is 2 Mbps.

A cable modem/CATV network is an FDM-based system that typically consists of computers with Ethernet adapter cards, televisions, splitters, distribution amplifiers, trunk amplifiers, the carrier's (cable company) Head-end and data network, and, of course, miles of coaxial cable (see Figure 4.9). CATV companies generally have substantial optical fiber installations as well. Cable modem technology operates as follows:

1. The subscriber transmits information toward the carrier's Head-end via an upstream channel.

2. Equipment within the Head-end demodulates the information and transmits it onto the carrier's data network.

3. The information is routed from the carrier's data network to the subscriber's place of employment or the Internet.

4. Reply information is routed from the subscriber's place of employment or the Internet to the carrier's data network.

5. The reply information is received by the Head-end equipment and modulated onto a downstream channel.

6. The subscriber receives the reply information via the appropriate downstream channel.

FIGURE 4.9

Cable modem.

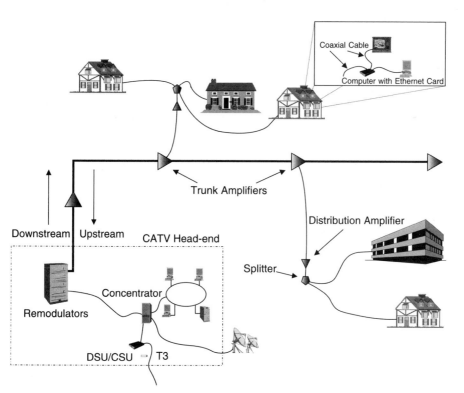

A cable modem network is a highly distributed Ethernet environment that employs the standard CSMA/CD access scheme. In other words, subscribers vie for bandwidth and thus transmission capacity. As the number of subscribers increases, the available capacity decreases.

Summary

As the term implies, the *backbone* constitutes the core infrastructure of a computer network. Connecting media, hubs, concentrators, and internetworking devices are included within the backbone. Backbone technologies, old and new, span the realms of the LAN, MAN, and WAN. Advances in software technologies, such as multimedia, video conferencing, and intranet applications, coupled with the converging technologies that have traditionally supported data, voice (telephony), and video (television and related media) demand advances in the technologies tasked with the transportation of the data traffic generated by these applications.

Traditional, or legacy, technologies are ill equipped to handle the emerging transportation requirements. Recent and nascent contenders of backbone technologies are "intelligent" enough to detect patterns in data traffic, referred to as *flows,* and/or the type of traffic in order to adjust the quality of service (*QoS*) required for the proper handling of such traffic. The QoS associated with a stream, or flow, of video information, for example, would require the allocation of a fixed amount of bandwidth, whereas the QoS for critical data would require high-priority transportation.

As the population of domestic web surfers and the virtual workforce (telecommuters, mobile workers, and remote administrators) increases the quantity and quality of access services must grow proportionally. Access technologies are devices, protocaols, and policies that provide access to the network backbone, and hence the desired service(s). Laptops, desktop computers, and PCS devices equipped with the appropriate modem constitute user access devices, whereas dialup, xDSL, ISDN, PCS, cable modem, and VPN constitute the access schemes, and associated protocols, used by these devices.

Primitive Applications

Chapter Learning Objectives:

- Understand the current and past roles of several Internet applications.
- Examine the usage of these applications.
- Examine the helper programs of these primitive applications.

"Old men and comets have been reverenced for the same reason: their long beards, and pretences to foretell events."

Jonathan Swift, Thoughts on Various Subjects

Primitive? Perhaps. Although the World Wide Web has rendered many primitive Internet applications (such as Gopher and WAIS) effectively defunct, Telnet and FTP are still used quite extensively. In the sections that follow, we examine these primitive applications to understand their role in the evolution of the Internet and how they are used today.

5.1 Telnet: Logging into a Remote Host

Telnet is a client application native to the TCP/IP protocol suite that allows a computer to emulate a terminal, log into a remote host, and run remote processes. TN3270 is a derivative of Telnet that allows a computer to emulate an IBM 3270

Telnet is a client application native to the TCP/IP protocol suite that allows a computer to emulate a terminal, log into a remote host, and run remote processes.

terminal and remotely log into an IBM host. Because the computer is emulating a terminal, it only receives screen updates from the remote host. In such a mode, it is not capable of actually running the process. To invoke the Telnet application from a command prompt (Microsoft DOS or Windows, or Unix), enter the following syntax:

```
telnet <remote_host> <port_number>
```

where <remote_host> is the Internet address of the desired, remote host, and <port_number> is an optional field that tells the remote host to start up a specific type of service.

Both a command prompt and a graphical version (see Figure 5.1) of Telnet (from Microsoft Corporation) are presented as follows. The first example illustrates a basic Telnet login and logout. Pertinent information such as the last unsuccessful login attempt and the last successful login are displayed at login. The Unix command *ps* (show processes) is typed on the local keyboard, yet executed on the remote host:

```
telnet (st6000.sct.edu)

login: tfallon
tfallon's Password:

Last unsuccessful login: Tue Sep 22 15:27:13 EDT 1998 on
/dev/pts/19 from 168.28
.178.218
Last login: Mon Nov 16 02:38:15 EST 1998 on /dev/pts/4 from
user-38lcfrr.dialup.
mindspring.com

[YOU HAVE MAIL]

tfallon [171] ps -a

   PID    TTY     TIME CMD
   19256  pts/2   0:04 tintin++
   22134  pts/1   0:00 elm
   22378  pts/4   0:00 ps
   23350  pts/1   0:01 pico
   24388  pts/0   0:00 elm
   26486  pts/3   0:01 pine
   27700  pts/5   0:01 elm

tfallon [172] logout
```

The next example illustrates a basic Telnet login from a DOS prompt with port option 13, date/time:

```
C:\> telnet st6000.sct.edu 13

Mon Nov 16 02:54:21 1998
```

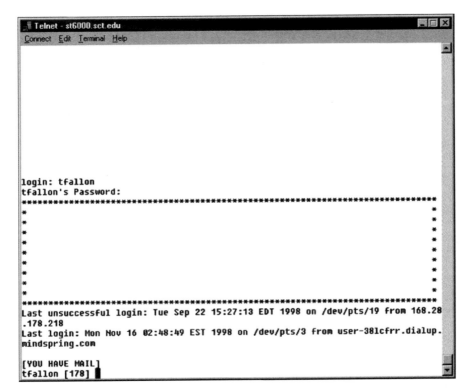

FIGURE 5.1
Graphical version of Telnet.

Telnet has two modes of operation: input and command. When a remote connection is established, Telnet defaults to input mode and is capable of receiving characters from the user's keyboard. However, when a logon attempt fails or if the word "Telnet" is typed by itself, a telnet> prompt appears, which indicates that the user is in command mode and can enter telnet commands.

Telnet Commands

? or help: Shows a list of available commands.

close: After exiting a remote host, the close command is used to terminate the connection.

open: Used to connect to a remote host. Syntax is: open <remote_host>.

quit: Terminates all connections and exits telnet program.

<enter>: Return to remote session or exit telnet, if none exists.

set echo: Echoes the character typed at the keyboard. If you can't see what you're typing, or if the character(s) you typed appear(s) doubled on the screen, then type "set echo" at the telnet prompt.

Hytelnet is still used to access Free-Nets, CWISs (Campus-Wide Information Services), OPACs, and many other sites. Hypertext links allow users to navigate screens of information until they find the desired remote host.

5.2 Hytelnet: An Aid to Telnet

Hytelnet (Hypertext Browser for Telnet) is a program that aids users in locating "Telnet-able" Internet sites, illustrates site login procedures, and frequently performs the Telnet login. Hytelnet is still used to access Free-Nets, CWISs (Campus-Wide Information Services), OPACs, and many other sites. Hypertext links allow users to navigate screens of information until they find the desired remote host. The following New York Public Library Telnet information was obtained via Hytelnet. The web was used to search for the keyword "Hytelnet" and to invoke its services (see Figure 5.2).

```
UNIX System V Release 4.2 (nyplgate) (pts/0)

login: nypl

UNIX System V/386 Release 4.2 Version 1.1.2
nyplgate
Copyright (c) 1992 UNIX System Laboratories, Inc.
Copyright (c) 1987, 1988 Microsoft Corp. All rights reserved.
Last login: Mon Nov 16 03:54:15 on pts000
```

```
          WELCOME TO THE NEW YORK
             PUBLIC LIBRARY
          NETWORK. (NYPLnet)
```

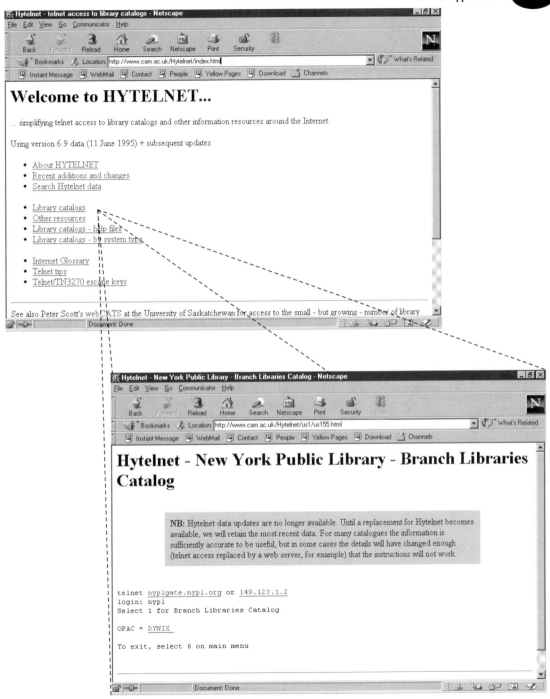

FIGURE 5.2

Hytelnet (hypertext browser for Telnet) example.

```
The following Databases are currently available:

        1 - NYPL Branch Libraries Catalog

        2 - NYPL Research Libraries Catalog
               (This includes the Dance Collection Catalog.
                Note instructions for Dance users once
connected.)

        3 - EXIT NYPLnet

        To return to this menu at any point, type 'q' and press
enter

                        SELECT DATABASE and press enter:
```

5.3 FTP (File Transfer Protocol)

FTP (File Transfer Protocol) is a client application native to the TCP/IP protocol suite that allows computer systems to exchange files via the Internet. Several hosts on the Internet are configured as *anonymous ftp* servers. As the name implies, these servers allow anyone to log in using the account name "anonymous." The required password is usually either "guest" or the user's e-mail address. Once a file is transferred, the user may need to uncompress it, use a converter program, or use the application in which it was developed to view and/or run it. To invoke the FTP application from a command prompt (Microsoft DOS or Windows, or Unix), enter the following syntax:

FTP (File Transfer Protocol) is a client application native to the TCP/IP protocol suite that allows computer systems to exchange files via the Internet.

```
ftp <remote_host> <port_number>
```

where the parameters are identical to those illustrated in the previous section.

Both a command prompt and graphical version (WS_FTP or Winsock FTP by Ipswitch, Inc., see Figure 5.3) of FTP are presented as follows. The first example illustrates a basic FTP login and logout. The Unix command *pwd* (print working directory) is used to determine the current remote directory. The Unix command *ls* (list subdirectory) and the FTP command *bin* (binary) are used to determine the name of the remote file (metropolis.gif) to be transferred and to set the transfer mode to binary.

```
tfallon [181] ftp st6000.sct.edu

Connected to st6000.sct.edu.
220 st6000.sct.edu FTP server (Version 4.1 Wed Nov 20 05:12:15
CST 1996) ready.
Name (st6000.sct.edu:tfallon): tfallon
331 Password required for tfallon.
Password:
```

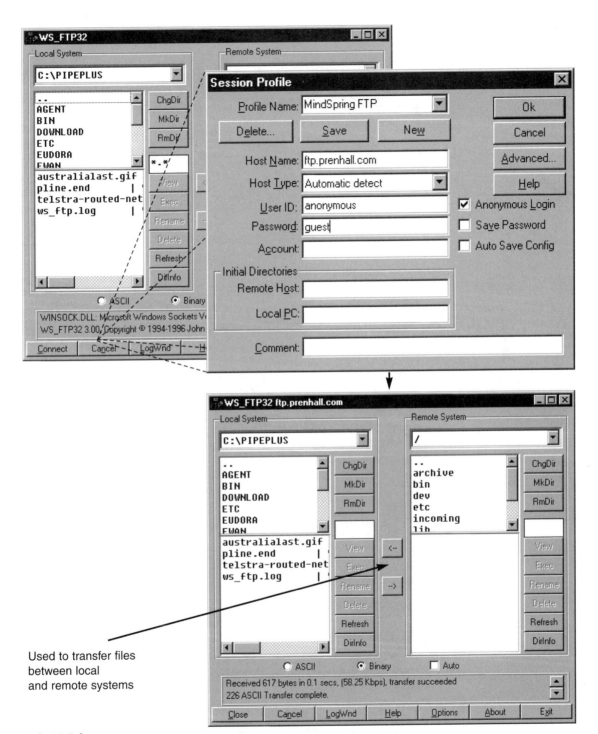

Used to transfer files
between local
and remote systems

FIGURE 5.3
WS_FTP example.

```
230 User tfallon logged in.
ftp> pwd
257 "/home/b/tfallon" is current directory.
tfallon [184] ftp st6000.sct.edu
Connected to st6000.sct.edu.
220 st6000.sct.edu FTP server (Version 4.1 Wed Nov 20 05:12:15
CST 1996) ready.
Name (st6000.sct.edu:tfallon): tfallon
331 Password required for tfallon.
Password:
230 User tfallon logged in.

ftp> ls -l
200 PORT command successful.
150 Opening ASCII mode data connection for /bin/ls.
07-07-98  12:48AM                    2181 metropolis.gif
226 Transfer complete.

ftp> bin
200 Type set to I.

ftp> get metropolis.gif
200 PORT command successful.
150 Opening BINARY mode data connection for
metropolis.gif(2181 bytes).
226 Transfer complete.
2181 bytes received in 0.0246 seconds (86.59 Kbytes/s)
local: metropolis.gif remote: metropolis.gif

ftp> close
221

ftp> quit
221 Goodbye.
```

FTP also possesses input and command modes that function similarly to those of Telnet. When a remote connection is established, FTP defaults to input mode and is capable of receiving characters from the user's keyboard. However, when a logon attempt fails or if the word "FTP" is typed by itself, an ftp> prompt appears, which indicates that the user is in command mode and can enter ftp commands.

FTP Commands

? or help: Shows a list of available commands. By typing "help <command>", a description of how to use that particular command is given.

close: After exiting a remote host, the close command is used to terminate the connection.

open: Used to connect to a remote host. Syntax is: open <remote_host>.

quit: Terminates all connections and exits ftp program.

ascii: Invokes ASCII transfer mode to transfer text files.

binary: Invokes binary transfer mode to transfer files such as executable, graphics, and audio (that is, non-ASCII).

pwd: Shows current directory.

cd: Changes to specified directory. Syntax is: cd <directory>.

get or mget: Retrieves file(s) from remote host.

put or mput: Stores file(s) to remote host.

5.4 Archie: An Aid to FTP

Although Archie servers are becoming more rare, several can still be located via the web.

Archie is a program that aids users when searching an Archie (archival) server database for files that can be retrieved via anonymous FTP. Archie does not retrieve the files for the user; rather, it indicates the file's location, size, modification date, and attributes. If an Archie client is not installed on the user's computer, Telnet can be used to log into an Archie server by using the account "archie." Although Archie servers are becoming more rare, several can still be located via the web. The following example depicts an interactive Archie session with the server archie.rutgers.edu. The Archie command "prog" was used to search for the phrase "space shuttle."

```
login: archie

Last login: Tue Nov 17 13:16:41 from unixs2.cis.pitt.
Sun Microsystems Inc.    SunOS 5.6      Generic August 1997
-------------------------- Network Services -----------------
-----------


                    Welcome to Archie!
                       Vers 3.5


# Bunyip Information Systems, Inc., 1993, 1994, 1995

# Terminal type set to 'vt100 24 80'.
# 'erase' character is '^?'.
# 'search' (type string) has the value 'exact'.

archie> prog space shuttle

# Search type: exact.
```

```
working...

>> space



Host ftp.seas.gwu.edu    (128.164.9.5)
Last updated 07:17  5 Apr 1998

    Location: /pub/rtfm/sci/space
       DIRECTORY      drwxr-xr-x              512  14:49  3 Mar 1998
shuttle


Host ftp.msc.edu         (137.66.1.3)
Last updated 18:08 27 Mar 1998

    Location: /pub/X
       FILE      -rw-r--r--          117632  05:00 20 Dec 1990
shuttle


Host nic.funet.fi        (128.214.248.6)
Last updated 20:00 22 Apr 1998

    Location: /pub/misc/old-hsu-
archive/publicdomain/texts/space
       DIRECTORY      drwxrwxr-x           8192  05:00 22 Mar 1995
shuttle

    Location: /pub/misc/old-hsu-archive/publicdomain/digest
       DIRECTORY      drwxrwxr-x           8192  05:00 22 Mar 1995
shuttle

    Location: /pub/mirrors/rtfm.mit.edu/pub/usenet-by-
hierarchy/sci/space
       DIRECTORY      drwxrwxr-x           8192  13:12  6 Jul 1997
shuttle

    Location: /pub/misc/old-hsu-archive/publicdomain/texts
       DIRECTORY      drwxrwxr-x           8192  05:00 22 Mar 1995
shuttle
archie> quit
# Bye.
```

Archie Commands

prog <search string>: Search command.

set search exact: Default search setting that forces the search to match the search string exactly.

set search sub: Allows for search of any occurence of search string (for example, <math> could mean mathematics, math, or mathworks).

set search regexp: Allows Unix expressions to be substituted for search string.

show search: Shows current search setting.

set pager: Views one screen at a time.

help: Help on command usage.

mail <address>: Mails results of search to specified address.

quit: Terminates archie session.

5.5 Gopher: Burrowing through the Internet

Gopher is a text-based, menu-driven client application that enables users to connect to Gopher servers, select an item of interest, and then tunnel through the Internet to find the item. Although approaching obsolescence, Gopher is still in use at some locations. By employing Telnet and FTP, Gopher automatically connects the user with the desired destination and, if necessary, retrieves files. Gopher is essentially an internationally distributed library card index that consists of several interconnected Gopher servers. Collectively, the menu items of all Gopher servers are called *gopher-space.* Perhaps the most practical manner in which to connect to a Gopher server is through the web (see Figure 5.4).

Gopher menu elements (end of line symbols):

/: Connects to another menu.

.: Accesses a file.

<?>: Connects to an index search server, where you will be asked to enter a keyword(s).

<TEL>: Causes you to Telnet somewhere.

Gopher commands:

?: Shows command key sequences.

a: Bookmarks a file.

A: Bookmarks a directory.

V: Shows bookmarks.

s: Saves menu item to file.

q: Quits Gopher.

Gopher is essentially an internationally distributed library card index that consists of several interconnected Gopher servers.

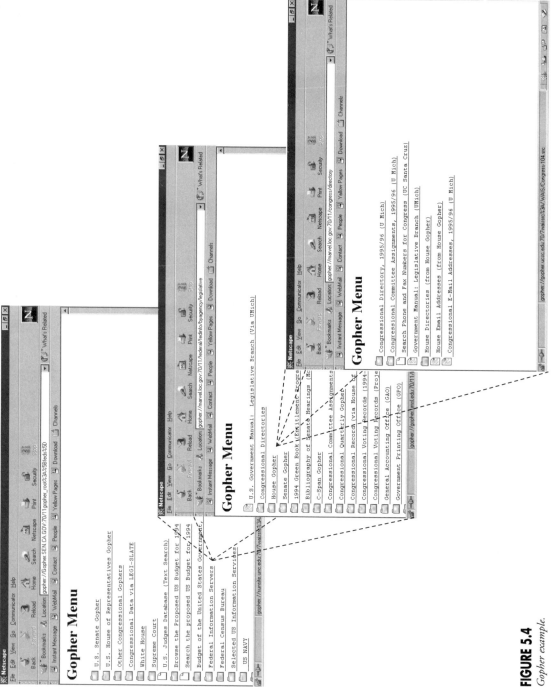

FIGURE 5.4
Gopher example.

5.6 Veronica: An Aid to Gopher

Veronica (Very Easy Rodent-Oriented Net-wide Index to Computerized Archives) is a program used to enhance searches in gopher-space. Veronica creates a customized menu consisting of items, found throughout gopher-space, related to the keyword(s) entered. Keyword searches allow the use of boolean operators. Veronica lives in gopherspace, all gopher commands apply.

Summary

Prior to the advent of the web, several popular client applications enabled users to login to remote hosts and exchange information. Telnet, FTP, e-mail, and other applications are still used for such purposes. Telnet enables the user to login to a remote host and invoke remote applications, whereas FTP is used to remotely store and retrieve files. Gopher is a search-and-retrieve application that has been largely superceded by the web.

●
Veronica creates a customized menu consisting of items, found throughout gopher-space, related to the keyword(s) entered.

The World Wide Web

Chapter Learning Objectives:

- Discuss some of the uses of the web.
- Understand web page design.
- Create and dissect web pages.

"The secret thoughts of a man run over all things, holy, profane, clean, obscene, grave, and light, without shame or blame."

Thomas Hobbes, Leviathan

6.1 Spinning the Web

The most popular of Internet services is the World Wide Web. The web, as it is commonly called, is rapidly changing the manner in which we present and manipulate information. It is used for a multitude of services including collaborative research, electronic commerce (e-commerce), advertising, multimedia broadcasting, database interactions, online education, and much more. So great is the impact of the web, that it is estimated that two to three trillion dollars ($2,000,000,000,000 to $3,000,000,000,000) in e-commerce transactions will occur over the next five years! Although significant, e-commerce represents only one area of growth of this relatively new medium.

As mentioned previously, the web is based on a client/server network model. A client program, referred to as a *browser*, is used to transmit a request for information to a web server. The web server, in turn, transmits a reply in the form of a document, commonly referred to as a *web page*. *HTTP* (Hypertext Transfer Protocol), a protocol within the TCP/IP protocol suite, is used to transport the user's request from browser

The web is rapidly changing the manner in which we present and manipulate information.

to server and the content and formatting information of the web page from server to browser. Web pages are merely text files that contain special markers, referred to as *tags*, that indicates formatting information and the inclusion of special features, such as an audio clip or a section of JavaScript, to the receiving browser. The de facto markup language that describes the proper usage of these tags is *HTML* (Hypertext Markup Language).

HTML is based upon *SGML* (Standard Generalized Markup Language), a more complex document formatting language. Successive versions of HTML are recommended and developed by the World Wide Web Consortium (*W3C*, www.w3.org). Although considered the official sanctioning body for HTML, the W3C, nevertheless, internally refers to HTML change proposals as Recommendations. The current Recommendation is HTML 4.0.

Web site developers, sometimes referred to as *webmasters*, create web pages by using text editors (such as vi or Notepad), HTML editors (such as Coffee Cup by Coffee Cup Software), HTML-enabled word processors (such as Microsoft Word), and/or advanced development tools (such as Allaire's Cold Fusion). Sites consist of web pages, objects embedded within the pages (such as animated GIFs or Java applets), and, possibly, back-end applications (such as databases). Generally, the first web page of a particular site encountered by an individual "surfing the Net" is referred to as the *home page*; the home page is usually designed to introduce the layout and contents of the web site. Individuals direct their browsers to a particular web site by entering the site's *URL* (Uniform Resource Locator), or web address, into the location or address field of their browser. The URL www.whitehouse.gov, for example, would be entered to visit the White House's web site.

Early web pages incorporated primitive formatting tags, referred to as *elements*, for paragraph delineation, italicization, header font size manipulation, and the interconnecting of web pages and/or sites via hypermedia references. Although these early tags are still commonly incorporated, web pages are now embellished with advanced features such as tables, forms, animated GIFs, multimedia clips, Java applets, JavaScripts, and ActiveX controls. Recent and nascent software innovations such as *DHTML* (Dynamic HTML), *CSS* (cascading style sheets), and *XML* (Extensible Markup Language) are enabling developers to create web sites that are feature-rich and dynamic in nature. In the subsequent sections of this chapter and the next, we will examine the intricate details of the World Wide Web.

6.2 Web Browsers and Servers

As we learned in Chapter 2, when requesting information from a server, a browser uses TCP/IP to establish a socket connection (host address and port number) on port 80 (HTTP). Once the connection is established, the browser issues a request line, one or more request headers, and a blank line. Upon receipt of the request, the server issues a response line, one or more response headers, a blank line, and the requested document. At this point, an HTTP 1.1 server waits for a subsequent request from the browser. An HTTP 1.0 server, however, would close the socket connection.

The three most commonly used HTTP request methods are GET, HEAD, and POST. POST is used to send information, such as data entered into an online form, to the server. This information is appended as a separate line(s) within the request. The GET and HEAD methods are used primarily to retrieve information from a server. Response headers and the requested document are returned in response to a GET request, whereas only the response headers are returned in response to a HEAD request. Both methods can be used to send information to the server by appending it to a question mark, which, in turn, is appended to the URL.

In the following example, Telnet was used to establish a manual interactive HTTP session (port 80) with the web server www.prenhall.com. The syntax of the single request line, GET / /HTTP1.1, is used to instruct the server to send the source code of the site's home page to the awaiting Telnet program. Received by the server are the response line, HTTP/1.1 200 OK, several response headers (for example, Server: Netscape-Enterprise/3.5.1c), and a partial listing of the source code; the entire code will be interpreted in a subsequent section. The response line status code 200 indicates that the request was successful.

```
tfallon[232] telnet www.prenhall.com 80

GET / /HTTP1.1

HTTP/1.1 200 OK
Server: Netscape-Enterprise/3.5.1C
Date: Tue, 01 Dec 1998 20:23:31 GMT
Content-type: text/html
Link: <http://www.prenhall.com/?PageServices>;
rel="PageServices"
Last-modified: Thu, 20 Nov 1997 14:18:39 GMT
Content-length: 2650
Accept-ranges: bytes

<html>
<head><title>Prentice Hall</title>
</head>

<frameset rows="0,100%" border=0>
<frame src="nothing.html" scrolling="NO">
<frame src="index_body.html">
</frameset>
<noframes>
<body bgcolor="FFFFFF">
<font face="arial, geneva"><b>
<h2>Prentice Hall<h2>
```

Similar to the previous example, the syntax of the single request line, HEAD / /HTTP1.1, is used to instruct the server to send only the response headers of the site's home page to the awaiting Telnet program. Received by the server are the response line,

HTTP/1.1 500 Server Error, and several response headers. The response line status code, 500 Server Error, indicates that request headers with specific information should have been sent along with the initial response line.

```
HEAD / /HTTP1.1

HTTP/1.1 500 Server Error
Server: Netscape-Enterprise/3.5.1C
Date: Tue, 01 Dec 1998 20:24:03 GMT
Content-type: text/html
```

At the time of this writing, the versions of the two most popular browsers are Netscape Navigator 4.7 (Netscape Communications Corporation) and Internet Explorer 5.0 (Microsoft Corporation). Current events should prove to be an interesting factor in the intense competition between these two great rivals. The U.S. Department of Justice and Microsoft are sparring over claims of antitrust practices, and AOL has recently acquired Netscape. Since the products of both companies are ubiquitous throughout the global workforce, the evolution of these events could create significant changes in the operational strategies of individuals and companies.

Netscape Communicator is a suite of Internet communication applications that include a web browser (Navigator), an e-mail client (Messenger), a newsgroup reader, an address book, and an HTML editor (Composer). Additional Communicator features include the AOL Instant Messenger, Symantec Corporation's Java Console (a code debugger), advanced security mechanisms, support for international users, support for web channels, support for plug-ins (Netscape enhancement utilities), and provisions for offline work. The default configuration for Communicator possesses the following prominent features (see Figure 6.1):

> Netscape Communicator is a suite of Internet communication applications that include a web browser, an e-mail client, a newsgroup reader, an address book, and an HTML editor.

Title Bar: Indicates the title of the application being used. In the case of Navigator, the name of the featured web site is also displayed.

Download Indicator: Indicates the download status of the contents of a specific web page. Streaking meteors indicate download in progress.

Application Toolbar: Used to select one of the Internet communication applications.

Status Bar: Indicates the download status, in bytes, of the contents of a specific web page.

View Field: Self-explanatory.

Personal Toolbar: A user-customized toolbar that includes the AOL Instant Messenger, a WebMail button, a web channels button, and personal entries.

Location Toolbar: Used to add and manipulate bookmarks and enter URLs.

Navigation Toolbar: Used to navigate through web pages, reload web pages, load the default home page, load a personal home page, search the Internet for desired documents, print web documents, view security information, and terminate web page downloading.

Title Bar

Download Indicator

Menu Toolbar →

Navigation Toolbar →

Location Toolbar →

Personal Toolbar →

View Field

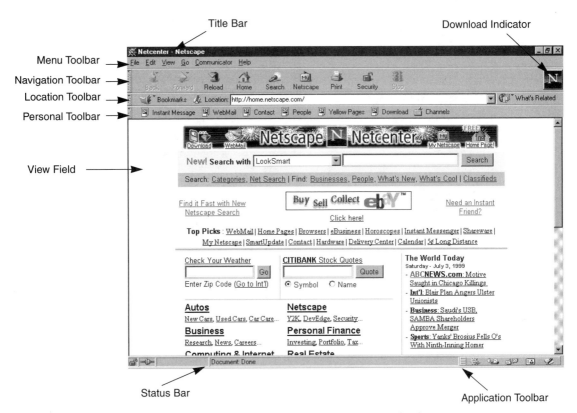

Status Bar

Application Toolbar

Netscape Communicator screenshot ©1999 Netscape Communication Corporation. Used with permission.

FIGURE 6.1
Netscape Communicator.

Menu Toolbar: Used to manipulate web pages, work offline, customize user preferences, show and hide various toolbars, select Internet communication applications, and provide context-sensitive help.

The intuitive design of Navigator's graphical user interface (GUI) enables one to quickly assimilate the most commonly used features. To exemplify this intuitive design, we electronically visit the White House by directing our browser to the URL www.whitehouse.gov (see Figure 6.2). Within the File menu of the Menu Toolbar we choose the entry Open Page. An Open Page dialog box appears. Type the URL www.whitehouse.gov in the centrally located blank field and click the button labeled Open. After a few moments, pertinent information and a graphic of the White House flanked by two waving American flags appear within the View field. The URL entry, http://www.whitehouse.gov/WH/Welcome.html, is displayed in the Netsite field of the Location Toolbar. In order to bookmark this web site, we choose the Bookmarks entry within the

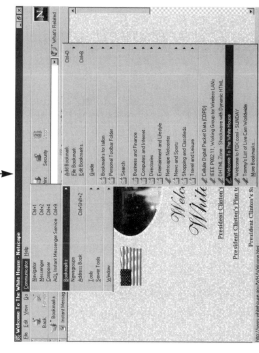

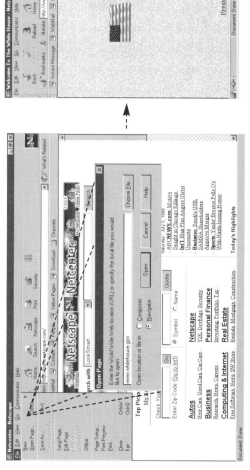

Netscape Communicator screenshot ©1999 Netscape Communication Corporation. Used with permission.

FIGURE 6.2

Using Navigator to visit the White House.

Communicator menu of the Menu Toolbar, or the Bookmarks button on the Location Toolbar. From the Bookmarks drop-down menu, we choose Add Bookmark. Choosing our newly created bookmark assists us in subsequent visits to the White House.

Microsoft Internet Explorer is a suite of Internet communication applications that include a web browser (IE), an e-mail client, a newsgroup reader, address book (Outlook Express), and an HTML editor (FrontPage Express). Additional IE features include advanced security mechanisms, support for international users, support for web channels, support for ActiveX controls and the Microsoft Windows Media Player (IE enhancement utilities), and provisions for offline work. The default configuration for IE also has several prominent features (see Figure 6.3):

Title Bar: Indicates the title of the featured web site.

Download Indicator: Indicates the download status of the contents of a specific web page. Ring rotating around "e" indicates download in progress.

Status Bar: Indicates the download status, in bytes, of the contents of a specific web page.

View Field: Self-explanatory.

Personal Toolbar: A user-customized toolbar that includes a Best of the Web button, a web Channels Guide, and personal entries.

Location Toolbar: Used to enter URLs.

Navigation Toolbar: Used to navigate through web pages, reload web pages, load the default home page, search the Internet for desired documents, add and manipulate Favorites (equivalent to bookmarks), invoke Outlook Express, print web documents, and terminate web page downloading.

Menu Toolbar: Used to manipulate web pages, work offline, customize user preferences, show and hide various toolbars, select Internet communication applications, and provide context-sensitive help.

IE's graphical user interface (GUI) enables one to quickly assimilate the most commonly used features. Again we electronically visit the White House by directing our browser to the URL, www.whitehouse.gov (see Figure 6.4). Within the File menu of the Menu Toolbar we choose Open. An Open dialog box appears. Type the URL www.whitehouse.gov in the centrally located blank field and click the OK button. After a few moments, pertinent information and a graphic of the White House flanked by two waving American flags again appear within the View field. The URL entry, http://www.whitehouse.gov/WH/Welcome.html, is displayed in the Address field of the Location Toolbar. In order to bookmark this web site, we choose the Add to Favorites entry from the Favorites menu of the Menu Toolbar, or the Favorites button on the Navigation Toolbar. From the Add Favorite dialog box, we choose OK to create the new bookmark.

Web server software exists for several operating systems including Unix, Windows NT, Macintosh, and Novell Netware. Several popular servers such as Netscape Enterprise Server, Microsoft Internet Information Server, O'Reilly & Associates WebSite, and

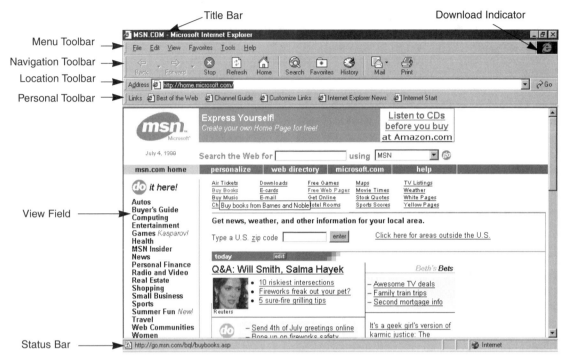

Screenshot reprinted by permission from Microsoft Corporation.

FIGURE 6.3

Microsoft Internet Explorer.

Apache Web Server (freeware) generally support the following features and software technologies, which will be discussed in subsequent sections:

1. Storage and distribution of web page content.
2. Support for content residing in multiple directories.
3. Account and station access restrictions.
4. Support for CGI (Common Gateway Interfaces) scripts.
5. Support for server APIs (Application Programming Interface).
6. Support for server-side includes (external data used to dynamically modify web page content).
7. Automated log files.
8. Provisions for e-commerce (directly or through third-party programs).
9. Provisions for security (such as authentication, encryption, and log files).
10. Provisions for creating and using cookies (collected user data files).
11. Provisions for server push technologies (dynamic web content that is continuously pushed toward a subscriber's browser).
12. Remote administration via the web.

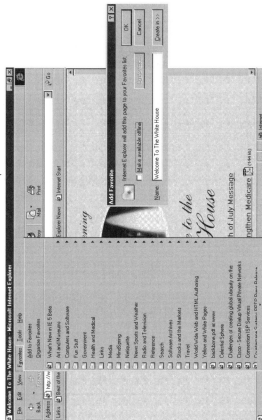

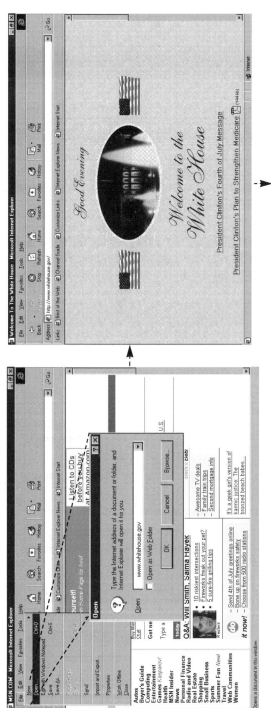

FIGURE 6.4

Using IE to visit the White House.

6.3 URL Formats

In its most popular format, a *URL* (Uniform Resource Locator) is essentially a web address comprising three parts: a protocol field, a host field, and a path/filename field. The complete format of the White House URL, for example, is actually http://www.whitehouse.gov/. A dissection of the URL reveals that the HTTP protocol, http://, is being used to request the home page (indicated by the trailing /) from the White House's web site, www.whitehouse.gov. By modern convention, the leading http:// and trailing / are dropped, leaving just the host field. Since most organizations direct people to their web site's home page, other derivatives of URL formats are seldom used. Hence addresses on the web, for the most part, are advertised to the planet as www.company.com, www.university.edu, www.institution.gov, etc.

Nuances, such as appending a country domain identifier (e.g., www.company.com.jp) to the host field or inserting a tilde before the name of a user's home directory in the path/filename field (e.g., www.university.edu/~tfallon/file.html), allow for a greater number of HTTP-type URL variations. However, there are many distinct URL formats (see Table 6.1). If one chooses to use the FTP protocol, for example, the general URL format is ftp://account:psswd@host.subdomain.domain/directory/fn. Depicted in Figure 6.5, the URL ftp://anonymous@newton.spsu.edu is used to open an FTP session with the host named newton.spsu.edu.

Table 6.1 URL Formats

Service	URL Format
HTTP	http://*host.subdomain.domain/directory/fn*
	or
HTTP with index.html as default	http://*host.subdomain.domain/directory/*
Anonymous FTP directory listing	ftp://*host.subdomain.domain/directory*
Anonymous FTP specific file	ftp://*host.subdomain.domain/directory/fn*
FTP	ftp://*account:psswd@host.subdomain.domain* /*directory/fn*
Local File	file://*directory/fn*
	or
Local File on different drive	file:///*drive//directory/fn*
Mail Document	mailto://*account@host.subdomain.domain*
Gopher	gopher://*gopher.subdomain.domain*
USENET	news:*newsgroup*
TELNET	telnet://*host.subdomain.domain*

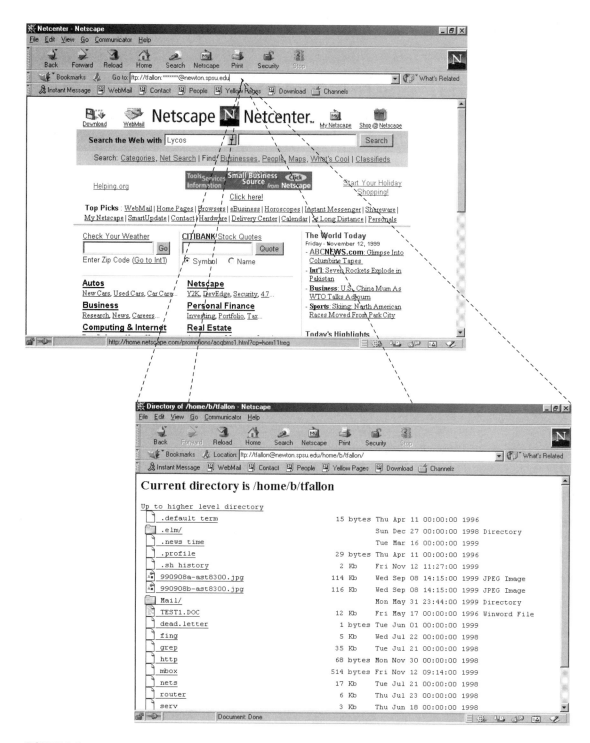

FIGURE 6.5

URL format example: FTP.

6.4 Examples of Web Usage

Although the Internet is used in many ways (for example, research collaboration, video conferencing, and Internet telephony), our focus here is on the creative uses of information sharing via the World Wide Web. Specifically, we will briefly explore examples in the areas of medicine, space science news, education, investing, electronic tax filing, online travel, and e-commerce. Other resources related to these and other areas of interest can be located using Internet research tools, commonly referred to as *search engines*. Research via search engines will be covered in the next section.

Suppose we are interested in learning more about diabetes. One online medical resource that can provide information is the National Medical Library (NLM) of the National Institutes of Health (NIH) (see Figure 6.6). The first URL (see Figure 6.6a), www.nlm.nih.gov/nlmhome.html, directs our browser to the feature-rich NLM web site that includes hyperlinks to Hot Topics, General Information, News, and the MEDLINE search engine. By clicking the Search MEDLINE button, followed by the PubMed hyperlink, we arrive at MEDLINE's PubMed search engine. After entering the keyword(s) to be searched, in our case, diabetes, we click on the Search button. After a few moments, a new page appears that contains search results, and a list of hyperlinks to useful, keyword-related resources.

If we are interested in space science news, a reasonable place to visit would be NASA's web site, www.nasa.gov (see Figure 6.7). Although the home page presents several interesting hyperlinks that cover various NASA-related topics, we follow a hyperlink trail that ultimately leads us to one of NASA's multimedia archives. A few of the intermediate hyperlinks leading to the Ames Research Center Hi-Bandwidth Zone web page (see Figure 6.7b) have been omitted in the figure, but we can directly enter the URL, www.arc.nasa.gov/enhanced/bandwidth.html. Scrolling down the page, we arrive at the section entitled Space (see Figure 6.7c). The 663KB MPEG file of the Galileo Orbiter (see Figure 6.7d) was played using the Microsoft Windows Media Player, which can be downloaded from www.microsoft.com.

Online universities,
departmental
intranets, and
global student
projects are a few
of the creative
ways in which the
web is used by
the academic
community.

Online universities, departmental intranets, and global student projects are a few of the creative ways in which the web is used by the academic community. For example, the Universities of Phoenix, www.uophx.edu/online/, and Northern Colorado, unconline.edu, offer online courses and degree programs that enable students to do course work on a schedule and at a location convenient to them (see Figure 6.8). Online universities may use several different software technologies to provide all of the standard services (such as admissions, registration, and faculty/student interaction) offered by traditional universities. Classroom participation, for example, may be conducted via online discussion forums using web-based or non-web-based conferencing software (see Figure 6.8a). Prior to participation, however, students must log in using a student ID or an alias (see Figure 6.8b).

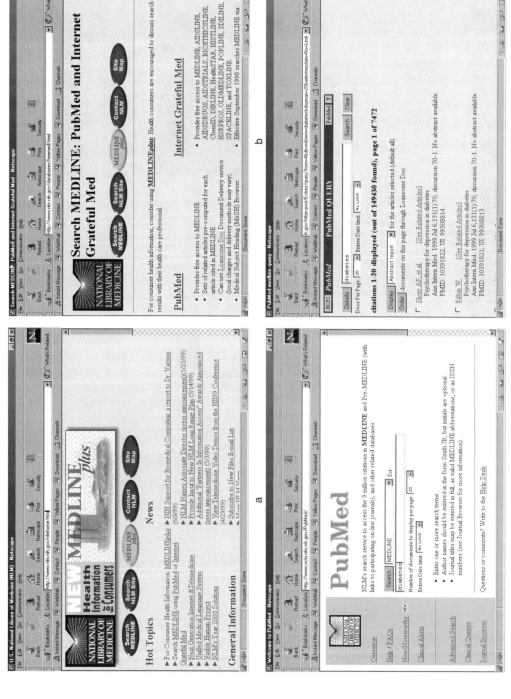

Source: National Institutes of Health.

FIGURE 6.6

Using the web for medical information.

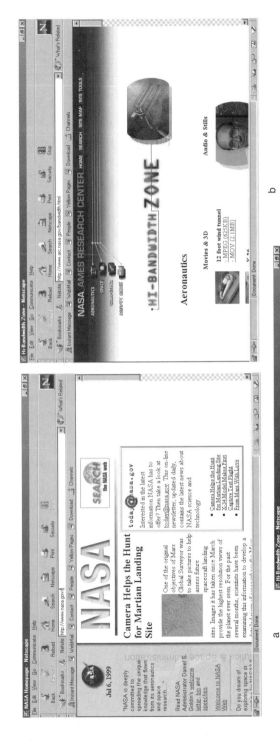

Screenshots courtesy of NASA Ames Research Center.

FIGURE 6.7

Using the web for scientific information.

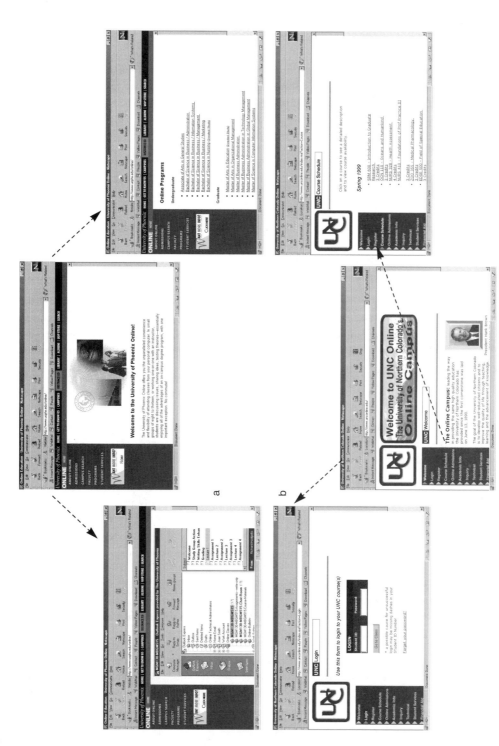

© 1999, University of Phoenix. All Rights Reserved; the Corporate logos and trademark appear with permission. UNC screen captures used with permission of UNC and e-college.com.

FIGURE 6.8
Using the web for online education.

Once online, students can access new assignments and lecture notes, upload previous assignments, take quizzes, receive immediate performance feedback, and interact with the teacher and other class members. Interaction via the forum usually involves the posting of questions and answers. Sequences of related questions and answers are referred to as *threads* and can be accessed real-time by any member of the class. Generally, threads are also archived so that they may be reviewed later. Other software (such as e-mail, audio streaming, and video streaming) may also be employed to enhance student learning.

Global Learning and Observations to Benefit the Environment (GLOBE), www.globe.gov, is a government-sponsored program that brings together students, teachers, and scientists from all over the world to collect and process environmental data (see Figure 6.9). Participating schools conduct soil, water, and air measurements and then enter the collected data into the GLOBE database (see Figure 6.9c). Raw data is processed to produce global visualization maps that are displayed on the web (see Figures 6.9d and e). Other utilities, such as chat rooms, are used to provide communication between the participating members.

Online investing is skyrocketing due, in part, to popular web sites such as the Motley Fool, www.fool.com (see Figure 6.10). Online advice, investment tips, stock quotes, portfolio tracking, and other pertinent data are common features encountered at most investment web sites. Some web sites have provisions for tracking the performance of a specific stock by entering the desired company's ticker symbol (see Figures 6.10b and c).

The URL www.irs.ustreas.gov/prod/cover.html refers to an online newspaper highlighting events within the IRS (see Figure 6.11). At the bottom of the page (see Figure 6.11c) is a hyperlink list of tax-related publications, utilities, and services. The hyperlink, Electronic Services, goes to the Electronic Services page where the e-file service and Electronic Payment Options can be found. The term *e-file* stands for electronic tax filing.

Although the Internet has enabled us to travel to virtually any place on the globe and beyond, the experience of being there in person is often preferred. In the case of personal travel, a virtual trip helps us choose preferred location, travel arrangements, and vacation activities. Let's say, for example, that we are planning a vacation from Atlanta, Georgia, to the tropical paradise of Honolulu. After a little research, we discover the tourist web site Planet Hawaii, planet-hawaii.com (see Figure 6.12). By clicking the Island hyperlink, we arrive at a map of Hawaii's archipelago (see Figure 6.12b). A simple double-click on the graphic of the island of Hawaii reveals all manner of information (history, services, activities, and tourist accommodations).

Prior to our grand voyage to the Big Island, we still have a few minor considerations: How do we get there? Where do we stay? How do we get around? Where do we eat? What can we do? Further online research yield's Fodor's Travel Online, www.fodors.com (see Figure 6.13).

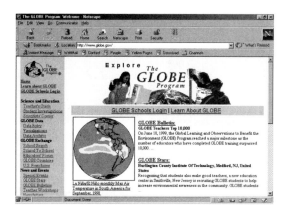

a

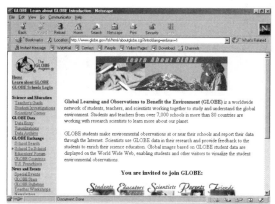

b

c

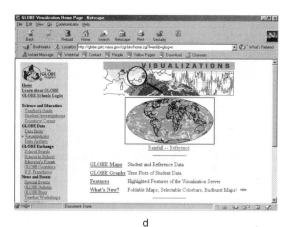

d

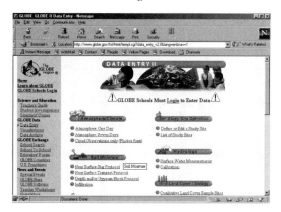

e

Screen captures used with permission of the Globe Program.

FIGURE 6.9

Using the web for environmental research.

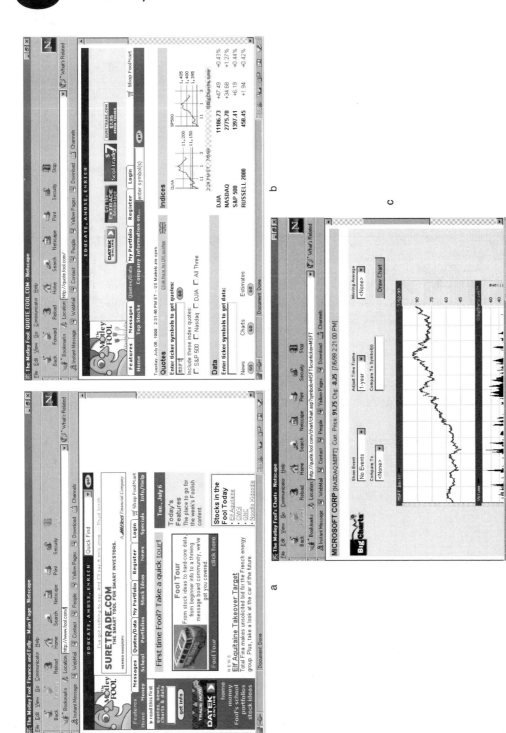

FIGURE 6.10
Using the web for investing.

Screen captures used with permission of www.BigCharts.com and The Motley Fool, Inc.

Courtesy Internal Revenue Service.

FIGURE 6.11

The Digital Daily site tracks the IRS.

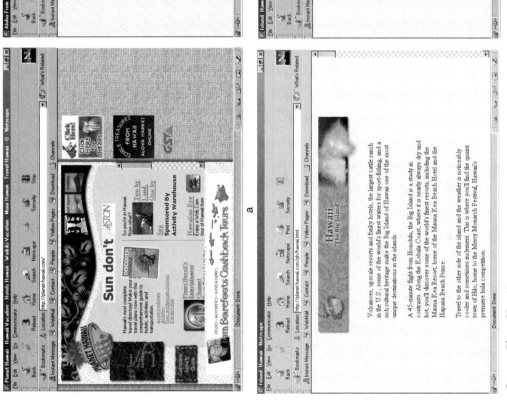

Courtesy Planet-Hawaii.

FIGURE 6.12
Using the web to make travel plans.

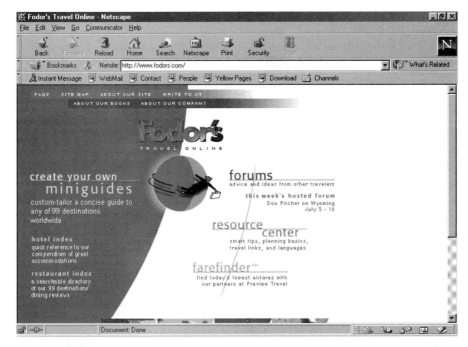

FIGURE 6.13
Using Fodor's Travel online site.

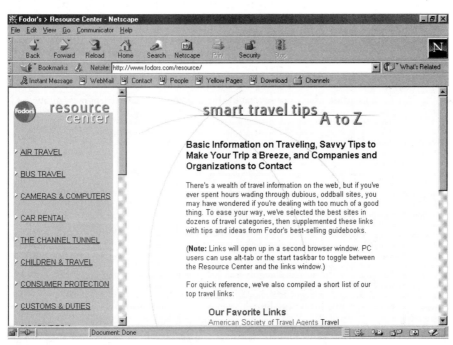

In anticipation of our big trip, we want a "live" view of our destination spot, which we'll get via a strategically located web cam (digital camera). Someone informs us of the web site, Tommy's List of Live Cam Worldwide, www.audible.com/wsj2/(see Figure 16.14). Scrolling down the page, we encounter and click the button labeled U.S.A. West. We locate the hyperlink Honolulu's Traffic Cams (see Figure 6.14b). A few more mouse clicks, and we view a "live" picture of Waikiki Beach (see Figure 6.14d).

Consumers who enjoy the competitive nature of auctions might consider visiting the Ebay web site, www.ebay.com (see Figure 6.15a). At Ebay, individuals can buy and sell goods, and individual items can be located via the search engine. For example, suppose we want to purchase a telescope. Entering "telescope" into the search field and clicking the Search button directs our browser to a web page containing a hypertext list of telescopes and related accessories (see Figure 6.15b). Included in the list is the item's value, the current number of bidders, and the amount of auction time remaining. Detailed information is retrieved by double-clicking the hyperlink of the desired item.

6.5 Using Search Engines

Search engines are software tools that match keyword search terms with web-related database entries. These entries consist of indexed web site data such as the name of the site, the author's name, titles of individual pages, and related keywords. Information from a specific web site is entered into the search engine database either manually or automatically. In either case, a webmaster generally registers their web site URL, and possibly an e-mail address, with a specific search engine(s). If the search engine's registration process is manual, then the webmaster enters specific information about the web site, such as keywords and an abstract. If it is automatic, then the registered web site information is collected at a predetermined time via a search engine program referred to as a *spider*. Most search engines employ the use of a spider. URLs of several of the most popular search engines follow:

> Information from a specific web site is entered into the search engine database either manually or automatically. In either case, a webmaster generally registers the web site URL, and possibly an e-mail address, with a specific search engine(s).

www.yahoo.com

www.altavista.com

www.lycos.com

www.webcrawler.com

www.hotbot.com

www.excite.com

www.infoseek.com

Directories and *keyword search fields* are the two common utilities by which users locate information on the web. Directories are categories of preselected web sites that are associated with web channels, bookmarks, and search engines. Netscape and Microsoft embellish their browsers with web channels and bookmark menus (that contain directories) to provide the user with a ready-reference to several popular web topics. A directory of web channels is different from a traditional directory of hyperlinks; *web channels* are pushed from a *push server* to the browser at scheduled intervals (discussed in a later section). Directories associated with search

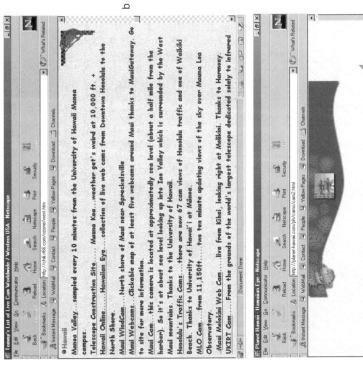

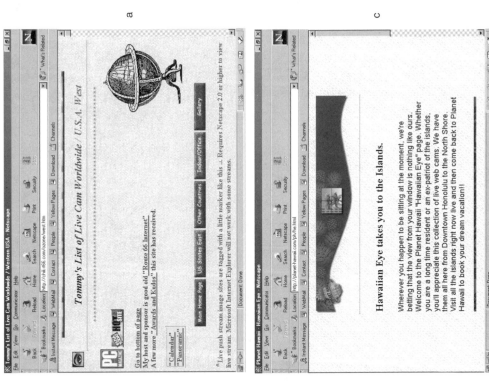

FIGURE 6.14

Web Usage: Travel.

Courtesy Route 66 Internet and Planet-Hawaii.

FIGURE 6.15

*The eBay online
auction site.*

a

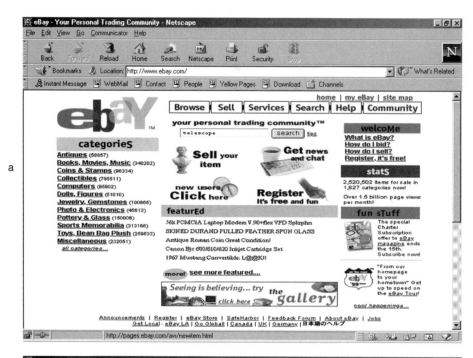

b

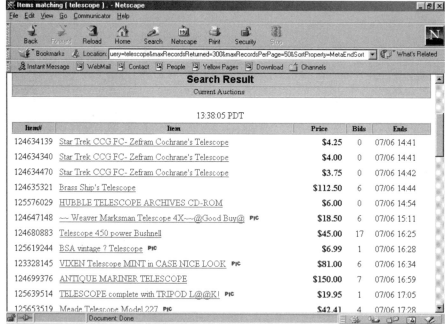

These materials have been reproduced by Prentice-Hall Inc. with the permission of eBay Inc.
Copyright ©eBay Inc. All rights reserved.

engines serve the same ready-reference purpose and are, therefore, useful for general research. Users conducting research on a specific topic should consider using keyword search fields.

After entering the desired keyword into the search field and clicking the search button, the search engine generates a web page of hyperlink references. These references are usually rated and ordered according to the accuracy with which they match the keyword(s). There are methods for refining the accuracy and, therefore, the results of a search. Enclosing the search term in quotations, for example, instructs the search engine to examine its index for the exact phrase, not the individual words constituting the phrase. For example, the phrase *Stars and Stripes* is searched for using the search engine www.hotbot.com. A hypertext list with approximately 42,000,000 entries is returned. By refining the phrase as *"Stars and Stripes,"* only 5600 entries are returned. Plus (+) and minus (-) characters can be used to include or exclude keywords from a search. For example, entering the keyword *airplane* into the search field of the search engine www.infoseek.com yields a hypertext list of approximately 547,000 entries. Using the same search engine and the phrase *airplane + jet* reduced the number of list entries to 400.

Most search engines possess an Options or an Advanced button that is usually adjacent to the search field. These buttons are used to refine a search per the specific features of the search engine. For example, using www.lycos.com, we conduct another search on the term *Stars and Stripes* (see Figure 6.16). With this search, however, we click on Lycos' Advanced Search hyperlink and select the drop-down menu option "All the words (adjacent, any order)" (see Figure 16.6b). Notice that we have modified our search phrase as "Stars and Stripes" or "The American Flag." The quote marks are used to delineate separate phrases. Our search results displayed several hypertext references from which to choose (see Figure 6.16c). We select the hyperlink "The American Flag Page—History" and the resulting page appears (see Figure 6.16d).

6.6 HTML 4.0

Several web sites and browsers in use today are based on HTML 3.2, which was developed to augment HTML 2.0 with the inclusion of support for tables, Java applets, text flow around images, subscripts, superscripts, and file upload. HTML 3.2, although feature-rich, marked the beginning, and end, of a diversion away from the original intent of HTML, which was to provide a language that enabled the author to describe a document's structure, by including several tags designed to modify a document's layout and presentation, or appearance.

(HTML 4.0 was developed as a stepping stone to the future of the web; it allows for the separation of a document's structure from its appearance, serves as a migration technology to nascent development languages, such as XML, and possesses a more sophisticated means by which to support multimedia objects.) A document's structure and appearance, for instance, are separated using style sheets. Style sheet rules are applied to HTML elements in order to control their appearance, and can be applied to a group of documents by adding a statement to each document that references a style sheet template file.

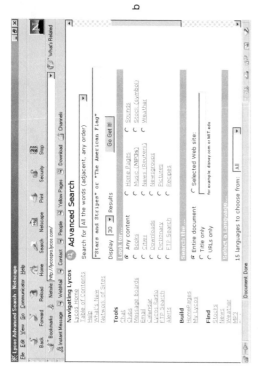

a

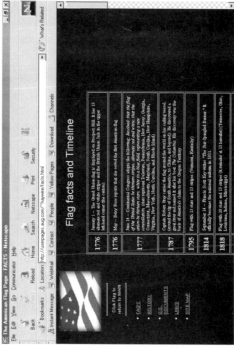

b

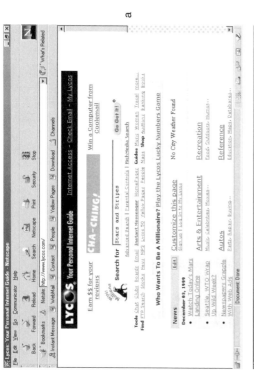

c

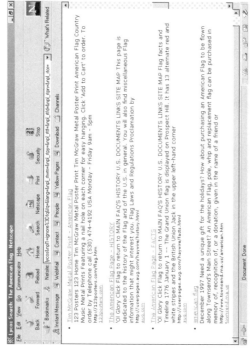

d

FIGURE 6.16

Doing research with search engines.

Changes made in the template cascade to all of the appropriate documents, hence the term *Cascading Style Sheets (CSS).* Other significant HTML 4.0 features are as follows:

Provisions for people with disabilities: Speech synthesizers or Braille readers for those who are visually impaired may render text of an HTML document.

Provisions for internationalization: Text may be rendered, for example, from right to left, instead of left to right.

Modification to table elements: The attributes of an entire table column, for example, may be modified as a single group.

Modification to form elements: Submission buttons, for example, may be used to start client-side scripts, or interpreted programs.

Formal support for several HTML extensions: Frames, for example, were initially developed and supported by Netscape as an extension to the HTML 2.0 element set.

Formal support for client-side scripts: Scripts may be used, for example, to create simple animation within the browser's view field.

Several elements incorporated into previous versions of HTML have been *deprecated,* or depreciated, due to the introduction of alternative elements or technologies, such as style sheets. Because many web browsers in use are still based on previous versions of HTML, both deprecated and alternative elements might be required when developing web pages. In subsequent sections, appropriate elements will be marked as deprecated.

6.7 A Cornucopia of Elements

Having previously established that the current genre of web page development owes its existence to HTML, we now ask, "What is a markup language and how does it function?" Recall that HTML is a progeny of the more general markup language SGML. SGML is an international standard (ISO 8879) used to define the structure of a document and the specific markup language used to create that structure. A specific markup language is identified by a unique *document type definition* (DTD). One particular DTD, HTML 4.0, defines the current version and level of functionality for HTML.

HTML's primary function is to provide the author of a web page(s) with the elements required to adequately describe the document's structure, such as the placement of headers, to a receiving browser. To help clarify this notion, consider the red paragraph, indentation, and other symbols strewn across a high school term paper. It had been "marked up" for your understanding. In HTML parlance, the symbols represent tags, whereas the teacher's intention such as indentation of a specific line, represent elements.

Tags are referred to as being single-sided or double-sided and are created by enclosing the tag name within a set of opposing angle brackets. *Single-sided tags* indicate that a certain function is to be enabled. The function is either a one-time event or is disabled when the browser encounters the subsequent tag. For example, the horizontal rule tag, <HR>, directs the receiving browser to draw a horizontal line across the screen. *Double-sided tags*

> HTML's primary function is to provide the author of a web page(s) with the elements required to adequately describe the document's structure, such as the placement of headers, to a receiving browser.

also indicate that a certain function is to be enabled and require two tags instead of one. The two tags surround and affect specific content within the web page, such as a paragraph of text. The first tag is referred to as the *opening tag,* and the second one is referred to as the *closing tag.* An element consisting of text and opening and closing italics tags, for example, might be entered as <I>seafood</I> within the source code of the web page. However, the same element would be displayed as *seafood* by the browser.

As a rule of thumb, tag syntax is case insensitive; that is, <i>seafood</i> is equivalent to <I>seafood</I>. However, tags can be modified by *attributes* and attributes can be assigned a specific *value.* The tag <IMG SRC="Euro.jpg">, for example, is a single-sided tag used to insert an image within the browser view field. The tag name is *IMG,* its attribute *SRC* indicates the source of the image, and the actual value assigned to the source is *Euro.jpg.* If *Euro.jpg* were inadvertently entered as *euro.jpg,* and if the web server's operating system were case sensitive, as Unix is, the file would not be found.

The three basic categories of HTML elements are the DTD and elements associated with the web page's head and body. The DTD element is identified by the <!DOC-TYPE> tag and must precede all other elements within an HTML document.

<! DOCTYPE HTML PUBLIC "-//W3C//DTD HTML 3.2 FINAL//EN">

The DTD element listed above is used to indicate that the document contains elements that are consistent with the W3C's approved, or final, recommendation for HTML 3.2. As a result of the introduction of style sheets, the deprecation of certain elements, and the formal adoption of frames, HTML 4.0 offers three distinct DTD elements.

<!DOCTYPE HTML PUBLIC "-//W3C//DTD HTML 4.0//EN" "http://www.w3.org/TR /REC-html40/strict.dtd">

"strict.dtd" in the DTD element listed above is used to indicate that the HTML 4.0 document is using style sheets to control its appearance. Documents that use deprecated elements to control appearance should use one of the following two DTD elements:

<!DOCTYPE HTMLPUBLIC "-//W3C//DTDHTML 4.0Transitional//EN" "http://www.w3.org/TR/REC-html40/loose.dtd">

<!DOCTYPE HTML PUBLIC "-//W3C//DTD HTML 4.0 Frameset//EN" "http://www.w3.org/TR/REC-html40/frameset.dtd">

The first DTD element indicates that the HTML 4.0 document contains deprecated elements *(Transitional)* consistent with previous HTML recommendations. The second DTD element is a superset of the first; it is augmented by the inclusion of frames *(Frameset).*

Prior to discussing the elements that constitute a web page's prologue and body, we briefly explore its overall basic structure using the following source code:

<!DOCTYPE HTML PUBLIC "-//W3C//DTD HTML 4.0 Frameset//EN" "http://www.w3.org/TR/REC-html40/frameset.dtd">
<HTML>

```
<HEAD>
<TITLE>This is a demo web page</TITLE>
⋮
additional prologue elements
⋮
</HEAD>
<BODY>
⋮
additional body elements
⋮
</BODY>
</HTML>
```

Immediately following the DTD element, we notice the three opening tags <HTML>, <HEAD>, and <TITLE>. All of these tags are double-sided, which means they require a corresponding closing tag. Double-sided tags can be used in a nested fashion but cannot be overlapped. The following partial listing of our source code represents an example of overlapped double-sided tags that violate proper HTML syntax:

```
<HEAD>
<TITLE>This is a demo web page
⋮
additional prologue elements
⋮
</HEAD>
</TITLE>
```

The web page's *prologue* is identified as all of the elements enclosed within the double-sided <HEAD> tag. Of these, only the title element, indicated by the double-sided <TITLE> tag, is mandatory. Information contained within the title element is displayed in a web browser's title bar and bookmarks. The body, indicated by the double-sided <BODY> tag, is that portion of the web page that contains the content presented to the user. A veritable cornucopia of body elements and objects are available to authors for the creation of highly effective web pages.

In the paragraphs that follow, we will discuss the elements commonly found within the prologue and body of a web page. Additional elements, especially those related to multimedia objects, will be introduced and analyzed in the next chapter. Although several elements (such as SCRIPT, STYLE, BASE, ISINDEX, and LINK) are allowed within the prologue, we focus our attention on TITLE and META.

The prefix META possesses several different meanings within the English language. With regard to HTML, however, META describes an element that is used to provide information about a web page or the content contained therein. META elements consist of a single-sided <META> tag, associated attributes and values, and the meta information. Examples of meta information include a list of keywords to be indexed by a visiting search engine and an expiration date used to inform a browser not to load a cached version of a particular web page. The three META tag attributes are CONTENT, NAME, and HTTP-EQUIV; META element semantics require the pairing of either the NAME and CONTENT or HTTP-EQUIV and CONTENT attributes. The definition and examples of proper syntax for these attributes are as follows:

CONTENT: The META attribute used to specify the value assigned to the named META variable or HTTP header response.

NAME: The META attribute used to declare META variables such as the author's name, the creation date, and document keywords.

```
<META NAME="AUTHOR" CONTENT="NANCY WOGSLAND">
<META NAME="DATE" CONTENT="19971201">
<META NAME="KEYWORDS" CONTENT="SOUTHEASTERN LIBRARY NETWORK,
SOLINET, LIBRARY, OCLC SERVICES, TRAINING">
```

HTTP-EQUIV: The META attribute used by a web server to generate and transmit nonreserved HTTP response headers (such as REPLY-TO, FROM, EXPIRES, and REFRESH) to the requesting browser. Encountered frequently on the web, the latter two are used to inform a browser of the expiration of a particular web page and that a refresh is required after the designated number of seconds, respectively. In the following example, the META element is used to indicate to the browser that the requested web page should be reloaded from its local cache, assuming the page had been loaded previously, until one minute after midnight on January 18, 1999. Thereafter, the web page should be reloaded from the web server.

```
<META HTTP-EQUIV="EXPIRES" CONTENT="Mon, 18 Jan 1999 00:00:01 GMT">
```

The second META element example, shown below, illustrates the manner in which a web page might be automatically refreshed after a ten-second delay. The third example further specifies that the browser is to be redirected to the new URL, http://www.any-where.com/redirected.html. A similarly constructed element might be used to redirect browsers to relocated web sites.

```
<META HTTP-EQUIV="REFRESH" CONTENT="10">
```

```
<META HTTP-EQUIV="REFRESH" CONTENT="10; URL=http://www.anywhere. com/redi-
rected.html">
```

The double-sided <BODY> tag delineates the body of a web page. Attributes associated with the opening <BODY> tag enable the author to modify the color of the page's background (BGCOLOR), text (TEXT), and hyperlinks; the three possible states of the hyperlink, unvisited (LINK), visited (VLINK), and active (ALINK) are generally represented with unique colors. Additional attributes are used to tile the background with an image (BACKGROUND) and/or play an audio clip (BGSOUND). The latter is a proprietary feature associated with Microsoft's Internet Explorer.

Hexadecimal-encoded RGB (Red/Green/Blue) colors or color names selected from a predefined palette are used to assign values to the first five attributes: BGCOLOR, TEXT, LINK, VLINK, and ALINK. Six hexadecimal numbers, preceded by a hash mark (#), are used to represent each RGB color. The range of possible values, or colors, extends from

$000000_{(16)}$ to $FFFFFF_{(16)}$, where the first two values represent the color red, the second two the color green, and the last two the color blue. The color black, for example, would be represented as #000000, whereas the color blue would be represented as #0000FF. The color names found within the predefined palette are assigned the following hexadecimal values:

Color	RGB Value	Color	RGB Value
BLACK	#000000	PURPLE	#800080
NAVY	#000080	OLIVE	#808000
BLUE	#0000FF	GRAY	#808080
GREEN	#008000	SILVER	#C0C0C0
TEAL	#008080	RED	#FF0000
LIME	#00FF00	FUCHSIA	#FF00FF
AQUA	#00FFFF	YELLOW	#FFFF00
MAROON	#800000	WHITE	#FFFFFF

By using various combinations of body attributes and assigned values within the opening <BODY> tag, the author can create a wide range of desired effects. The following body element, for example, would yield a web page consisting of a white background, black text, blue unvisited hyperlinks, and lime green visited hyperlinks:

```
<BODY BGCOLOR="WHITE" TEXT="BLACK" LINK="BLUE" VLINK="LIME">
```

If one were interested in replacing the bland white background with an image of the Space Shuttle augmented with three iterations of an audio clip of an actual launch, one might construct the following two body elements:

```
<BODY BACKGROUND="Shuttle.gif" TEXT="BLACK" LINK="BLUE" VLINK="LIME">
```

```
<BGSOUND SRC="http:/www.nasa.gov/ficticious_directory/launch.au" LOOP=3>
```

In addition to the LOOP attribute, the BGSOUND element also supports the BALANCE (values between −10,000 for left speaker and 10,000 for the right speaker) and VOLUME (values between −10,000 for minimum and 0 for maximum) attributes.

BODY elements are generally classified as being either block-level or text-level. Block-level elements operate on blocks of information, such as a paragraph or a list; they are delineated with paragraph breaks. Text-level elements, on the other hand, operate on individual items of text, such as a word or a sentence, or other commonly associated items, such as an inline image or a Java applet. In the following examples, we examine the syntax and functionality of several salient block-level elements (see Table 6.2). Different browsers, such as Netscape Navigator and Microsoft Internet Explorer, might not render HTML elements exactly alike. It is, therefore, prudent to examine one's web pages within the view fields of multiple browsers prior to publishing on the web. This book generally uses Netscape Navigator in browser-related figures.

Six different header elements, H1 through H6, are available for use within the body of a web page. H1, the most prominent header, renders the enclosed text in a large font with

Table 6.2 Block-level Elements

Block-Level Element	Description
<H1></H1>	Primary Header
<H2></H2>	Secondary Header
<H3></H3>	Third-level Header
<H4></H4>	Fourth-level Header
<H5></H5>	Fifth-level Header
<H6></H6>	Sixth-level Header
<HR>	Horizontal Rule
 	Line Break
<NOBR></NOBR>	No Line Break
<WBR>	Word Break
<P>	Paragraph Break
<UL></UL>	Unnumbered List
<OL></OL>	Numbered or Ordered List
<LI>	List Item
<DIR></DIR>	Short List (Deprecated>
<MENU></MENU>	Menu List (Deprecated)
<DL></DL>	Glossary
<DT>	Glossary Item
<DD>	Glossary Item Definition
<PRE></PRE>	Preformatted Text
<DIV></DIV>	Document Divisions
<CENTER></CENTER>	Text Alignment (Deprecated)
<BLOCKQUOTE><BLOCKQUOTE>	Quote

bold characters, whereas H6, the least prominent header, renders the enclosed text in a small font with bold characters. ALIGN is a deprecated attribute that is used to horizontally position the header; it is assigned one of three possible values: LEFT, CENTER, or RIGHT. To position an H1 header entitled "My dog has fleas" on the left-hand side of the screen use the following syntax:

<H1 ALIGN="LEFT">My dog has fleas</H1>

Although quite different from header elements, the horizontal rule element, HR, can also be used to delineate distinct subsections of a web page. The HR element consists of the single-sided <HR> tag and one or more of the following four deprecated attributes:

SIZE: thickness of a horizontal rule in pixels.

WIDTH: width of the horizontal rule in either pixels or percentage of the page width.

ALIGN: Horizontal alignment assigned the value LEFT, CENTER, or RIGHT.

NOSHADE: Disable default shade effect.

Paragraph breaks are inserted into a web page by using the single-sided <P> tag. <P> can also be modified using a deprecated ALIGN attribute, the values of which are either LEFT, CENTER, or RIGHT. If the <P> tag is inadvertently excluded, separate paragraphs will be rendered as one contiguous block of information.

Of the five types of lists defined in Table 6.2, we will discuss only unnumbered (UL) and numbered/ordered (OL) lists. UL and OL elements consist of either the double-sided <UL> or <OL> tag, one or more single-sided <LI> tags (list items), and one or more list attribute. The <UL> tag can be modified by the deprecated TYPE attribute with the following values: DISC, CIRCLE, or SQUARE. In order to generate a three-item unnumbered list with square bullets, for example, one might enter the following lines of code:

```
<UL TYPE=""SQUARE">
<LI>Shaggy dog</LI>
<LI>Dog named Shag</LI>
<LI>Shag wears a flea tag</LI>
</UL>
```

The <OL> tag is modified using either of the deprecated attributes TYPE or START. One of five values may be ascribed to the TYPE attribute: 1, A, a, I, or i. The first type, 1, is used to create lists, the items of which are delineated with integers. The second two types, A and a, indicate that the letters of the alphabet, upper- or lowercase, are to be rendered. The last two, I and i, indicate that large or small Roman numerals are to be rendered. The START attribute specifies the first number or letter to be used within the list. For example, to create the same list illustrated previously using integers that started at the number 4 instead of square bullets, enter the following lines of code:

```
<OL TYPE="1" START="4">
<LI>Shaggy dog</LI>
<LI>Dog named Shag</LI>
<LI>Shag wears a flea tag</LI>
</OL>
```

Using the deprecated TYPE and/or VALUE attributes, list items (LI) can be individually modified. The TYPE attribute is described in the preceding paragraph. The VALUE attribute is equivalent to the START attribute associated with the <OL> tag. Whereas the START attribute is applied to the whole list, the VALUE attribute modifies the current and subsequent list items.

Combining several of the HTML elements we have discussed, we write the following source code for a simple web page. By saving this code as a separate text file, we are able to immediately view our work within a web browser. Using Netscape Navigator, for example, select the Open Page menu item found under File within the menu bar (see Figure 6.17). Additionally, the source code can be viewed by selecting the Page Source menu item found under View within the menu bar. Incidentally, viewing the source code of the pages of different web sites is an excellent way to enhance web page coding skills.

```
<!DOCTYPE HTML PUBLIC "-//W3C//DTD HTML 4.0 Transitional//EN"
"http://www.w3.org/TR/REC-html40/loose.dtd">
<HTML>
<HEAD>
```

FIGURE 6.17

A simple web page and its HTML source code.

```
<TITLE>Block-level Elements</TITLE>
</HEAD>
<BODY>
<H1 ALIGN="CENTER">My dog has fleas</H1>
<UL TYPE="SQUARE">
<LI>Shaggy dog</LI>
<LI>Dog named Shag</LI>
<LI>Shag wears a flea tag</LI>
```

```
</UL>
<HR SIZE="25" NOSHADE>
<P>
```
If I had a shaggy dog named Shag who roamed around the woods without a flea tag,
my house would become infested, until Shag of fleas had divested, at which time his
tail would again begin to wag.
```
</BODY>
</HTML>
```

Three of the listed text-level elements (see Table 6.3), FONT, A (anchor), and IMG, will
be discussed in the following paragraphs. Additional text-level elements, such as MAP
and APPLET are discussed in the next chapter. The deprecated FONT element consists

Table 6.3 Text-level Elements

Text-Level Element	Description
<FONT></FONT>	Font (Deprecated)
<BASEFONT>	Default Font Size (Deprecated)
<A></A>	Anchor (Hyperlink) Element
<IMG>	Image
<I></I>	Italic
<B></B>	Bold
<BIG></BIG>	Big Font
<SMALL></SMALL>	Small Font
<U></U>	Underline Id (Deprecated)
<S></S>	Strikeout Text (Deprecated)
<TT></TT>	Monospaced Text
<EM></EM>	Emphasized Text (Deprecated)
<STRONG></STRONG>	Strongly Emphasized Text
	Subscript
	Superscript
<VAR></VAR>	Variable
<DEL></DEL>	Deleted Text
<INS></INS>	Inserted Alignment
<KBD></KBD>	Keyboard Input
<CITE></CITE>	Citation
<DFN></DFN>	Definition
<SAMP></SAMP>	Sampled Output
<CODE></CODE>	Computer Code
<ACRONYM></ACRONYM>	Acronym
<ABBR></ABBR>	Abbreviation

of the double-sided <FONT> tag, three possible FONT attributes (SIZE, COLOR, and FACE), and the enclosed text. The FONT attributes are as follows:

SIZE: The absolute or relative font size applied to the enclosed text. Absolute sizes are assigned a value within the range of one to seven, where three is the default value. Relative sizes consist of a + or - sign preceding a number. The rendered size is calculated by either adding or subtracting the designated number to a predetermined base font as defined by the BASEFONT element.

COLOR: The color applied to the enclosed text. Colors are chosen the same way they are for BODY tags.

FACE: The font type ascribed to the enclosed text. Typical types include Arial and Helvetica.

For example, to render text with a font size of 25, color blue, and type Arial, use the following line of code.

```
<FONT SIZE="25" COLOR="BLUE" FACE="ARIAL">If I had a shaggy dog named Shag</FONT>
```

The *hyper* in the term *hyperlink* is made possible by the inclusion of the anchor element within web pages. Anchor elements are used to redirect one's browser to another web page, an anchor (fixed reference point) within a web page, or a separate frame within the current web page. We shall limit our discussion of the anchor element to the first two uses; frames are discussed in the next chapter. Anchor elements consist of the double-sided <A> tag, anchor attributes (such as HREF, NAME, or TARGET), and the enclosed object, such as text or an image.

The HREF (hypertext reference) attribute contains the redirection information required by the browser in response to a clicked hyperlink. If the hyperlink refers to another web page, then the HREF attribute is assigned the URL of the web page. If, however, the hyperlink refers to an anchor within a web page, the HREF attribute is assigned the URL and anchor name, joined by the hash mark (#). Anchors within the current web page merely require the assignment of the anchor name to the HREF attribute. Examples of the three scenarios follow:

```
<A HREF="www.shaggydog.com">The Shaggy Dog</A>
```

```
<A HREF="www.shaggydog.com#bone">Popular Shaggy Dog Bones</A>
```

```
<A HREF="bone">Local Bones</A>
```

The NAME attribute is assigned the name of an anchor. HREF assignments that contain a reference to an anchor redirect the browser to the object surrounded by the anchor element possessing the proper NAME attribute. When one clicks on the hypertext *Popular Shaggy Dog Bones*, for example, one's browser is redirected to the Top Ten Shaggy

Dog Bones section of the www.shaggydog.com web site. The anchor element associated with that section might appear as follows:

```
<A NAME="bone">Top Ten Shaggy Dog Bones</A>
```

Images to be inserted into a web page can be obtained in many different ways, including purchasing a CD-ROM(s) collection, downloading free images from the web, downloading images from a digital camera or photo-CD, scanning static images, or embedding an image file that is located on another web site. Once obtained, images can be modified, if needed, by using graphical editors such Adobe Photoshop or MMedia Research's Lview Pro. GIF, JPEG, and PNG file formats are supported by current versions of Netscape Navigator and Microsoft Internet Explorer. Other file formats, such as Adobe PDF files, generally require the use of an external viewer when downloaded.

The IMG element consists of the single-sided <IMG> tag and one or more IMG attributes. Provisions for text-only browsers, such as Lynx, image alignment and sizing, and embedding are controlled via the following attributes:

ALT: Values assigned to this attribute are rendered as text by text-only browsers.

ALIGN: This attribute can be assigned one of five possible values: TOP, MIDDLE, BOTTOM, LEFT, or RIGHT. The first three values indicate text positioning relative to the image, while the last two indicate image positioning relative to the browser view field or frame.

HSPACE: Values assigned to this attribute indicate the amount of horizontal spacing, in pixels, to the left and right of the image.

VSPACE: Values assigned to this attribute indicate the amount of vertical spacing, in pixels, above and below the image.

WIDTH: Values assigned to this attribute indicate the desired rendered width, in pixels, of the image.

HEIGHT: Values assigned to this attribute indicate the desired rendered height, in pixels, of the image.

SRC: This attribute is used to indicate the source of the image to be displayed. URLs assigned to this attribute indicate the location of an embedded image to be downloaded.

To insert a right-justified, local (same folder as the web page) dog image possessing a width and height of 100 pixels, along with the alternate text-only message "Shag the Dog," use the following code:

```
<IMG SRC="shag.gif" WIDTH="100" HEIGHT="100" ALIGN="LEFT" ALT="Shag the Dog">
```

Incorporating examples of the three text-level elements into the body of our previously established web page, we modify our source code as shown following, and note the changes displayed in our browser view field (see Figure 6.18). The two <BR> tags

FIGURE 6.18

The modified web page and its HTML source code.

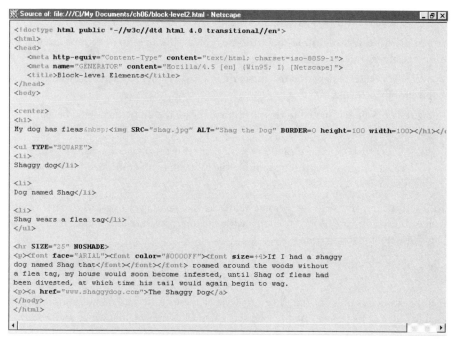

inserted prior to "The Shaggy Dog" hyperlink are used to force line breaks between the paragraph and the hyperlink.

```
<!DOCTYPE HTML PUBLIC "-//W3C//DTD HTML 4.0 Transitional//EN"
"http://www.w3.org/TR/REC-html40/loose.dtd">
<HTML>
<HEAD>
<TITLE>Block-level Elements</TITLE>
</HEAD>
<BODY>
<H1 ALIGN="CENTER">My dog has fleas</H1>
<IMG SRC="shag.jpg" WIDTH="100" HEIGHT="100" ALIGN="RIGHT" ALT="Shag
the Dog">
<UL TYPE="SQUARE">
<LI>Shaggy dog</LI>
<LI>Dog named Shag</LI>
<LI>Shag wears a flea tag</LI>
</UL>
<HR SIZE="25" NOSHADE>
<P>
<FONT SIZE="25" COLOR="BLUE" FACE="ARIAL">If I had a shaggy dog named
Shag that</FONT> roamed around the woods without a flea tag, my house would
soon become infested, until Shag of fleas had been divested, at which time his tail
would again begin to wag.
<BR>
<BR>
<A HREF="www.shaggydog.com">The Shaggy Dog</A>
</BODY>
</HTML>
```

The ADDRESS element is typically used for displaying contact information; it consists of the double-sided <ADDRESS> tag and pertinent address information. Such information is rendered in italic and is usually located at the bottom of a web page. The ADDRESS element can be used in conjunction with the MAILTO URL (see Table 6.1) to provide the user with a feedback mechanism via e-mail. An ADDRESS element is constructed as follows:

```
<H6> For additional information, please contact:</H6>
<ADDRESS>
Patrick Shag<BR>
Phone: (800) 123-4567<BR>
E-mail:<A HREF="MAILTO://patrick@shaggydog.com">patrick@shaggydog.com</A>
<BR>
</ADDRESS>
```

Comments that the author chooses not to have displayed online can be included within the source code of a web page by using the single-sided comment tag, <!--*this is a comment*-->. One common use of such embedded comments is the inclusion of copyright information. For example, the comment <!--Copyright 1999, Fallon--> would be seen only by individuals viewing the web page's source code. Comments are also used for documenting key elements or features of a web page.

ISO Latin-1, also referred to as ISO 8859-1, is an ISO standard that defines a set of special characters that can be inserted into a web page. The copyright symbol, ©, for example, can be inserted by including the special character &copy at the appropriate location within the body section of the source code. The ampersand (&) indicates to the receiving browser that the appended code is to be rendered as an ISO Latin-1 character. These special characters may also be represented in a decimal or hexadecimal format. For instance, the characters &#169 and &#xA9 are the decimal and hexadecimal (respectively) equivalents of © note the preceding hash mark (#) for both formats and the additional character x within the hexadecimal format. The ISO Latin-1 character set can be located within the HTML 4.0 specification section of the W3C web site, www.w3.org.

6.8 Dissecting a Web Page

One method of learning to write HTML is to study the source code developed by others (copyrights should be recognized and honored). In order to view a particular web site's source code, direct your browser to the web site via its URL and click the Page Source (Netscape Navigator), or Source (Microsoft Internet Explorer) entry under the View menu. We shall dissect the source code of SOLINET's (Southeastern Library Network, Inc.) home page, for example, by using this method. By entering the URL, www.solinet.net, we direct our browser to SOLINET's home page (see Figure 6.19a), from which we can view the associated source code (see Figure 6.20).

By moving the mouse pointer around the SOLINET home page, we discover several hyperlinks. The source code reveals that there are actually two active areas of hyperlinks, those associated with the top rectangular image and those associated with the central rectangular image. Each active area and associated image constitute a client-side imagemap; individual hyperlinks within an area are referred to as *hot spots*. Next, we focus primarily on the web page content that is visible within the view field shown in Figure 6.19a.

Referring to Figure 6.20, we notice that the web page is enclosed within opening and closing <HTML> tags, lines 1 and 59. Similarly, the prologue of the web page is enclosed within opening and closing <HEAD> tags, lines 2 and 14. Within the prologue, we notice the TITLE element, line 5, and several META elements. The META element on line 4 informs us that this web page was generated using the HTML editor Microsoft FrontPage 3.0. The META element on line 8 is used to provide search engines with keywords and phrases suitable for indexing.

The contents of the SOLINET home page is contained within the opening and closing <BODY> tags, lines 15 and 58. The opening body tag is modified by the use of several attributes: BGCOLOR, TEXT, LINK, VLINK, ALINK, TOPMARGIN, and LEFT-MARGIN. The BODY tag plus attributes specify that the body of the SOLINET home page is to be rendered with a white background, black text, and light blue hyperlinks. As we click a hyperlink, we notice that it changes color to olive green: ALINK="999966."

One method of learning to write HTML is to study the source code developed by others (copyrights should be recognized and honored).

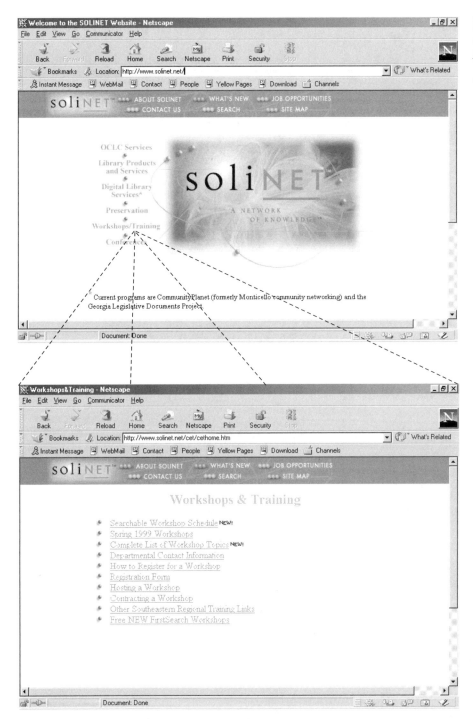

FIGURE 6.19
*a) SOLINET home
page b) Hyperlink to
Workshop & Training
web page.*

FIGURE 6.20

*Source code for the
SOLINET home page.*

```
1.  <html>
2.  <head>
3.  <meta HTTP-EQUIV="content-type" CONTENT="text/html;charset=iso-
8859-1">
4.  <meta NAME="GENERATOR" CONTENT="Microsoft FrontPage 3.0">
5.  <title>Welcome to SOLINET</title>
6.  <meta NAME="TITLE" CONTENT="SOLINET Home Page">
7.  <meta NAME="AUTHOR" CONTENT="NANCY WOGSLAND">
8.  <meta NAME="KEYWORDS" CONTENT="SOUTHEASTERN LIBRARY NETWORK,
SOLINET, LIBRARY, OCLC SERVICES, LIBRARY PRODUCTS, LIBRARY SERVICES,
PRESERVATION, TRAINING, ELECTRONIC LIBRARY SERVICES, LIBRARY NETWORK,
ELECTRONIC INFORMATION">
9.  <meta NAME="DESCRIPTION" CONTENT="homepage for SOLINET">
10. <meta NAME="PUBLISHER" CONTENT="SOLINET">
11. <meta NAME="DATE" CONTENT="19971201">
12. <meta NAME="RESOURCE TYPE" CONTENT="HTML">
13. <meta NAME="LANGUAGE" CONTENT="ENG">

14. <meta name="Microsoft Border" content="t"></head>

15. <body BGCOLOR="#FFFFFF" TEXT="#000000" LINK="#6666CC"
VLINK="#660099" ALINK="#999966" topmargin="0" leftmargin="0">

16. <table border="0" cellpadding="0" cellspacing="0"
width="100%"><tr><td><p ALIGN="left">
17. <MAP NAME="FrontPageMap">
18. <AREA SHAPE="RECT" COORDS="440, 26, 549, 46"
HREF="http://athena.solinet.net/solinet/site.htm">
19. <AREA SHAPE="RECT" COORDS="430, 6, 571, 25"
HREF="http://athena.solinet.net/hr/jobs.htm">
20. <AREA SHAPE="RECT" COORDS="317, 25, 429, 45"
HREF="http://athena.solinet.net/search.htm">
21. <AREA SHAPE="RECT" COORDS="313, 4, 426, 24"
HREF="http://athena.solinet.net/solinet/new.htm">
22. <AREA SHAPE="RECT" COORDS="194, 24, 307, 43"
HREF="http://athena.solinet.net/solinet/contact.htm">
23. <AREA SHAPE="RECT" COORDS="180, 5, 305, 25"
HREF="http://athena.solinet.net/solinet/aboutus.htm">
24. <AREA SHAPE="RECT" COORDS="52, 3, 177, 44"
HREF="_borders/default.htm" TARGET="_top"></MAP>
25<img usemap="#FrontPageMap" border="0" alt="links2.jpg (8545 bytes)"
src="images/links2.jpg"></p>
26. </td></tr><!--msnavigation--></table><!--msnavigation--><table
border="0" cellpadding="0" cellspacing="0" width="100%"><tr><!--
msnavigation--><td valign="top">

27. <p align="center"> 

28. <p align="center"><br>
29. <!--webbot bot="ImageMap" rectangle="(2,18) (140, 44)
oclcserv/oclc.htm##_top" rectangle="(2,49) (140, 85)
products/discount.htm##_top" rectangle="(3,90) (141, 126)
30. eis/access.htm##_top" rectangle="(3,133) (141, 154)
presvtn/preshome.htm##_top" rectangle="(3,159) (142, 195)
LAS/las.htm##_top" rectangle="(2,201) (142, 223)
31. cet/cethome.htm##_top" rectangle="(2,228) (142, 250)
conferences/conf.htm##_top" SRC="images/home.jpg" ALT="solinet
homepage image" BORDER="0" align="center" startspan -->
32. <MAP NAME="FrontPageMap1">
33. <AREA SHAPE="RECT" COORDS="2, 18, 140, 44"
```

```
HREF="oclcserv/oclc.htm">
34. <AREA SHAPE="RECT" COORDS="2, 49, 140, 85"
HREF="products/discount.htm">
35. <AREA SHAPE="RECT" COORDS="3, 90, 141, 126" HREF="eis/access.htm">
36. <AREA SHAPE="RECT" COORDS="3, 133, 141, 154"
HREF="presvtn/preshome.htm">
37. <AREA SHAPE="RECT" COORDS="3, 159, 142, 195" HREF="LAS/las.htm">
38. <AREA SHAPE="RECT" COORDS="2, 201, 142, 223"
HREF="cet/cethome.htm">
39. <AREA SHAPE="RECT" COORDS="2, 228, 142, 250"
HREF="conferences/conf.htm"></MAP>
40. <img align="center" usemap="#FrontPageMap1" border="0"
height="258" alt="solinet homepage image" src="images/home.jpg"
width="530"><!--webbot bot="ImageMap" endspan i-checksum="48769" -->

41. <p align="center"><br><br>                        (visible in view field)

42. <p align="center"><font FACE="Times     (not visible in view field)
New Roman,Times,serif" SIZE="2"><a HREF="solinet/aboutus.htm"
TARGET="_top">About SOLINET</a>
43. <a HREF="solinet/contact.htm" 42.
TARGET="_top">Contact Us</a> / <a HREF="solinet/new.htm"
TARGET="_top">What's New</a> / <a HREF="hr/jobs.htm"
TARGET="_top">Job Opportunities</a>
44. <a HREF="search.htm" TARGET="_top">Search</a> / <a
HREF="solinet/site.htm" TARGET="_top">Site Map</a>
<br>
45. <a HREF="oclcserv/oclc.htm" TARGET="_top">OCLC Services</a>
46. <a HREF="products/discount.htm"
TARGET="_top">Discounted Library Products</a> / <a
HREF="eis/access.htm"
TARGET="_top">Electronic Information Access</a> <br>
47. <a HREF="presvtn/preshome.htm" TARGET="_top">Preservation</a> / <a
HREF="LAS/las.htm"
TARGET="_top">Library Automation Services</a>
48. <a HREF="cet/cethome.htm" TARGET="_top">Workshops&amp;Training</a>
/ <a HREF="conferences/conf.htm" TARGET="_top">Conferences</a>
</font><br></p>
49. <p align="center"><font FACE="Times New Roman,Times,serif"><img
SRC="images/line.GIF" WIDTH="479" HEIGHT="4"><br>
50. <a HREF="default.htm" TARGET="_top"><img SRC="images/logosm2.gif"
BORDER="0" ALT="SOLINET logo" WIDTH="128" HEIGHT="38"></a></font>
51. <font FACE="Times New Roman,Times,serif" SIZE="2"><br>
52. 1438 West Peachtree Street, NW, Suite 200, Atlanta, GA 30309-
2955<br></p>

53. <p align="center"><font FACE="Times New Roman,Times,serif"
SIZE="1">Any comments,
54. questions, or suggestions should be sent to <a
HREF="mailto:webmaster@solinet.net">webmaster@solinet.net</a><br>
55. Any system related questions should be sent to <a
HREF="mailto:system_support@solinet.net">system_support@solinet.net</a
></font></p>

56. <p align="center"><i><font face="Times New Roman,Times,serif"
size="1">updated on 1/4/99</font></i>
57. <!--msnavigation--></td></tr><!--msnavigation--></table>
58. </body>
59. </html>
```

Upon revisiting the home page, we notice that the previously visited hyperlink is now rendered in purple: VLINK="660099." The attributes TOPMARGIN and LEFTMARGIN are used for positioning the body of the web page. The attribute settings TOPMARGIN="0" and LEFTMARGIN="0" specify that the body of the web page is to be indented 0 pixels from the view field's top and left margins.

The source code of the content located between lines 17 and 25 (top rectangular image) follows the TABLE element found on line 16; the associated closing </TABLE> tag is located on line 26. The <TABLE> element (discussed in the next chapter), in this case, is used to create a single-cell table, the content of which is a client-side imagemap. Imagemaps are created by associating URLs with specific areas (coordinates) of an image. Such associations are contained within a mapfile and are created either manually or by use of an imagemap editor such as MapThis! or MapEdit. Mapfiles that reside on a web server are used with server-side imagemaps, whereas mapfiles that are embedded within a web page are used with client-side imagemaps. We shall restrict our discussion to the latter.

Imagemaps can be used in many creative ways. An imagemap of the southeastern U.S., for example, might redirect a browser to Georgia's Chamber of Commerce home page when one clicks within the border of the image of Georgia. Similarly, Tennessee's Chamber of Commerce home page would appear if one were to click on the image of Tennessee. In our current example, the mapfile is established by the element <MAP NAME="FrontPageMap">, line 17. The mapfile name is assigned using the attribute NAME; it is used in conjunction with the IMG element attribute USEMAP, line 25. Following the MAP element are the AREA elements, lines 19–24, that are used to define the hotspots within the image.

The first AREA element, <AREA SHAPE="RECT" COORDS="440, 26, 549, 46" HREF="http://athena.solinet.net/solinet/site.htm">, line 18, is used to associate a rectangular hotspot of the image links2.jpg, line 25, with the URL, athena.solinet.net/solinet/site.htm. The area enclosed by the hotspot is defined by two pairs of (x,y) coordinates: (440, 26) and (549,46). The first coordinate represents the rectangle's upper left-hand corner, while the second coordinate represents the lower right-hand corner. Each coordinate, measured in pixels, is referenced to the upper left-hand corner (0,0) of the browser's view field.

Lines 19 through 24 define the other six hotspots that constitute the top rectangular image. The central rectangular client-side imagemap is created in an identical manner, lines 32–40; the hotspot associated with line 38, for example, is a hyperlink to SOLINET's Workshops & Training web page (see Figure 6.19b). Other values that may be assigned to the SHAPE attribute are CIRCLE (center coordinate (x,y), radius), POLY (multiple coordinates), and DEFAULT. DEFAULT is generally included as the last AREA element and serves as a catch all for mouse clicks outside the intended hotspots.

In this chapter, we have considered the basics of the web including its operation, URL formats, typical usage, search engines, and the creation of web pages. In the next chapter, we investigate the technologies and techniques used to enhance the functionality and aesthetics of this revolutionary medium.

6.9 Parental Safeguards

Section 501 of Subtitle A of Title V of the Telecommunications Act of 1996 (www.fcc.gov/telecom.html) defines all related sections of Title V as the Communications Decency Act (*CDA*) of 1996. A portion of section 502 essentially states that individuals who knowingly transmit obscene or indecent material to persons under the age of 18 may be fined and/or be imprisoned "whether the maker of such communication placed the call or initiated the communication." First Amendment challenges to the CDA have been upheld by the Supreme Court and thus have rendered the act unconstitutional. Parents, however, have several options for protecting their children from unsavory regions of cyberspace.

Parents have several options for protecting their children from unsavory regions of cyberspace.

These options include limitations to the physical access of computer systems, the employment of filtering software, and adoption of safe surfing practices. The former might include adult supervision, time constraints, and/or avoidance of unmonitored systems. Filtering software, such as CyberPatrol, NetNanny, or SurfWatch, can be installed by parents to block access to designated regions or related material inadvertently downloaded. Such software typically examines information received from or transmitted to chat rooms, FTP sites, newsgroups, and web sites. This information is correlated with a database of objectionable sites, character strings, and/or content ratings and is either filtered or accepted. Online Service Providers, such as AOL, generally employ parental control features based upon the same techniques or programs.

The U.S. Department of Education publishes an online pamphlet (www.ed.gov/pubs/parents/internet/) that includes several relevant tips regarding safe surfing practices for children. Similarly, the Federal Trade Commission publishes a pamphlet (www.ftc.gov) entitled "Site-Seeing on the Internet." With a little effort and research, parents can expose their children to the myriad positive aspects of cyberspace and simultaneously protect them from the negative.

Summary

The most popular of Internet services is the World Wide Web. The web is rapidly changing the manner in which we present and manipulate information. It is used for a multitude of services including collaborative research, electronic commerce (e-commerce), advertising, multimedia broadcasting, database interactions, online education, and much more.

The web is based on a client/server network model. A client program, referred to as a browser, is used to transmit a request for information to a web server. The web server, in turn, transmits a reply in the form of a document, commonly referred to as a web page. *HTTP* (Hypertext Transfer Protocol), a protocol within the TCP/IP protocol suite, is used to transport the user's request from browser to server and the content and formatting information of the web page from server to browser.

Web pages are merely text files that contain special markup language, referred to as *tags*, that indicates formatting information and the inclusion of special features, such as an audio clip or a section of JavaScript, to the receiving browser. The de facto markup language that describes the proper usage of these tags is *HTML* (Hypertext Markup Language). Early web pages incorporated primitive tags that enabled formatting features, referred to as elements, such as paragraph delineation, italicization, header font size manipulation, and the interconnecting of web pages and/or sites via hypermedia references.

When requesting information from a server, a browser uses TCP/IP (see Figure 2.11) to establish a socket connection (host address and port number) on port 80 (HTTP). Once the connection is established, the browser issues a request line, one or more request headers, and a blank line. Upon receipt of the request, the server issues a response line, one or more response headers, a blank line, and the requested document.

A URL (Uniform Resource Locator) is a web address comprising three parts: a protocol field, a host field, and a path/filename field. The complete format of the White House URL, for example, is actually http://www.whitehouse.gov/. A dissection of the URL reveals that the HTTP protocol, http://, is being used to request the home page (indicated by the trailing /) from the White House web site, www.whitehouse.gov.

Search engines are software tools that match keyword search terms with web-related database entries. These entries are comprised of indexed web site data such as the name of the site, the author's name, titles of individual pages, and related keywords. Information from a specific web site is entered into the search engine database either manually or automatically. In either case, webmasters generally register their web site URL, and possibly an e-mail address, with a specific search engine(s). If the search engine's registration process is manual, then the webmaster enters specific information about the web site, such as keywords and an abstract. If it is automatic, then the registered web site information is collected at a predetermined time via a search engine program referred to as a spider.

Several web sites and browsers in use today are based on HTML 3.2, the previous version, or W3C Recommendation, of HTML. HTML 3.2 was developed to augment HTML 2.0 with the inclusion of support for tables, Java applets, text flow around images, subscripts, superscripts, and file upload. HTML 3.2, although feature-rich, marked the beginning and end of a diversion away from the original intent of HTML, which was to provide a language that enabled the author to describe a document's structure, by including several tags designed to modify a document's layout and presentation.

HTML 4.0 was developed as a stepping stone to the future of the web. It allows for the separation of a document's structure from its appearance; serves as a migration technology to nascent development languages, such as XML; and possesses a more sophisticated means by which to support multimedia objects.

One method to learn HTML is to study the source code developed by others (copyrights should be recognized and honored). In order to view a particular web site's source code, select the Page Source (Netscape Navigator) or Source (Microsoft Internet Explorer) entry from the View menu.

Breathing Life into the Web

Chapter Learning Objectives:

- Understand tables, cascading style sheets, and frames.
- Understand embedded objects.
- Explore various multimedia technologies used on the web.
- Discuss push and pull technologies.
- Understand web database connectivity.

"True ease in writing comes from art, not chance, as those move easiest who have learned to dance."

Alexander Pope, An Essay on Criticism

In the previous chapter we learned to create the basic structure of a web page. Several objects, including tables, cascading style sheets, frames, and JavaScript, may be employed to enhance web page functionality and aesthetics. The inclusion of multimedia presentations and advanced database connectivity provides an even greater set of web site possibilities for the webmaster. Search engines, e-commerce, and online registration systems are based upon these technologies.

With the advent of *XML* (eXtensible Markup Language), authors of web pages will be able to design their own elements, store information within these elements, and exchange style and content information between web pages and applications. With push technologies, information can be pushed in the form of channels, such as the news or stock quotes, to one's browser at specified times or from specified sources. The web is teeming with feature-rich technologies that can be used to create highly compelling web sites. One must consider, however, that the embellishment of web pages with some of the aforementioned technologies, such as multimedia, may result in the degradation of download performance. Always evaluate a web site from the perspective of the visitor.

7.1 Tables, Style Sheets, and Frames
Tables

●
Tables, like spreadsheets, are comprised of rows and columns.

Tables, like spreadsheets, are comprised of rows and columns. The spaces enclosed by these rows and columns are referred to as cells. The primary tags used in the creation of tables are the double-sided <TABLE>, <TR> (table row), <TH> (table header), and <TD> (table data) tags. Captions may be added to tables by using the double-sided <CAPTION> tag. Building upon our previous web page example (see Figure 6.21), we create a new web page that contains the following source code, which has been saved in a text file named shaggydog.html:

```
<!doctype html public "-//w3c//dtd html 4.0 transitional//en">
<html>
<head>
  <meta http-equiv="Content-Type" content="text/html; charset=iso-8859-1">
  <meta name="GENERATOR" content="Mozilla/4.5 [en] (Win95; I) [Netscape]">
  <title>Tables, Style Sheets, and Frames</title>
</head>
<body>
<center>
<h1>
<img SRC="pyramid.gif" BORDER=0 height=18 width=18>  Other Dogs 
<img SRC="pyramid.gif" BORDER=0 height=18 width=18></h1></center>
<center>There are several categories of dogs. <i>Sporting dogs</i>, for
instance, are dogs that are used in hunting, racing, and herding.
<p><img SRC="bluebar.gif" BORDER=0 height=11 width=768></center>
<br> 
<center>
<table BORDER=2 WIDTH="60%" >
<caption ALIGN="TOP"><b><i><font size=+1>A Few Sporting
Dogs</font></i></b></caption>
<tr><th>Setters</th><th>Retrievers</th></tr>
<tr><td ALIGN=CENTER>Irish Setter</td><td ALIGN=CENTER>Golden
Retriever</td></tr>
<tr><td ALIGN=CENTER>English Setter</td><td ALIGN=CENTER>Labrador
Retriever</td></tr>
<tr><td ALIGN=CENTER>Gordon Setter</td><td
ALIGN=CENTER>Weimaraner</td></tr>
```

```
</table>
</center>
</body>
</html>
```

Modifying the hyperlink reference in our previous web page example from www.shaggy-dog.com to shaggydog.html and the hyperlink text from The Shaggy Dog to Other Dogs, we create the hyperlink relationship depicted in Figure 7.1. Referring to the source code, we notice the H1 header, Other Dogs, that is flanked by the two icons, pyramid.gif, and the sentence containing the italicized phrase *sporting dogs*. Separating the sentence and the table is a blue bar, with height and width attributes adjusted to span the view field.

We notice that the overall table structure is contained within a double-sided <CEN-TER> tag, hence the table's orientation with respect to the view field. The border and width of the table are modified by the opening <TABLE> tag attributes: BORDER and WIDTH. The BORDER attribute is assigned a value from zero (no border) to N, where N denotes pixels; the default value for N is one. As N increases, the border of the table exhibits a greater degree of three-dimensional relief. The WIDTH attribute is either assigned a value of N (in pixels) or a percentage (V%), where V% represents the span of the view field. The line of code, <TABLE BORDER=2 WIDTH="%60">, indicates that the table is to possess a slightly raised border and span 60% of the view field.

The CAPTION element follows the opening <TABLE> tag. It is to be aligned with the top of the table. The syntax associated with the text, <B><I><FONT SIZE=+1>A Few Sporting Dogs</FONT></I></B>, yields a bold, italicized caption the size of which is one greater than the baseline font. Tables are constructed one row at a time. Rows are delineated by the double-sided <TR> tag. Similarly, column headers and cells are delineated by the double-sided <TH> and <TD> tags, respectively. Comparing the graphic (see Figure 7.1b) to the source code, one recognizes the alignment of cell data beneath the appropriate column header. Furthermore, the data is aligned within the cell's center.

The ALIGN attribute is associated with both the TABLE and TD elements and may be assigned the values LEFT, RIGHT, or CENTER. The TD element possesses the additional ALIGN value, JUSTIFY. Other attributes are BGCOLOR, COLSPAN, and ROWSPAN. BGCOLOR (background color) is also used with the TABLE and TD elements, and its syntax is constructed in an identical manner to the BODY element. The COLSPAN and ROWSPAN attributes are used exclusively with the TD element to indicate the number of columns and rows, respectively, that an individual cell spans. <TD COLSPAN=2>*span two cells*</TD>, for instance, would yield a cell that spans two columns.

Other attributes associated with the TABLE element are CELLSPACING and CELL-PADDING. Both attributes are assigned an integer value from one to N, in pixels. CELLSPACING defines the amount of space to be inserted between the edges of adjacent cells and the table's border. CELLPADDING defines the amount of space to be inserted between the edge of a cell and the information contained within the cell.

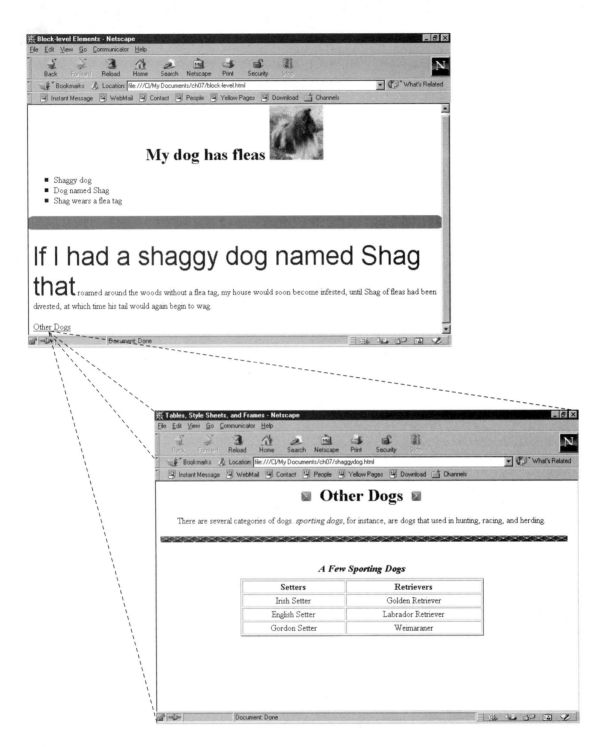

FIGURE 7.1

a) Shaggy Dog home page. b) Hyperlink to Other Dogs.

Style Sheets

The original intention of the web was to create a system whereby information could be formatted and presented in a logical, efficient manner. Earlier versions of HTML had no provisions to accommodate presentational style. In time, however, companies that developed web browsers, primarily Netscape and Microsoft, created a multitude of presentational elements and an interdependence between a web page's format and style. Such an interdependence forces an author to manipulate individual lines of code. Enter cascading style sheets.

In late 1996, the W3C published its Recommendation for CSS1 (Cascading Style Sheets, Level 1), which defines an extensive set of presentational rules that can be applied to the content of a web page. CSS has caused the deprecation of several presentational elements and attributes. In 1998, the W3C published its second Recommendation for style sheets, CSS2. CSS2 is a superset of CSS1, adding several new features.

Style sheet rules are comprised of three parts: a selector, one or more properties, and one or more corresponding values. Selectors are, for the most part, element names such as BODY, H6, and LI that are used to indicate the element selected for modification. Similarly, the property indicates the specific characteristic to be modified, such as background color or font family; the amount or type of modification is determined by the assigned value, such as red or Helvetica (see Table 7.1).

> Style sheet rules are comprised of three parts: a selector, one or more properties, and one or more corresponding values.

Table 7.1 Common CSS properties: bold, italic values denote user selected.

Classification	Property	Inherited	Values
Font	font-weight	Yes	100 (lightest)–900(heaviest) normal bold bolder lighter
	font-family	Yes	times helvetica serif sans-serif cursive arial palatino courier monospace
	font-size	Yes	*specified* *percentage of default* xx-small x-small

(Continued on next page)

Table 7.1 *(Continued)*

Classification	Property	Inherited	Values
			small
			medium
			large
			x-large
			xx-large
			larger
			smaller
	font-style	Yes	normal
			italic
			oblique
Text	letter-spacing	Yes	*defined unit of length*
			normal
	word-spacing	Yes	*defined unit of length*
			normal
	text-decoration	No	none
			underline
			line-through
			overline
			blink
	text-transform	Yes	none
			lowercase
			uppercase
			capitalize
	text-align	Yes	left
			right
			center
			justify
	text-indent	Yes	*defined unit of length*
			percentage of default
			negative value
Text	vertical-align	No	top
			middle
			bottom
			text-top
			text-bottom
			percentage of default
			baseline
			sub
			super
	line-height	Yes	normal
			specified
			percentage of default
			defined unit of length
	white space	No	normal
			pre
			nowrap

Table 7.1 *(Continued)*

Classification	Property	Inherited	Values
Foreground/ Background	color	Yes	***defined color (text)***
	background-color	No	***defined color***
			transparent
	background-image	No	none
			URL
	background-repeat	No	repeat
			repeat-x
			repeat-y
			no-repeat
	background-attachment	No	scroll
			fixed
	background-position	No	left/center
			left/right
			center/right
			top/middle
			top/bottom
			middle/bottom
			percentage of default
			defined unit of length
Images	width	No	auto
			percentage of default
			defined unit of length
	height	No	auto
			defined unit of length
Positioning	float	No	left
			right
			none
			inherit
	clear	No	both
			left
			right
			none
Positioning	z-index	No	auto
			integer
			inherit
	position	No	static

(Continued on next page)

Table 7.1 *(Continued)*

Classification	Property	Inherited	Values
			relative
			absolute
			fixed
Lists	list-style-image	Yes	none
			URL
	list-style-type	Yes	square
			disc
			circle
			decimal
			lower-alpha
			upper-alpha
			lower-roman
			upper-roman
	list-style-position	Yes	inside
			outside
Margin/Border/ Padding	margin-left	No	auto
			defined unit of length
			percentage of default
	margin-right	No	auto
			defined unit of length
			percentage of default
	margin-top	No	auto
			defined unit of length
			percentage of default
	margin-bottom	No	auto
			defined unit of length
			percentage of default
	border-width	No	thin
			medium
			thick
			defined unit of length
	border-color	No	defined color
	border-style	No	none
			dotted
			dashed
			groove
			double
			solid
			inset
			outset
			ridge
	padding	No	*defined unit of length*
			percentage of default

Properties are generally classified as Font, Text, Foreground/Background, Images, Positioning, Lists, and Margin/Border/Padding. Elements nested within another element are said to inherit the new properties of their parent element, unless that specific property is incapable of being inherited. For example, an italicized phrase (delineated by the double-sided <I> tag) embedded within a paragraph would be rendered in bold, if its parent element (delineated by the single-sided <P> tag) were modified by the rule, P {font-weight: bold}.

The basic syntax of a style sheet rule is: selector {property: value; property: value}. For example, the rule H1 {font-family: cursive} would indicate to the receiving browser to render all H1 elements in a cursive font, unless otherwise specified. Multiple elements that are to possess the same property can be included within a single rule by using commas to separate them. For example, to have all H1, H2, and P (paragraph) elements rendered in a green Arial font, construct the following rule:

H1, H2, P {font-family: arial; color: green}

In the context of style sheets, a *class* is an author-defined, common set of property:value pairs that are applied to an element on an as-needed basis. The basic syntax for a class is: .class_name {property: value; property: value}. Note the period (.) that precedes the class name. For example, to render specific sections of text as blue and underlined, construct the following class:

.blue_underline {color: blue; text-decoration: underline}

The class would then be applied to a section of text by using the CLASS attribute and an appropriate element, such as SPAN; SPAN is used to span style sheet rules across web page content, such as text, that is otherwise independent of HTML elements. For example, to apply the class blue_underline to the phrase "shaggy dog," modify the source code to <SPAN CLASS="blue_underline">shaggy dog</SPAN>. In order to associate a class with one specific element, append the element name to the front of the class definition. The following example would allow H1 elements to acquire the blue_underline properties:

H1.blue_underline {color: blue; text-decoration: underline}

Similar to a class, an ID is also an author-defined, common set of property:value pairs that are applied to an element. IDs and classes are different, however, in their syntax (ID declarations begin with a hash mark, #) and manner in which they are used; IDs should occur only once within a web page. For example, an ID used to set the height and width of a specific image to 50 pixels by 75 pixels is constructed as follows:

#dog_image {height: 50px; width: 75px}

The original source code associated with the image would be modified from <IMG SRC="dog.jpg"> to <IMG ID="dog_image" SRC="dog.jpg">.

Style sheets are categorized as being either inline, internal, or external. *Inline style sheets* are applied directly to the element to be modified using the STYLE attribute. In order to render the bullet of a particular list item as a lowercase Roman numeral, for instance, include the following line of code:

<LI STYLE="list-style-type: lower-roman">*list item*</LI>

Internal style sheets are included within the web page's prologue and are delineated by the double-sided <STYLE> tag. They can include individual rules, classes, IDs, and comments. Style sheet comments are delineated using */* comment */*. Using an internal style sheet, we build upon our previous web page (see Figure 7.2).

```
<!doctype html public "-//w3c//dtd html 4.0 transitional//en">
<html>
<head>
<meta http-equiv="Content-Type" content="text/html; charset=iso-8859-1">
<meta name="GENERATOR" content="Mozilla/4.5 [en] (Win95; I) [Netscape]">
<title>Tables, Style Sheets, and Frames</title>
<style type="text/css">
<!--
/* Internal Style Sheet Rules */
H1 {font-family: arial; font-size: 175%}
I {font-weight: bold; font-style: oblique; font-size: 130%}
TABLE {padding: .1in}
BODY {background-color: yellow}
-->
</style>
</head>
<body>
<center>
<h1>
<img SRC="pyramid.gif" height=18 width=18 >  Other Dogs 
<img SRC="pyramid.gif" height=18 width=18></h1></center>
<center>There are several categories of dogs. <i>Sporting dogs</i>, for
instance, are dogs that are used in hunting, racing, and herding.
<p><img SRC="bluebar.gif" height=11 width=768></center>
<br> 
<center>
<table BORDER=2 WIDTH="60%" >
<caption ALIGN="TOP"><b><i><font size=+1>A Few Sporting
Dogs</font></i></b></caption>
<tr><th>Setters</th><th>Retrievers</th></tr>
<tr><td ALIGN=CENTER>Irish Setter</td><td ALIGN=CENTER>Golden
Retriever</td></tr>
<tr><td ALIGN=CENTER>English Setter</td><td ALIGN=CENTER>Labrador
Retriever</td></tr>
<tr><td ALIGN=CENTER>Gordon Setter</td><td
ALIGN=CENTER>Weimaraner</td></tr>
</table>
</center>
</body>
</html>
```

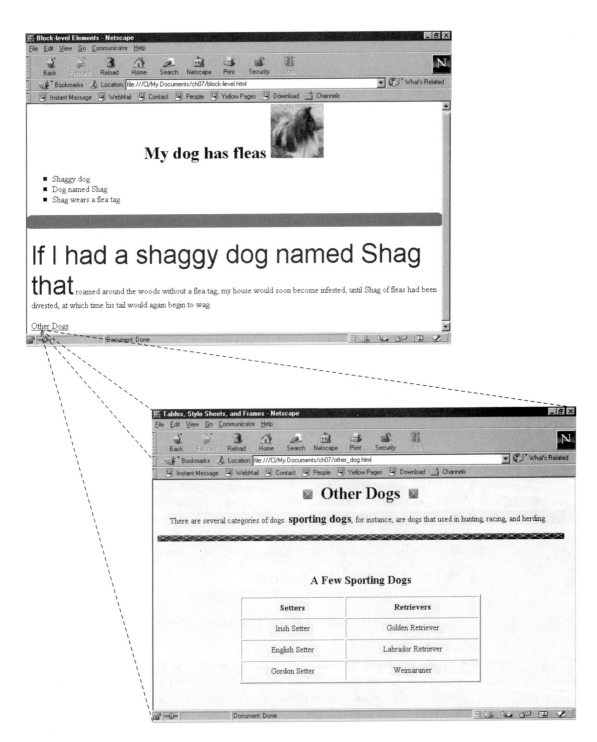

FIGURE 7.2

a) Shaggy Dog home page. b) Hyperlink using CSS to Other Dogs.

The internal style sheet is represented in bold. The rules comprising this style sheet account for the changes in appearance between Figures 7.1b and 7.2b. Notice that the opening <STYLE> tag is modified by the attribute TYPE; the default value is MIME type text/css. The style sheet rules are enclosed within an HTML comment tag, <!- - *rules* - ->, to accommodate browsers that don't support CSS. Such browsers will interpret the style sheet as a comment.

The first rule is used to render H1 elements in an Arial font that is 175% greater in size than the default font size. Similarly, the second rule is used to render I elements in a bold font that is 130% greater in size. Scrutinizing the italicized phrase "sporting dogs" and the caption "A Few Sporting Dogs," however, one discovers that the italic font style has been overridden and replaced with an oblique font style. In other words, the style sheet rule associated with the I element possesses a greater precedence than the double-sided <I> tag. Indeed, the term *cascading* in cascading style sheets is derived from the application of a hierarchical precedence of rules.

The TABLE element is modified to provide a .1 inch padding between the contents of each cell and the cell wall. In the parlance of CSS, a margin defines the entire rectangular area that an element might occupy. The table in Figure 7.2b, for instance, possesses a rectangular region that includes the visible table (rows and columns) and caption. The table's border lies within this margin. Similarly, the padding surrounding the contents of each table cell is contained within the border. Several of the margin, border, and padding properties associated with this "box" structure are listed in Table 7.1.

External style sheets are internal style sheets, less the double-sided <STYLE> tag, that are contained within a separate file. This separation of the style sheet from the web page enables the author to simultaneously control the style of several web pages. Modifications to rules within the external style sheet are immediately incorporated into web pages that are linked to the style sheet. Links are created between web page and external style sheet by the inclusion of a LINK element within a web page's prologue. To insert a link to an external style sheet named shaggy_style.css, for example, type the following:

```
<LINK REL=STYLESHEET TYPE="text/css"
HREF="http://www.shaggydog.com/shaggy_style.css">
```

The REL attribute is used to indicate the relationship between the web page and the external style sheet.

CSS employs two different units of measure: absolute and relative. Absolute units of measure, of which there are five {mm (millimeter), cm (centimeter), in (inch), pt (points), and pc (picas)}, are weighted by an integer or a decimal floating-point number. To specify a font size of one inch, for example, type {font-size: 1in}. Relative units of measure, of which there are three {px (pixels), em (width of the character M), and ex (width of the character x)}, vary relative to a specific pixel or font characteristic.

Frames

The view field of a browser may be subdivided into multiple, smaller fields called *frames*; a collection of such frames is called a *frameset*. Each frame is loaded with an individual web page that can be linked to other web pages in other frames. Although frames were initially introduced in version 2 of Netscape Navigator, they were not officially adopted by the W3C until its current Recommendation, HTML 4.0.

Framed web pages differ significantly in structure from nonframed web pages. In order to illustrate these differences, we examine the following source code, which will be used to simultaneously display both of our previous web pages within the same view field (see Figure 7.3).

> The view field of a browser may be subdivided into multiple, smaller fields called frames; a collection of such frames is called a frameset.

```
<!DOCTYPE    HTML    PUBLIC    "-//W3C//DTD HTML 4.0 Frameset//EN"
"http://www.w3.org/TR/REC-html40/frameset.dtd">
<html>
<head>
<title>Examining Frames</title>
</head>
<frameset cols="50%,50%">
<frame src="shaggydog.html">
<frame src="other_dog.html">
</frameset>
<noframes>
<body>
<p>This information is for browsers that do not support frames.
</body>
</noframes>
</html>
```

The DTD element of our framed web page is of type Frameset, whereas the two non-framed web pages displayed within the frames are of type Transitional. Additionally, the BODY element has been replaced by the FRAMESET element, indicating that the content of the web page is a framing structure, not a typical web page. Contained within the double-sided <NOFRAMES> tag is the content to be presented within the view field of a browser that does not support frames.

Subdivision of the view field is determined by the values assigned to the COLS and ROWS attributes of the FRAMESET element. The portion of source code, <FRAME-SET COLS="50%,50%">, indicates to the receiving browser that the view field is to be vertically divided into two columns of equal width. Acceptable values are number of pixels, remaining view field indicated by an asterisk (*), and percentage of view field. In order to subdivide the view field into four equally sized quadrants, for example, include either <FRAMESET ROWS="50%,50%" COLS="50%,50%"> or <FRAMESET ROWS="*,*" COLS="*,*">. It is possible to further subdivide frames by the nesting of FRAMESET elements.

FIGURE 7.3

a) A framed web page.
b) Source code for framed web page.

a

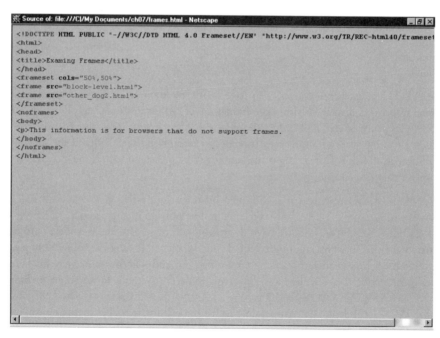

b

If a view field is subdivided into two or more frames, then each frame should receive an individual web page. Web pages are loaded into individual frames in the order in which they are listed. For example, the web page block-level.html is loaded into the left column (see Figure 7.3) because its FRAME element, <frame src="block-level.html">, is listed first. FRAME possesses the following attributes, some of which also apply to the FRAMESET element:

SRC: Indicates the URL of the source file to be loaded into the frame.

NAME: Assigns a name to the frame for updating purposes.

FRAMEBORDER: Used by both the FRAME and FRAMESET elements to enable or disable borders. Acceptable values are YES and NO.

MARGINWIDTH: Sets the width, in pixels, of the left and right margins.

MARGINHEIGHT: Sets the width, in pixels, of the top and bottom margins.

SCROLLING: Enables/disables frame scrolling bars. Acceptable values are YES, NO, and AUTO; the default value is AUTO.

NORESIZE: Used to prevent the user from manipulating the frame dimensions with the mouse.

Assigning a frame's name to a TARGET attribute within a web page's hyperlink redirects the referenced web page to a specified frame, or target. To subdivide a browser's view field into two columns, use the COLS attribute assignment. For example, COLS="25%,75%" creates a thin left navigation column, and the right column could be used to load the content. A few hyperlinks within the web page (named index.html) might be constructed in the following manner; the target frame is to be named "selection":

```
<A HREF="small.html" TARGET="selection">Small dogs</A>

<A HREF=" medium.html" TARGET="selection">Medium dogs</A>

<A HREF="tall.html" TARGET="selection">Tall dogs</A>
```

The general structure of the associated frameset web page might be constructed as follows:

```
<!DOCTYPE HTML PUBLIC "-//W3C//DTD HTML 4.0 Frameset//EN"
"http://www.w3.org/TR/REC-html40/frameset.dtd">
<html>
<head>
<title>Indexed Archival System</title>
</head>
<frameset cols="25%,75%">
<frame src="index.html">
<frame src="initial_page.html">
</frameset>
<noframes>
<body>
```

```
<p>This index archival system requires the use of ...
</body>
</noframes>
</html>
```

The BASE element is used to specify a default target name for all hyperlinks that do not include the TARGET attribute. The basic syntax for this element is <BASE TAR­GET="target_name">, where "target_name" is specified by the author. Four predefined hierarchical target names are used to define a hierarchical relationship between frames: _top, _parent, _self, and _blank. Referring to Figure 7.3, the target name _top represents the entire view field, _parent represents both frames (in this case, also the entire view field); and _self represents either the left or the right frame. The target name _parent will always represent the entire view field, unless nested framesets are being employed; for example, the web page loaded into the right frame is further subdivided into two or more other frames. The target name _blank causes the referenced web page to be loaded into a new unnamed window.

7.2 Embedded Objects

●

Several types of software objects can be embedded within a web page to alter its appearance and/or behavior.

Several types of software objects can be embedded within a web page to alter its appearance and/or behavior. In this section, we will briefly investigate some of these objects including Java applets, ActiveX controls, JavaScript scripts, VRML (Virtual Reality Modeling Language) worlds, animated GIFs, and multimedia technologies. In our discussion, we will encounter new HTML elements (APPLET, SCRIPT, and EMBED) created explicitly for the inclusion of these objects. We will also introduce the OBJECT element that was designed to supercede the APPLET, SCRIPT, EMBED, BGSOUND, and IMG elements.

Java Applets

Initially named "Oak," Java was created by a design team headed by James Gosling of Sun Microsystems. Its original purpose was to provide a communications language to be used by microprocessors embedded within common household appliances. However, for marketing reasons, in May of 1995 Sun introduced Java as a platform-independent, object-oriented programming (OOP) language suitable for distributed networking environments, such as the web. A few months later, Java would be unleashed on the world by being integrated into Netscape's Navigator 2.0. Within a relatively short period of time, Java programmers would use this powerful language to develop an entire spectrum of applications and applets.

Since its inception, Java has undergone significant changes and has spawned other Java-related technologies. The current version, Java 2, provides improved security and performance and was designed to address the needs of the modern business environment. A few significant Java-related technologies include JavaBeans and Jini. JavaBeans is a collection of Java software components (such as a form or a control bar) that can be incorporated into applications to provide immediate functionality. Jini technology, on the other hand, is software that uses the Java language to interconnect all manner of digitally enabled devices (such as laptops, coffee pots, and TVs), thus fulfilling Java's original design purpose.

Although standalone, executable applications can be developed using Java, we will focus on portable, lightweight applications referred to as *applets*. Both applications and applets can be developed using any manner of development tools. Sun Microsystem's Java Development Kit (JDK), for example, can be downloaded from their Java web site, www.javasoft.com. The JDK includes a Java compiler, an interpreter for running applications, the Applet Viewer for running applets, a program debugger, and several application/applet demos.

Java is an object-oriented programming language that is very similar to C++. An *object* is a software model of a real-world item. A coffee pot, for instance, can be virtually created and programmed to behave as the physical machines located on our kitchen countertops. By including a separate instance, or copy, of the coffee pot object into a program, the programmer need not create it from scratch. In fact, only the initial state and/or behavior of the coffee pot need be modified.

The blueprint that defines an object is referred to as a *class*. Common classes are organized into libraries such as AWT (Abstract Windowing Tool), LANG (Java Language), APPLET, and IO (input/output). A class, in turn, is comprised chiefly of *variables* (operational data) and the *methods* that act upon them. Several preexisting methods enable a programmer to quickly add the desired functionality (such as opening a new window, interpreting a mouse click, or initializing an applet) to an application or applet. Because methods are located within classes and predefined classes are located within libraries, programmers generally import one or more classes into their programs.

In a hierarchy of classes, a *subclass* possesses its own characteristics and inherits the characteristics of its *superclass*. Physics and chemistry, for example, are subclasses of science. By similar reasoning, all applets are created as a subclass to the APPLET class library. In fact, they are said to *extend* the APPLET class library.

The life cycle of an applet consists of essentially three phases. In the first phase, the programmer writes the applet's source code as a standard text file. The file is saved as applet_name.java, where applet_name is assigned by the programmer. In the second phase, the newly generated source code file, applet_name.java, is compiled using a Java compiler, where the applet's source code is converted into a format referred to as *Java bytecodes*. The output of this phase produces a file named applet_name.class. In the third phase, the applet is loaded into an interpreter program, where the bytecode is verified as being secure and then run.

The verifier and interpreter program is referred to as a *Java Virtual Machine* (JVM). Although more common as an embedded program, such as that found within a Java-enabled web browser, JVMs can also be implemented in hardware as Java chips. Sun Microsystem's Hot Java, Microsoft's Internet Explorer, and Netscape's Navigator web browsers all possess integrated JVMs. Because versions of these browsers exist for platforms running Windows, MacOS, and Unix, Java applets can run virtually anywhere. In other words, the platform-specific JVM is responsible for converting Java bytecodes into a format suitable to the local platform. Regarding Java, Sun Microsystems has coined the phrase, "Write once, run anywhere."

In order to illustrate some of the basic features common to all applets, we create a slightly modified version of the ever-popular introductory program "Hello World." However, our modified version, listed below, will be used to display the phrase "Hello Shaggy" within our web page:

```
import    java.applet.Applet;
import    java.awt.*;

public class HelloShaggy extends Applet {
        private String message;

        public void init() {
                setBackground(Color.yellow);
                // Retrieve message included within PARAM element.
                message=getParameter("input");
        }

        public void paint(Graphics g) {
                // Check for input string. If one exists, display it.
                if (message != null)
                        g.drawString(message, 5, 15);
        }
}
```

At the beginning of our source code are two lines that begin with the keyword "import." These lines of code instruct the compiler to include specific classes which, in turn, contain collections of common methods. Some of these methods will be called from within the applet to provide specific functionality. For example, the first line, import java.applet.Applet; causes the class Applet of the class library applet to be included as part of the completed applet, HelloShaggy.class. The * in the second line instructs the compiler to include all classes of the awt class library.

In the third line of code, public class HelloShaggy extends Applet, we create a new Applet subclass called HelloShaggy. The term *public* is used to indicate that our new subclass can be accessed by other classes and applets. Note the opening brace { immediately following the subclass declaration in line three and the closing brace } located on the last line. These braces are used to delineate one class from another within the same applet.

They are also used in the delineation of methods, such as public void init( ) {…} located on the fifth line.

On the fourth line, the statement "private String message"; is used to create a variable called message that is used to store a string of text characters. This string is declared *private,* which means that it is to be accessed only by methods within the HelloShaggy subclass. The next statement, public void init( ), is used to initialize our applet by setting the background color to yellow (setBackground(Color.yellow)) and initializing our string variable message to the value retrieved by the method getParameter. By inserting two slashes // before the text string "Retrieve message included within PARAM element of W3 page," we insert a comment into our source code.

In the last few lines of our applet, the "paint" method is invoked by the statement, public void paint(Graphics g). This method is used to repaint the area of the screen associated with the applet; the graphics variable, g, is used to define this area. As we shall see, the statement, g.drawString(message, 5, 15), is used to write the text string contained within the "message" variable to the (x,y) coordinates (5,15) of the applet area. If the variable "message" is empty, or null, then the "drawString" method call would never occur.

The completed source code is saved as the text file named HelloShaggy.java. This file is then compiled using the compiler Javac, where the applet, HelloShaggy.class, is placed in the designated folder (see Figure 7.4a). In order to embed the applet into one of our previously developed web pages, we use the double-sided APPLET (used for insertion) and single-sided PARAM (used to pass author-defined parameters to the applet) tags.

The bold font in the following source code (see Figure 7.4b) illustrates the syntax required to embed the applet; the resulting web page is shown in Figure 7.4c. The CODE attribute of the APPLET tag is set equal to the name of the applet, or class file. The NAME attribute of the PARAM tag is used to indicate the parameter name that is to be retrieved by the embedded applet. In this case, the parameter is called "input," and it is associated with the source code line: message=getParameter("input"). The VALUE attribute of the PARAM tag is used to assign a real value to the named parameter and, therefore, to the applet so that it might be displayed.

```
<!doctype html public "-//w3c//dtd html 4.0 transitional//en">
<html>
<head>
   <meta http-equiv="Content-Type" content="text/html; charset=iso-8859-1">
   <meta name="GENERATOR" content="Mozilla/4.5 [en] (Win95; I) [Netscape]">
   <title>Tables, Style Sheets, and Frames</title>
<style type="text/css">
<!--
H1 {font-family: arial; font-size: 175%}
I {font-weight: bold; font-style: oblique; font-size: 130%}
TABLE {padding: .1in}
BODY {background-color: yellow}
-->
```

```
</style>
</head>
<body>
<center>
<h1>
<img SRC="pyramid.gif" height=18 width=18 > 
<applet code="HelloShaggy.class" width=80 height=20>
<param name="input" value="Hello Shaggy">
</applet>
 
<img SRC="pyramid.gif" height=18 width=18></h1></center>
<center>There are several categories of dogs. <i>Sporting dogs</i>, for
instance, are dogs that are used in hunting, racing, and herding.
<p><img SRC="bluebar.gif" height=11 width=768></center>
<br> 
<center>
<table BORDER=2 WIDTH="60%" >
<caption ALIGN="TOP"><b><i><font size=+1>A Few Sporting
Dogs</font></i></b></caption>
<tr><th>Setters</th><th>Retrievers</th></tr>
<tr><td ALIGN=CENTER>Irish Setter</td><td ALIGN=CENTER>Golden
Retriever</td></tr>
<tr><td ALIGN=CENTER>English Setter</td><td ALIGN=CENTER>Labrador
Retriever</td></tr>
<tr><td ALIGN=CENTER>Gordon Setter</td><td
ALIGN=CENTER>Weimaraner</td></tr>
</table>
</center>
</body>
</html>
```

JavaScript

During the production of a movie, actors follow scripts describing what lines and actions they must perform. Computer-based scripts developed with languages, such as Perl (Unix), Microsoft's VBScript, and Netscape's JavaScript, behave in a similar manner. Sequential lines of code are interpreted in order that an action might be performed. Although scripts can be executed on the same system as the web server (server-side), in this section we will discuss client-side JavaScript. JavaScript 1.3, the current version, is generally supported by current versions of Microsoft Internet Explorer and Netscape Navigator.

Developed by Netscape and initially called LiveScript, JavaScript made its debut in 1996 as an integral part of Netscape Navigator 2.0. JavaScript is similar to the Java programming language in that it is also an object-oriented language and possesses the term "Java"; however, the two languages have little else in common. JavaScript can enhance web pages in several ways, such as validating web-based forms, providing animation, acting upon user-generated events (mouse clicks, keyboard inputs, etc.), and creating on-the-fly HTML code.

a

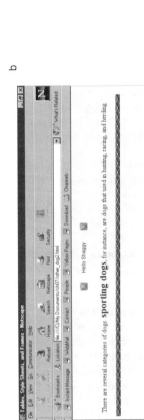

b

c

FIGURE 7.4

a) Compilation of HelloShaggy.java using Jacav. b) HTML source code including HelloShaggy.class. c) Resulting web page.

Unlike the extensive collection of class libraries available to the Java programmer, JavaScript possesses a set of predefined objects, the properties of which can be manipulated using predefined methods, such as date, math, string, document, and location. User-generated events are handled using event handlers. For instance, an image might be highlighted while a user's mouse passes over it (onMouseOver = highlight_function( )).

To illustrate some of the features of JavaScript, we modify our existing web page to include a time stamp that shows the exact time the web page is loaded; the lines of JavaScript are accented in bold:

```
<!doctype html public "-//w3c//dtd html 4.0 transitional//en">
<html>
<head>
   <meta http-equiv="Content-Type" content="text/html; charset=iso-8859-1">
   <meta name="GENERATOR" content="Mozilla/4.5 [en] (Win95; I) [Netscape]">
   <title>Tables, Style Sheets, and Frames</title>
<style type="text/css">
<!--
H1 {font-family: arial; font-size: 175%}
I {font-weight: bold; font-style: oblique; font-size: 130%}
TABLE {padding: .1in}
BODY {background-color: yellow}
-->
</style>
<script language="JavaScript">
<!--
//HTML comment tag is used to hide script from non-JavaScript
browsers
function time_of_day() {
        var date_info = new Date();
        var hours = date_info.getHours();
        var minutes = date_info.getMinutes();
        var seconds = date_info.getSeconds();
        var time = hours + ":" + minutes + ":" + seconds;
        return time;
}
-->
</script>
</head>
<body>
<center>
<h1>
<img SRC="pyramid.gif" height=18 width=18 > 
<applet code="HelloShaggy.class" width=80 height=20>
<param name="input" value="Hello Shaggy">
</applet>
 
<img SRC="pyramid.gif" height=18 width=18></h1></center>
```

```
<center>There are several categories of dogs. <i>Sporting dogs</i>, for
instance, are dogs that are used in hunting, racing, and herding.
<p><img SRC="bluebar.gif" height=11 width=768></center>
<br> 
<script language="JavaScript">
document.write("<b>The current time is: </b><i>" + time_of_day() +
"</i>");
</script>
<center>
<table BORDER=2 WIDTH="60%" >
<caption ALIGN="TOP"><b><i><font size=+1>A Few Sporting
Dogs</font></i></b></caption>
<tr><th>Setters</th><th>Retrievers</th></tr>
<tr><td ALIGN=CENTER>Irish Setter</td><td ALIGN=CENTER>Golden
Retriever</td></tr>
<tr><td ALIGN=CENTER>English Setter</td><td ALIGN=CENTER>Labrador
Retriever</td></tr>
<tr><td ALIGN=CENTER>Gordon Setter</td><td
ALIGN=CENTER>Weimaraner</td></tr>
</table>
</center>
</body>
</html>
```

Similar to CSS, JavaScript scripts can be either internal or external. External scripts, for example, might be included as the value assigned to the HREF attribute found within an anchor tag. Internal scripts, on the other hand, are contained solely within the web page's HTML code. Furthermore, they can also be included within the web page's prologue and/or its body. Scripts located within the prologue are fully loaded prior to the user content that is located in the body. The first script in our HTML code is embedded prior to the closing </HEAD> tag and is, therefore, part of the prologue of the web page. The second script is embedded within the body, prior to the table entitled "A Few Sporting Dogs."

Typically, scripts are embedded using the double-sided SCRIPT tag, the primary attribute of which is LANGUAGE. Scripts can be embedded, and, therefore, effectively hidden from browsers that do not support JavaScript, by enclosing them within the double-sided HTML comment tag, <!-- ... -- >. JavaScript comments, like Java comments, are created by preceding the comment string with a double slash //, such as "//HTML comment tag is used to hide script…"

The time_of_day( ) method used to retrieve the time stamp information is user-defined and begins with the line: function time_of_day( ). The contents of the method are enclosed within braces {…}. A variable named date_info is created and assigned to a new instance of the predefined Date object by use of the statement: var date_info = new Date( ). In other words, the variable date_info represents a user-defined version of the Date object, which can be modified. A variable named "hours" is created to store hour information retrieved using the date_info instance of the Date object method gethours(). In a similar manner, minutes and seconds information is retrieved and stored to the variables, minutes and seconds, respectively.

The last two lines of the method time_of_day create and format a variable named "time," and then return this information to the method that made the call. In this case, the calling method is located within the second script. In fact, the only method within this script is used to invoke the write method associated with the document object that, in turn, calls the time_of_day method. The write method is used to display information to the screen; the embedded + symbols in the argument ("The current time is: <i>" + time_of_day() + "</i>") are used to join the various pieces of information together (see Figure 7.5).

ActiveX Controls

Microsoft initially introduced ActiveX in the spring of 1996 to compete directly with the burgeoning popularity of Java applets. Akin to Java Beans, ActiveX controls are software components (objects designed for a specific purpose), such as a web page formatting device or an audio volume control, that can be used to enhance the functionality and appearance of a web page. Whereas Java Beans are highly portable between operating environments, ActiveX controls are restricted to the specific operating environment for which they were developed, such as Windows NT or 98. However, because ActiveX controls are written using programming languages, such as Microsoft's Visual C++ or Visual Basic, as unrestricted executable code, they generally possess greater access to the local system resources, such as the hard drive.

ActiveX controls are merely components conforming to a predefined set of standards referred to as the *Microsoft Component Object Model* (COM). In the present context, ActiveX controls are embedded within a web page using the OBJECT and PARAM elements and associated attributes. ActiveX controls, like Java applets, are not integrated into the HTML source code of a web page; instead they are invoked by a specific reference within the source code. Although ActiveX plug-ins exist for Netscape Navigator, direct support for the technology is incorporated into Microsoft's Internet Explorer version 3.0 and greater.

In order to illustrate how an ActiveX control is embedded within a web page, we construct a new page with the aid of Microsoft's ActiveX Control Pad (see Figure 7.6a), which is downloadable from Microsoft's web site, www.microsoft.com. For this example, our ActiveX control is the Microsoft Media Player, which will be used to play an MPEG movie showing a partial eclipse of the Sun (see Figures 7.6b and 7.6c). Modifications and key elements are shown in bold in the following HTML source code:

```
<!doctype html public "-//w3c//dtd html 4.0 transitional//en">
<HTML>
<HEAD>
<TITLE>X-ray Solar Eclipse</TITLE>
</HEAD>
```

```
<BODY BGCOLOR="Yellow">

<P ALIGN="Center"><b>This stunning video of the Moon eclipsing the
Sun was captured by the Soft X-ray Telescope (SXT) aboard the
Japanese Yohkoh spacecraft on October 24th, 1995. Video courtesy of
Jim Lemen of the Lockheed Palo Alto Research Labs</b><br><br>

<OBJECT ID="MediaPlayer1" WIDTH=287 HEIGHT=225
CLASSID="CLSID:22D6F312-B0F6-11D0-94AB-0080C74C7E95">
    <PARAM NAME="AudioStream" VALUE="-1">
    <PARAM NAME="AutoSize" VALUE="-1">
    <PARAM NAME="AutoStart" VALUE="-1">
    <PARAM NAME="DisplayForeColor" VALUE="16777215">
    <PARAM NAME="DisplayMode" VALUE="0">
    <PARAM NAME="DisplaySize" VALUE="0">
    <PARAM NAME="Enabled" VALUE="-1">
    <PARAM NAME="EnableContextMenu" VALUE="-1">
    <PARAM NAME="EnablePositionControls" VALUE="-1">
    <PARAM NAME="EnableFullScreenControls" VALUE="0">
    <PARAM NAME="EnableTracker" VALUE="-1">
    <PARAM NAME="Filename"
VALUE="c:\Mydocu~1\ch07\eclipse.mpg">
    <PARAM NAME="Rate" VALUE="1">
</OBJECT>

</BODY>
</HTML>
```

The background color was set to yellow and a caption provided. The Media Player
control is identified by the OBJECT tag attribute CLASSID, as in the line CLASSID=
"CLSID:22D6F312-B0F6-11D0-94AB-0080C74C7E95". A handle, to be used for access
by other objects, is assigned to the CLASSID by using the ID attribute, ID="MediaPlayer1."
Several of the PARAM elements, used to initialize and define the behavior of the control,
have been eliminated for clarity and succinctness; for example, audio parameters were of little value in Figure 7.6. The AutoStart and Filename parameters were modified to automatically play (PARAM NAME="AutoStart" VALUE="-1") the MPEG file (PARAM NAME=
"Filename" VALUE="c:\Mydocu~1\ch07\eclipse.mpg") after the web page is loaded.

Thousands of predeveloped ActiveX controls exist for virtually every conceivable industry, including software development, multimedia providers, engineering, and medical
information services. However, because controls are not necessarily restricted like Java
applets, some measure of security, when downloading a control, must be provided. The
downloading of controls and Java applets can be prevented by properly configuring
browser security settings. An additional, and perhaps more palatable, solution is to have
controls digitally "signed" prior to release. The signature can be used to verify that the
control to be downloaded was, indeed, created by a particular person or company.

FIGURE 7.5
a) Web page with JavaScript. b) A partial listing of its HTML source code.

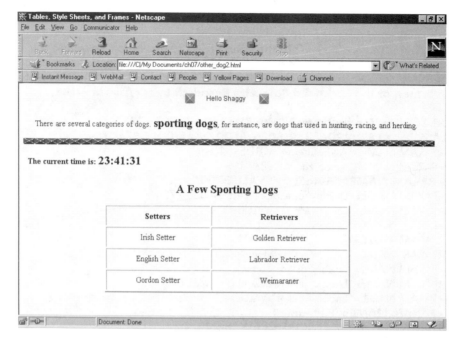

a

b

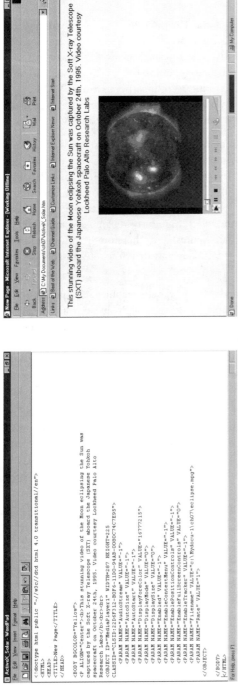

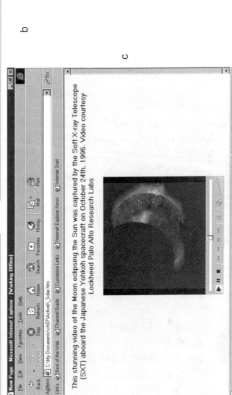

a

b

c

FIGURE 7.6

Web page created using ActiveX Control Pad. b) Web page with embedded ActiveX Control. c) Same web page two seconds later.

The solar x-ray images are from the Yohkoh mission of ISAS, Japan. The x-ray telescope was prepared by the Lockheed Palo Alto Research Laboratory, the National Astronomical Observatory of Japan, and the University of Tokyo with the support of NASA and ISAS. ActiveX® screen shots reprinted with permission from Microsoft Corporation.

VRML Worlds

Introduced by Mark Pesce and Tony Parisi at the 1994 World Wide Web Conference, *VRML* (Virtual Reality Modeling Language) has evolved into a global standard for 3D interactive multimedia on the Internet. The first official version of VRML, version 1.0, was based upon Silicon Graphics' Open Inventor Language. Improvements to VRML 1.0, such as animation, enhanced interactivity, and scripting were incorporated into VRML 2.0, which was based upon the Moving Worlds proposal by Sony, SGI (Silicon Graphics, Inc.), Mitra, et al. VRML97, the current version, is a slightly refined version of VRML 2.0.

VRML worlds are the 3D interactive environments that one visits by using a web browser plug-in and/or VRML browser, such as Intervista's WorldView, SGI's CosmoPlayer, or Netscape's Live3D. Like web pages, they are located via their URL and classified by their MIME type (x-world/w-vrml). In fact, VRML worlds can be embedded within web pages by using the HTML element EMBED; for example, <EMBED src="http://www.worlds_r_us.com/my_world.wrl"). Some worlds are very simplistic in design (such as a collection of basic geometric figures) and, therefore, require very little source code. Such worlds generally download quickly and therefore, are suitable for use over traditional modems.

Other worlds, however, are highly complex and may incorporate graphics and multimedia to effect a more realistic setting. Imagine, for example, "walking through" an electronic shopping mall as a three-dimensional virtual being. As you walk into a sporting goods store, a set of virtual fishing poles catches your eye. You pick one up and practice casting with it. As you are casting, a virtual store manager walks over and asks, "Would you like to purchase this fishing pole?" You nod, walk over to the virtual checkout counter, and purchase the pole. Of course, you actually purchased the pole via electronic commerce; the real pole arrives two weeks later.

Although worlds similar to the fishing pole scenario exist, the amount and type of information associated with such a world would render it impractical for downloading over modems, which eliminates most of the home shopping market. The world's source code would download very quickly because it is merely a text, or ASCII, file; the delay is caused by the associated graphical and multimedia information. The following source code is used to construct a simple 3D model of the Sun-Earth-Moon system. The associated file, sphere.wrl, was created with a simple text editor and displayed using InterVista's WorldView VRML browser (see Figure 7.7).

```
#VRML V2.0 utf8

Separator {
     #Create image of the Sun
     Material{       emissiveColor   1 1 0}
     PointLight{ intensity    1.5   }
     Sphere {        radius      14   }

Separator {
     #Create image of the Earth
```

```
       Transform{      translation              350 0 0}
       Material{       diffuseColor      0  0  1
                       specularColor     0  1  4
                       shininess                     .85}
       Sphere {        radius    2}

Separator{

       #Create image of the Moon
       Transform{      translation              3 9 0}
       Material{       diffuseColor      1 1 3
                       specularColor     1 1 1
                       shininess                     .5}

       Sphere{         radius    .8}
             }
       }
}
```

The first line of code, #VRML 2.0 utf8, indicates to the receiving browser that the following information describes a VRML 2.0 world that conforms to an encoding scheme
known as UTF-8. The three separators, highlighted in boldfaced type, are used to hold
VRML objects (such as a sphere or the material used to describe the sphere), referred to
as *nodes,* within a common group. The contents of a separator are contained within
opening and closing curly braces, {...}. Separators can contain one or more nodes and/or
other separators. When separators are nested, as in our example, attribute modifications
to nested nodes are made with reference to the outermost separator. A change in position
of a nested node, for example, would be made relative to the position of the first node
within the outermost separator. When nodes are contained within a unique separator,
they function independently of other nodes.

In the outermost separator, we create a new instance of a sphere that will be used to represent the Sun. Since the Sun is an object that emits light, we assign the value 1 1 0 (RGB
encoding for yellow) to the field name emissiveColor within the Material node. The
color of the Earth and Moon are set in a similar way using the field names diffuseColor
(an object's natural color) and specularColor (an object's reflected color).

The PointLight node and Intensity field are used to specify that the sphere is to radiate in
all directions equally with a relative intensity of 1.5. The Sphere node is used to create a
yellow ball with a radius of 14. The Earth and Moon are constructed in a similar manner,
and then positioned relative to the Sun by assigning the proper coordinate values (x,y,z)
to the translation field within the Transform node. Finally, we are ready to "fly" through
our virtual world by using our mouse to manipulate the desired navigational controller
(see Figures 7.7b and 7.7c). Modern VRML browsers and plug-ins incorporate several
types of controllers that are used to control different modes of travel, such as walk, spin,
look, slide, and point (fly in a specific direction).

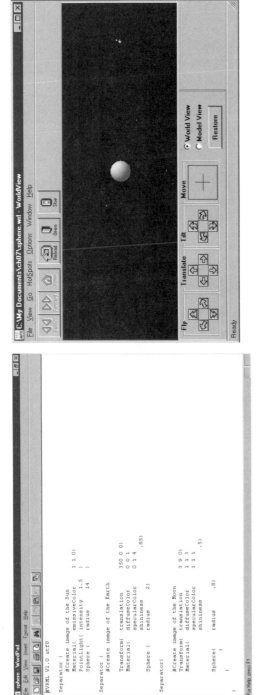

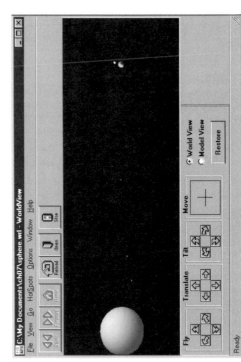

Graphics courtesy Computer Associates.

FIGURE 7.7

a) Source code for VRML world sphere.wrl. b) Resulting VRML world. c) Close-up perspective of same VRML world.

Animated GIFs

By playing a related sequence of images and/or sounds at a predetermined rate, the illusion of fluid motion, or animation, is created. Animated sequences may be as simple as a series of stick figure drawings on a set of flip cards, or as complex and awe-inspiring as a Disney movie. Ubiquitous to the web, animation is often used as an efficient and popular means to add liveliness to web pages. Web-based animations can be created using one of several different types of technologies, including Java, JavaScript, push, pull, or animated GIFs. Proprietary animation development technologies, such as Macromedia's Director and Authorware programs and corresponding Shockwave plug-in, are also available.

Perhaps the easiest animation technology to implement, an animated GIF is a set of images sequenced and stored into a single file, the format of which is GIF89a; the standard format for a static GIF file is GIF87. Animated GIF tools, such as Ulead's GIF Animator or the GIF Construction Set by Alchemy Mindworks, are used to order the sequence of images, modify their color, configure sequence timing and looping count, and export the new file in the GIF89a format with the extension .gif.

An animated GIF file is embedded into a web page in the same manner as a static GIF file. Suppose, for example, that we have created an animated GIF of the Earth rotating about its axis. In order to embed the file into a web page, we enter the following line of HTML code: <IMG SRC=earth.gif>. Depending upon the looping configuration, the downloaded animated GIF will play once, play a specified number of times, or play continuously.

Audio and Video

Imagine downloading and playing a new song within hours of its initial recording by your favorite artist. Actually, this phenomenon occurs daily throughout the world using a very popular audio technology known as MP3 (MPEG Layer-3). MP3 is an audio *codec* (coder/decoder) used in the compression/decompression and streaming of CD-like quality audio information. On the client side, one needs to download and install an audio plug-in, such as the WinAmp audio player by winamp.com, prior to downloading music. The following are several audio formats used to encode standalone and streaming audio files; corresponding audio players must be used for specific formats:

Audio Format	File Extension
AIFF (Audio Interchange File Format from Apple Computer)	.aiff
WAV (Microsoft)	.wav
μLaw	.au
MIDI (Musical Instrument Digital Interface)	.mid
RealAudio (RealNetworks)	.ra or .ram
MPEG Layer-3	.mp3

ANCHOR (hyperlinks), OBJECT, and EMBED elements are used to embed references to audio and video files within a web page. To include a hyperlink that, when clicked, would download and play an MP3-encoded version of "The Blue Danube," include the following HTML code:

```
<A HREF="http://www.somewhere.com/music_folder/blue_danube.mp3"><IMG
SRC="notes.gif" HEIGHT="20" WIDTH="20"></A>
```

To use the EMBED element instead, include the following line of code:

```
<EMBED SRC="http://www.somwhere.com/music_folder/blue_danube.mp3">
```

Depending upon the player used, additional attributes, such as looping count, play upon download, and volume control might be included within the EMBED element. For the most part, video is handled in the same manner as audio. The following are several video formats used to encode standalone and streaming video files; corresponding video players must be used for specific formats:

Video Format	File Extension
QuickTime (Apple Computer)	.mov, .qt
Audio-Video Interleaved (Microsoft)	.avi
VIVO (Vivo Software)	.viv
MPEG (ISO video standard)	.mpeg, .mpe, or .mpg

To include a hyperlinked image of a violin that, when clicked, would download and play a QuickTime-encoded movie depicting Beethoven composing music, include the following HTML code:

```
<A  HREF="http://www.somewhere.com/movie_folder/beethoven.qt"><IMG
SRC="notes.gif" HEIGHT="20" WIDTH="20"></A>
```

If the movie were Audio-Video Interleaved-encoded and the browser used were Internet Explorer, one might embed the movie reference into the web page using proprietary IMG attributes: DYNSRC, START, or LOOP. The following line of code, for example, specifies that the file beethoven.avi is to be downloaded and played three times when the mouse cursor is positioned over the image:

```
<IMG SRC="beethoven.gif" DYNSRC="beethoven.avi" LOOP="3"
START="MOUSEOVER">
```

7.3 Streaming Technologies

Rather than fully downloading a multimedia file prior to playing, the process of streaming involves the immediate playing of information upon reception.

Real-time video and audio feeds from news agencies, talk shows, and astronauts aboard the Space Shuttle are a few examples that use streaming technologies. Rather than fully downloading a multimedia file prior to playing, the process of *streaming* involves the immediate playing of information upon reception. Actually, the initial process is not immediate. As the stream of information begins to arrive, a small buffer, or queue, within the client system is filled. The rate at which this buffer fills indicates to the streaming server the required data rate and, therefore, the quality of the information to be transmitted.

Streaming technologies employ the use of UDP instead of the more common TCP protocol to transport IP packets from the server to the client system. Recall that UDP, a connectionless protocol, does not possess fields for sequencing and error recovery, as does TCP. Therefore, UDP is a more efficient transport protocol for time-sensitive information such as video and audio.

Both audio and video streaming-based systems are comprised of client (player) and server components, such as the product suite RealAudio, RealVideo, and RealServer by RealNetworks. Other factors that affect the quality of the presentation received include the server's disk, processor, and I/O performance; the nature of the network connections between the server and client; the codecs used; and the client's processor and I/O performance. Evolving standards, such as RTSP (Real-Time Streaming Protocol) and IP Multicasting, promise to further refine performance and delivery issues associated with streaming technologies. RTSP, for example, has provisions for inter-vendor compatibility and multicasting to a specific audience, the latter being accomplished via IP Multicasting.

In order to illustrate how streaming technologies operate, we tune to a live broadcast of the BBC (British Broadcast Corporation) by redirecting our browsers to the URL http://www.broadcast.com/bbc (see Figure 7.8a). This is the BBC web page of the popular web site, www.broadcast.com. By clicking the hyperlink "RealAudio 28.8k ENGLISH feed," our browser is redirected to the BBC's streaming audio server and audio information begins to stream across the Internet to our audio player, RealPlayer (see Figure 7.8b). Upon selecting the Statistics item under RealPlayer's View menu, a window showing the UDP connection statistics is presented (see Figure 7.8c).

7.4 Push versus Pull Technology

Push and Pull technologies are essentially opposites. Information is either *pushed* from the server to the client, or *pulled* by the client from the server. These technologies neither coexist nor serve the same function. With Push technology, the user subscribes to a specific set of information referred to as a *channel*. Although these channels are pushed to the client on a scheduled basis, they are different from television channels because the user can generally customize the channel's schedule and content to be received. Information is downloaded from a channel to the client system's local drive and, therefore, can be read offline.

News, weather, and stock market information are typical subscription channels. Developers use HTML source code, images, audio, Java applets, ActiveX components, and other technologies when creating the contents of a channel. Push clients receive this information as a multipart stream and, therefore, must be able to interpret the MIME type multipart/mixed. Clients are Push-enabled browsers, plug-ins, or proprietary programs, such as Marimba's Castanet. Netscape Navigator and Microsoft Internet Explorer are Push-enabled and refer to the technology as *Netcasting* and *Webcasting*, respectively.

Another good example of Push technology is EntryPoint's Push client (see Figure 7.9a). EntryPoint channels are customized within the Personalize Channels window by selecting

Push and Pull technologies are essentially opposites. Information is either pushed from the server to the client, or pulled by the client from the server.

FIGURE 7.8

a) Broadcast.com BBC web page. b) Live BBC broadcast using RealPlayer. c) RealPlayer UDP connection statistics.

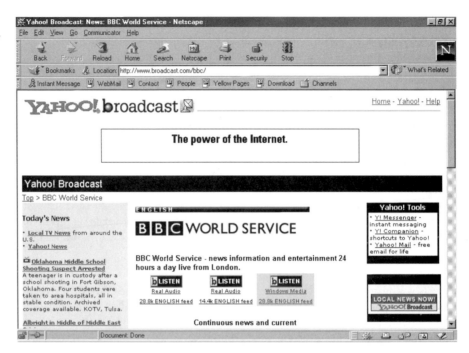

Used with permission from BBC World Service, Broadcast.com, and Yahoo! Inc.

the tab that corresponds to the desired channel and modifying the appropriate entry. Access to the EntryPoint Network is accomplished via the EntryPoint Login dialog box (see Figure 7.9b). EntryPoint includes a personalized information ticker that scrolls information from specified sources at a user-defined rate (see Figure 7.9c).

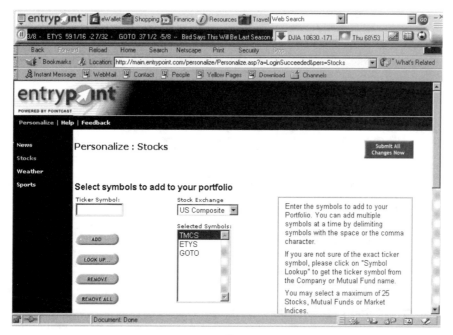

a

FIGURE 7.9

*a) EntryPoint
Network client.
b) EntryPoint Login
dialog box. c) Entry-
Point personalized
entry ticker.*

b

c

Used with permission of EntryPoint, Inc.

Client Pull technologies require the client, usually a web browser, to periodically request new data from the web server. In a previous section, we discussed web page refresh using the META element. Such a function might be useful if, for example, a user visited a defunct web site. The user's browser could be automatically redirected to an updated or related web site after an arbitrary three-second delay with the following line of HTML code:

```
<META HTTP-EQUIV="Refresh" Content="3" URL="http://www.new_site.com/">
```

7.5 Forms, CGI Scripts, and Database Connectivity

Although increasingly sophisticated technologies are being used to design interactive user-to-application interfaces, the traditional HTML form and CGI combination still constitute a viable design mechanism.

Although increasingly sophisticated technologies, such as Java, ActiveX, and XML, are being used to design interactive user-to-application interfaces, the traditional HTML form and CGI (Common Gateway Interface) combination still constitute a viable design mechanism. In this section, we will briefly investigate one of the more common form/CGI applications, web database connectivity.

Forms are essentially data-gathering devices, or front ends, for interactive web-based applications. Forms come in many different shapes and sizes and may possess a single entry field, multiple entry fields, radio buttons, checkboxes, pull-down menus, and more. They are found in many locations throughout the web, including search engines, airline ticket reservation systems, poll-based web sites, and online magazine subscriptions. The interactive process of transmitting a request to a particular application and receiving a response from that application is as follows:

1. Having completed the form, the user submits it by clicking the appropriate button.
2. The submitted information is received by the web server and relayed to the CGI script.
3. The CGI script parses the received information into key fields and either immediately acts upon it, or formats it and presents it to the recipient application, such as a database.
4. If appropriate, the CGI sends a formatted response (such as another form, a report, or a spreadsheet) back to the web server, whereupon it is transmitted to the user.

A basic text input form is constructed using the FORM element and associated attributes. We shall discuss key features (shown in boldfaced type) of the following HTML code as we compare it to the form depicted in Figure 7.10b:

```
<!doctype html public "-//w3c//dtd html 4.0 transitional//en">
<html>
<head><title>Input Form Sample</title></head>
<body bgcolor="yellow">
```

```
<h3>Basic Text Input Example</h3>
<form method="post" action="http://www.somewhere.com/form.cgi">
<pre>
Your Name      <input type="text" name="person" size="25">
Your Address  <textarea name="address" rows=4
cols=40></textarea><p>
Your Phone #  <input type="text" name="telephone" size="10" maxlength="12">
</pre><p>
<input type="submit" value="submit">
<input type="reset" value="clear form">
</form>
</body>
</html>
```

The opening FORM tag is modified by the METHOD and ACTION attributes. Either POST or GET can be assigned to the METHOD attribute. The POST method is used to transmit the gathered information as NAME/VALUE pairs, or tuples, contained in a single file, whereas the GET method is used to append the gathered information to the CGI's URL by preceding the information with a question mark. The following extended URL, for example, would be generated by the GET method after Bob submits the completed form:

http://www.somewhere.com/form.cgi?person="bob"&address="123+La+La+Lane" &telephone="8001234567"

The segment person="bob" illustrates the meaning of NAME/VALUE pairs. The NAME attribute is assigned the name of a variable to be parsed by the CGI script, whereas the VALUE, in this case, describes the actual data entered. However, a VALUE attribute does exist and is used to set default values, such as the label "clear form" on the reset button.

The ACTION attribute specifies the location of the CGI to be used for processing the submitted information. Opening and closing <PRE> tags surround three distinct input elements, which are used to create input fields, in order to fix their position relative to one another. Although there are more elegant ways of positioning these fields, <PRE> tags are simple and efficient.

The first input field, Your Name, is established by using the INPUT element with the value "text" assigned to the corresponding TYPE attribute; it is 25 characters in length. The second input field, Your Address, is established by using the double-sided <TEXTAREA> tag and associated ROWS and COLS attributes; it is rectangular in shape with a width of 40 characters and a height of 4 characters.

By setting the TYPE attribute of the INPUT element to either "submit" or "reset," one creates submit and reset buttons, respectively. Similarly, setting the TYPE attribute to "password" can create a password field. When a user enters information into a password field, only asterisks are displayed. Several form-related tags and attributes are listed in Table 7.2.

CGI scripts can be developed using one of several scripting languages including Javascript, VBScript, Perl, and Applescript. The completed script is usually placed in a specific folder,

FIGURE 7.10

a) Source code for a basic input form. b) Resulting web form.

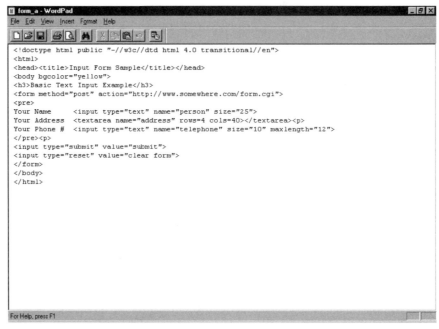

a

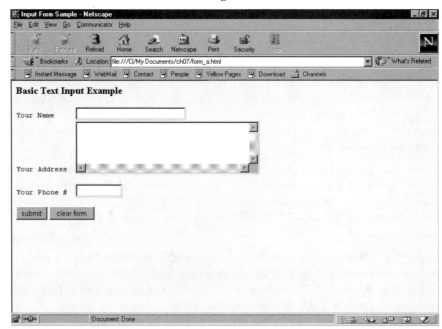

b

Table 7.2 Form Tags and Attributes

Form Tags	Description
<FOR<>—</FORM>	Enclose all form elements in thes tags (required)
ACTION	**Form tag attribute** indicates URL of script.
METHOD	**Form tag attribute** indicates how data is sent to the script: POST or GET.
<INPUT>	Single-sided, used to input user data.
TYPE	**Input tag attribute** indicates type of input element. Options include text, textarea, radio button, checkbox, password, submit, hidden, and reset.
NAME	**Input tag attribute** indicates variable to be sent to script.
SIZE	**Input tag attribute** indicates size of text-related input fields.
MAXLENGTH	**Input tag attribute** indicates maximum number of characters for text-related input fields.
VALUE	**Input tag attribute** indicates default value of an input element.
CHECKED	**Input tag attribute** indicates preselected radio button or checkbox.
ROWS	**Textarea tag attribute** indicates number of rows in textarea.
COLS	**Textarea tag attribute** indicates number of columns in textarea.
<SELECT>—</SELECT>	Creates a multi-line text selection box.
MULTIPLE	**Select tag attribute** allows multiple user selections.
<OPTION>	Single-sided tag used in conjunction with select tag to create options.
SELECTED	**Option tag attribute** indicates a preselected option in a selection box.

such as cgi-bin, on the web server to provide better security. In the case of database connectivity via the web, CGI scripts must be able to communicate with the specific database environment. Several database languages, such as SQL (Structured Query Language), JDBC (Java Database Connectivity), and ODBC (Open Database Connectivity), enable CGI scripts to issue various database commands such as open, modify, compare, and close.

In its most fundamental form, a *database* is nothing more than a table comprised of rows and columns. Columns represent a common field, whereas rows represent a common record. Oracle, Sybase, and Microsoft produce three popular database management systems (DBMS). A *relational database management system* (RDBMS) is a collection of tables, the fields of which can be inter-related, thus providing the possibility for complex relationships between the various tables. An *object relational database management system* (ORDBMS) stores information as discrete objects, rather than in a tabular format.

To better understand the relationship between the fields of an HTML form and a small database, we will examine the following source code as it relates to Figure 7.11. Salient features appear in boldfaced type:

```
<!doctype html public "-//w3c//dtd html 4.0 transitional//en">
<html>
<head>
<title>Data Input Form</title>
</head>
<body bgcolor="yellow">
<h3>Data Input Form for Customer Database</h3>
<pre>
<form method="post" action="http://www.somewhere.com/cgi-bin/database.cgi">
<input type="hidden" name="_Table" value="Customers">
<input type="hidden" name="_activity" value="insert">
<input type="hidden" name="_fieldname" value="[Company Name]">
Company Name:      <input name="_fieldvalue" value=""><br>
<input type="hidden" name="_fieldname" value="[Contact First Name]">
Contact First Name: <input name="_fieldvalue" value="">
<input type="hidden" name="_fieldname" value="[Customer Last Name]">
Customer Last Name: <input name="_fieldvalue" value="">
<input type="hidden" name="_fieldname" value="[Billing Address]">
Billing Address:   <input name="_fieldvalue" value="">
<input type="hidden" name="_fieldname" value="[City]">
City:              <input name="_fieldvalue" value="">
<input type="hidden" name="_fieldname" value="[State/Province]">
State/Province:    <input name="_fieldvalue" value="">
Username:          <input name="_username" size=8 maxlength=15 value="">
Password:          <input type="password" name="_password" size=8 maxlength=8
value="">
<br><br>
<input type="submit" value="Process Data">
</form>
</pre>
</body>
</html>
```

When the TYPE attribute of the INPUT element is set to "hidden," the input field does not appear within the web page. Such fields are used in the submission of static data. The NAME attribute of the first boldfaced INPUT element is set to _Table, and the VALUE

FIGURE 7.11

a) Source code for a basic database input form. b) Resulting web form. c) The associated database.
Used with permission by Microsoft Corporation.

attribute is set to Customers. This particular name/value pair is used to specify the database, or table, named Customer (see Figure 7.11c). Similarly, the value/name pairs of the two subsequent INPUT elements are used to initiate an insert function and associate the first field of the HTML form with the first field of the database.

7.6 Cookies

Many web sites collect information about your surfing habits as you travel through cyberspace. Some information, such as an account name and password, is asked for directly, while other information is not. By default, most browsers allow the visited web server to deposit this small amount of information onto your hard drive in the form of a *cookie*. This feature can generally be disabled or modified. Cookies are text files or entries within a single text file that are web site–dependent. In other words, only the specific web site that deposited the cookie can read or update it.

Although cookies can be useful for automatically supplying web servers with required information upon subsequent visits, they are also considered by many to be a privacy concern. (In addition to account names and passwords, cookies might also be used to glean information about sites visited, frequency of visits, and spending habits.) As with any new technology, there are pluses and minuses. The convenience of cookies, for example, might offset one's concerns about loss of privacy.

Summary

The purpose of this chapter was to build upon the fundamental knowledge of the web established in Chapter 6. We began by discussing the purpose and creation of tables, style sheets, and frames. Tables, like spreadsheets, are comprised of rows and columns and their primary purpose is the positioning and formatting of data. Cascading style sheets consist of a set of rules used to describe and control the presentation of a web page; they were initially introduced to allow for the separation of web page format and presentation. The term cascading refers to the fact that style sheets obey a hierarchical order of precedence as they are applied.

You can embed several different types of software technologies into the pages of a web site to add a significant amount of presentational aesthetic value and functionality. Java applets, for example, can be used to create software objects with advanced interactive capabilities. Javascript, on the other hand, can be used to insert powerful scripts inline with HTML code. ActiveX can be used to include predeveloped components such as multimedia players, forms, buttons, and much more.

The 3-D version of cyberspace can be incorporated into web sites by using VRML worlds, which can be hyperlinked to traditional flat-space web sites. One might, for example, "fly" through a three-dimensional window and land upon a two-dimensional dinosaur. Animated GIFs, and audio/video technologies can greatly enhance a web site. However, the latter two require network connections of significant capacity. Fortunately, streaming technologies, which begin to play audio/video information as they are downloaded, enable users with low-speed connections to fully participate in multimedia-laden web sites.

Push and Pull technologies are essentially opposites of one another. In Push technology, a web server pushes user-defined content, referred to as a channel, toward the browser. In Pull technology, the browser periodically pulls content from a specified web server. Forms and CGI scripts are still widely used to provide interactivity between the end user and specific applications associated with a particular web server. One of the primary uses of forms and CGI scripts is interfacing web-based forms to database systems.

Cookies are pieces of information deposited on the visitor's hard drive by the web server. Although usually innocuous, they do raise concerns over issues of privacy. Cookies can be used to automatically pass on required information to web servers, prior to entry. They can also be used to track visitors' habits as they travel throughout cyberspace.

Modes of Communication

Chapter Learning Objectives:

- Explore e-mail concepts and operation.
- Understand listservs.
- Understand USENET.
- Explore IRC (Internet Relay Chat).
- Understand video conferencing.
- Understand Internet telephony.

"We never touch but at points."

Ralph Waldo Emerson, Journals

In the previous chapters, we discussed the Internet and the underlying technologies that have enabled such phenomenal creations as the web. We now turn our attention to some of the services and technologies associated primarily with two-way communications between people. As cybercitizens, we witness humanity becoming more connected with each passing day. In reality, however, relatively few people have access to the communications systems and services that are commonplace to individuals in affluent nations. Spotty infrastructures, political restrictions, prohibitively expensive equipment cost and access fees, and cultural beliefs are some of the impediments that prevent cyberspace from being an omnipresent reality.

8.1 E-mail

It is estimated that two billion e-mail transactions traverse the vast web of Internet connections daily, and that the volume of data traffic on the Internet doubles every six months! The global transport and delivery system that processes this staggering amount of e-mail is primarily based upon *SMTP* (Simple Mail Transfer Protocol), which is part of the *TCP/IP* protocol suite. SMTP is responsible for transporting e-mail from the originating system to its associated e-mail server and among all intermediate e-mail servers to the recipient's e-mail server. In other words, SMTP is the transport vehicle used for accessing the entrance ramps and highways of the global e-mail system.

Because of its simplistic nature, SMTP is a relatively easy protocol to understand and manipulate. In order to illustrate this simplicity, we manually open an SMTP session (TCP port 25) with an e-mail server using Telnet; the port number is entered into the port number field when using a graphical version of Telnet. We will then compose an e-mail message, send it to a recipient account (tfallon@st6000.sct.edu), and view the received message using the e-mail client Eudora (see Figure 8.1).

The following set of SMTP commands and corresponding responses were entered manually in the Telnet window, captured in a log file, and manually enumerated (C indicates command and R indicates response). Figure 8.1a does not show the commands entered; rather, it only shows the echoed responses.

R1:   220 newton.SPSU.edu ESMTP Sendmail 8.9.2/8.9.2; Mon, 10 May 1999 11:30:09 -0400

C1:   HELO st6000.sct.edu

R2:   250 newton.SPSU.edu Hello user-38lcdka.dialup.mindspring.com [209.86.54.138], pleased to meet you

C2:   MAIL From:<tfallon@st6000.sct.ed>

R3:   250 <tfallon@st6000.sct.edu>... Sender ok

C3:   RCPT To:tfallon@st6000.sct.edu

R4:   250 tfallon@st6000.sct.edu... Recipient ok

C4:   DATA

R5:   354 Enter mail, end with "." on a line by itself

Subject: SMTP Demo

This is a test message to demonstrate how SMTP operates.

R6:   250 LAA28518 Message accepted for delivery

C5:   QUIT

R7:   221 newton.SPSU.edu closing connection

Note that the initial response, R1, appears to have no corresponding initial command, C1. R1 is actually an acknowledgment from the e-mail server, which informs our simulated e-mail client that a communications end point, or socket, has been established and that commands may be transmitted. Although we requested communication with a server named st6000.sct.edu, a server named newton.spsu.edu responded. The two servers are actually one and the same; st6000.sct.edu is an alias for newton.spsu.edu.

Five commands, HELO, MAIL, RCPT, DATA, and QUIT, were used to create and transmit the message. The first command, HELO, is used to establish a dialog between our simulated client and the e-mail server, st6000.sct.edu. MAIL identifies the originator of the message, and RCPT its recipient. For convenience, the account tfallon@st6000.sct.edu is both originator and recipient. The various elements of the message (subject, timestamp, body, etc.) follow the DATA command. A period following the last line of the message is used to inform the server that the message is complete and ready for delivery. The connection is closed using the QUIT command.

Currently, the two contending protocols responsible for the delivery of messages from the destination e-mail server to the recipient's e-mail client are *POP-3* (Post Office Protocol version 3) and *IMAP-4* (Internet Message Protocol version 4). Similar to our SMTP analogy, POP-3 and IMAP-4 represent the transport vehicle for messages exiting the global e-mail system. POP-3 is a client-side protocol that downloads all of a recipient's messages from the e-mail server before they are read. IMAP-4, on the other hand, is a server-side protocol that allows the recipient to selectively download messages.

Although virtually any e-mail client can communicate with any e-mail server that supports its access protocol, POP-3 or IMAP-4, optimal client-server combinations exist. Qualacomm's Eudora and Netscape's Messenger, for example, were designed for Internet-based communications, whereas Microsoft's Outlook Express and Lotus Notes Mail were designed for LAN-based communications with their associated servers, Exchange and Notes, respectively. Some e-mail clients are bundled together with collaboration, schedule, and calendar utilities to produce groupware programs such as Novell Groupwise, Microsoft Exchange, and Lotus Notes.

Most e-mail clients share several common features, including folders for organizing received messages, online and offline modes of operation, message status flags, message filtering, and e-mail account address books. Such features provide the recipient with sufficient tools to effectively manage e-mail. Message filtering, for example, can be used to eliminate SPAM, or junk mail, as it is received. Address books are used to readily locate and insert e-mail addresses into a newly composed message. When coupled with an online directory (e-mail addresses, phone numbers, location, etc.) via a directory access protocol, such as LDAP (Lightweight Directory Access Protocol), address books become much more powerful.

FIGURE 8.1

a) SMTP transmission using Telnet port 25.
b) Using Eudora to receive message.

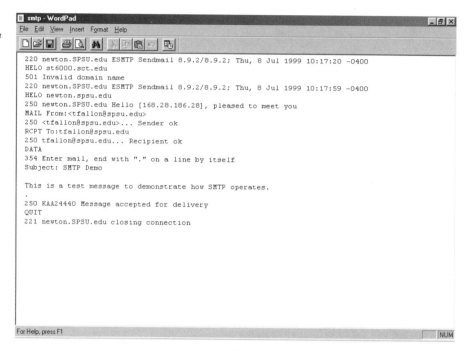

a

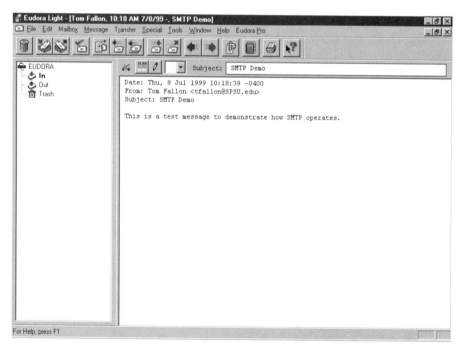

b

Eudora Pro aand Eudora Light are registered trademarks of Qualcomm Incorporated. Used with permission of Qualcomm, Inc.

SMTP-based e-mail messages are encoded in a seven-bit ASCII format. Such a format is ideal for text-based messages. Binary attachments, however, must be converted to ASCII prior to transmission and back to binary upon reception; otherwise they will be rendered unusable. The most popular scheme used to accomplish the conversion is *MIME* (Multipurpose Internet Mail Extensions).

Several different files and media types may be included as attachments. Among these are word processor files, audio clips, graphic files, and movies. Although traditional text-based e-mail messages are incapable of carrying viruses, their binary attachments can carry viruses. Infected attachments remain inert until they are opened. Therefore, it is considered good practice to scan all received attachments with anti-virus software prior to opening.

The main elements of a typical e-mail message are the addresses of the originator and recipient, the subject, the body, a signature, and attachments. E-mail addresses are comprised of two parts: an account name and the e-mail server's *Fully Qualified Domain Name* (FQDN). The two parts are joined using the at (@) symbol, as in tfallon@st6000.-sct.edu. Although usually text, the body of the message can contain other elements such as hyperlinks and HTML code. One possible evolutionary path for e-mail messages is based upon the IETF standard VPIM (Voice Profile for Internet Mail), which defines a MIME-based means to integrate e-mail, voice, and fax that is commonly referred to as *unified messaging*.

Traditional e-mail is a relatively insecure technology. Since the body of e-mail messages are ASCII-encoded and the view field of most network analyzers display information in hexadecimal and ASCII formats, a properly located network analyzer can, in many cases, be used to capture an e-mail transmission and view it. In order to prevent this from occurring, security protocols based upon public-key cryptography have been developed to guarantee the secure delivery of messages from originator to recipient. The two contending e-mail security protocols are PGP (Pretty Good Privacy) and *S/MIME* (Secure MultiPurpose Internet Mail Extensions).

Public-key cryptography uses cryptographic algorithms and keys to encrypt, decrypt, and authenticate e-mail messages. These algorithms use two keys, referred to as the *public key* (available to anyone) and the *private key* (unique to the individual), to enable the encryption/decryption process (see Security Issues in Chapter 9). Either key can be used in the encryption process, but the other key must be used in the decryption process. For example, an individual sending an e-mail message would encrypt the message using the recipient's public key. The recipient would, in turn, use his or her private key to decrypt the message.

PGP and S/MIME use two distinct methods to ensure the validity of a recipient's public key. E-mail clients that employ PGP collect digital signatures by trusted users to validate the trustworthiness of a particular public key. E-mail clients that employ S/MIME, on the other hand, use a digital certificate hierarchy, known as the X.509 standard, in the validation process. A digital certificate is comprised of the public key and the digital signature of a validating body, referred to as a *certificate authority* (CA).

8.2 Listservs

Mailing lists are often used in the creation of electronic discussion groups that address common themes, such as becoming an astronaut candidate or preparing sushi. Mailing lists are either moderated (controlled by a list administrator) or unmoderated (unrestricted). The server software that manages the distribution of messages to the members of a list is referred to as a *listserv*. One becomes a member of a particular list by subscribing to its listserv. Having subscribed, the new member automatically receives every message posted to the list, and may contribute to a particular conversational thread by posting a message directly to the list.

One can subscribe to a particular list by sending an e-mail message to the listserv with a blank subject field and the body of the message containing the single phrase: subscribe <listname> <first_name> <last_name>. In order to subscribe to the astronaut candidate list, for example, transmit the following message:

To: majordomo@sauron.msfc.nasa.org

Subject:

subscribe   astronaut-candidates   first_name   last_name

Majordomo is a commonly used listserv program. sauron.msfc.nasa.org is the FQDN of the listserv's host, and the name of the actual list is astronaut-candidates. After subscribing to the list, the listserv sends a reply welcoming one to the list. Thereafter, the new member participates in or begins a threaded conversation by sending e-mail directly to the list. Continuing our previous example, the message might be constructed as follows:

To: astronaut-candidates@sauron.msfc.nasa.org

Subject: Introduction to the list

Greetings,

My name is Luna Walker and I would like to formally introduce myself. I am currently a Ph.D. candidate in Astrophysics at...

Additional commands can be sent to the listserv to obtain information or modify your list member status. When going on vacation, for example, you could issue the nomail command to the listserv to inform the listserv to stop sending messages. Upon returning, issue the mail command to reverse the process. A list of typical listserv commands follows:

Help: Return available listserv commands.

Subscribe: Join a particular list.

Nomail/Mail: Cease e-mail transmission/resume e-mail transmission.

Digest/Index: Accumulate messages (Digest) or message headers (Index) prior to transmission.

Confirm: Confirm subscription.

List: Return names of listserv's lists.

Ack/Noack: Enable or disable acknowldgement of transmitted messages.

8.3 USENET

USENET is an electronic global forum where thousands of threaded discussions are collected and posted in the form of newsgroups; and mailing lists are generally cross-posted to the appropriate newsgroups. USENET servers manage all aspects of newsgroups including storage, delivery to client programs (referred to as *news readers*), and distribution to other USENET servers, referred to as a *feed*. The specific news feeds transmitted to and received from other USENET servers are determined by the administrator of each server.

Like mailing lists, newsgroups can be moderated or unmoderated, require that the member subscribe prior to automatic delivery of information, and generally consist of threaded discussions. Additionally, they are hierarchically organized as cateogory.subcategory.sub-subcategory. For example, using the popular news reader, Free Agent by Forte, we scroll through the list of newsgroups offered by our USENET server until we locate the amateur astronomy newsgroup, sci.astro.amateur (see Figure 8.2a).

A double-click of the mouse displays a dialog box offering subscription to the newsgroup and viewing of message headers (see Figure 8.2b). Clicking the button labeled Sample Message Headers produces, in this case, the headers of the first so messages posted within the newsgroup (see Figure 8.2c). Double-clicking any of the headers produces the associated message in the lower view field. You can post messages to a newsgroup whether or not you have subscribed to it.

8.4 IRC (Internet Relay Chat)

IRC (Internet Relay Chat) is an Internet service that enables users to converse in cyberspace via their keyboards. Like other Internet services, IRC is based on client/server technology. IRC servers within an IRC network, such as IRCnet, EFnet, or Undernet, relay conversational information between users participating within a common channel, or topical discussion. One uses web plug-ins or IRC clients, such as mIRC, ICQ (I Seek You), or ircII (Unix), to join a channel and converse with the entire group or with a specific individual in a side conversation. When someone types a question or comment, it is immediately relayed to everyone present within the channel.

Prior to joining a channel, the user typically configures a client with information such as a list of IRC servers, the user's nickname, and an alternate name (see Figure 8.3a). A nickname is used to give the user an online identification. Once the client is configured, a connection is made to the desired IRC server and IRC commands are issued (see Figure 8.3b). Although graphical IRC clients allow you to issue commands with the mouse, IRC commands can be manually entered by preceding the command with a slash (/) character.

> USENET is an electronic global forum where thousands of threaded discussions are collected and posted in the form of newsgroups; and mailing lists are generally cross-posted to the appropriate newsgroups.

> IRC (Internet Relay Chat) is an Internet service that enables users to converse in cyberspace via their keyboards. Like other Internet services, IRC is based on client/server technology.

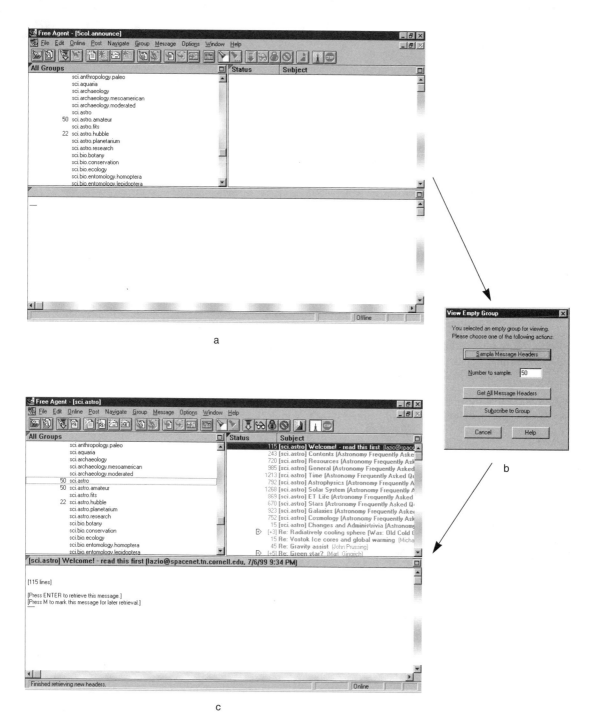

Used with permission by Forté.

FIGURE 8.2

a) USENET news reader. b) Newsgroup dialog box. c) First 50 message headers for the newsgroup, sci.astro.amateur.

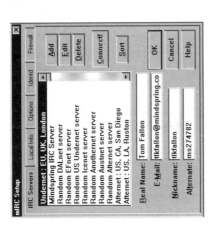

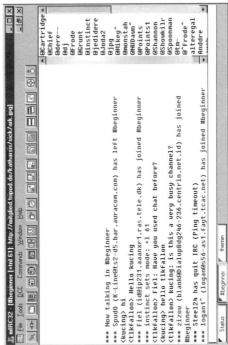

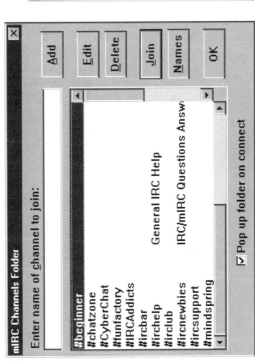

FIGURE 8.3

a) mIRC setup dialog box. b) Connecting to Mindspring IRC Network. c) Joining the Channel #beginner. d) Participating in Channel Dialog.

Used with permission of Tjerk Vonck and mIRC Co. Ltd.

Some of the IRC commands include join, ping, dcc chat, msg, and quit. The command /join #beginner is used, for example, to join the discussion associated with the channel named beginner. Channel names that span all servers within an IRC network are preceded by a hash mark (#). Those associated with a single server are preceded by an ampersand (&). After joining a channel, you can participate in the current discussion (see Figure 8.3d).

Ping is used to determine the round-trip delay time between the current user and another user within the same channel. Dcc chat is used to establish a direct, or one-on-one, conversation with another user within the same channel, and msg is used to transmit messages. IRC also employs several emoticons (smiley faces, frowns, etc.) and acronyms, such as lol (laughing out loud), ttfn (ta ta for now), and wb (welcome back), to provide users with a greater ease of expression.

8.5 Video Conferencing

●
Video conferencing is the real-time exchange of video and audio information via a network to enable two or more parties to meet face to face.

Video conferencing is the real-time exchange of video and audio information via a network to enable two or more parties to meet face to face. Standards-based video conferencing programs augmented by whiteboards, chat windows, binary file exchange, and security features are created from several different vendors including CU-See-Me by White Pines, NetMeeting by Microsoft, and ProShare by Intel. Modern video conferencing solutions generally include one of these programs, a digital video camera (such as Connectix's QuickCam), a computer, and a network connection (for example, dialup ISP or LAN connection).

Several standardized video formats are used to determine the color and spatial resolution of the received images. The Common Intermediate Format (CIF), for example, defines a standard image size to be 352 by 288 pixels. Other common variations are Quarter CIF (QCIF) and Subquarter CIF (SQCIF), which are 176 by 144 and 128 by 96 pixels, respectively. In order to gauge the required network capacity for a video conferencing session, we calculate the data rate required to support the transmission of uncompressed, 16-bit color, full-broadcast quality (30 frames per second) CIF as $16 \times 30 \times 352 \times 288 = 4,294,967,296$ bits per second! This rate doesn't even include audio.

Fortunately, significant compression can be achieved prior to transmission using the proper codecs. Although a number of standards that incorporate various codecs exist, we shall discuss the *ITU* (International Telecommunications Union) standards H.323 and T.120, which can be used for Internet-based video and data conferencing, respectively. The H.323 standard, a modified version of H.320 (video conferencing over ISDN), is comprised of the audio codecs H.263 and H.261; the video codecs H.711, H.722, H.723, and H.728; the channel control protocol H.245; and the signaling protocol Q.931. T.120, on the other hand, is a data conferencing standard that complements H.323 by offering additional services such as whiteboards (T.126), binary file exchange (T.127), and data security and conference management (T.124).

Both H.323 and T.120 are well suited for the Internet because they can operate within an IP multicast network, such as the Internet's Multicast Backbone (MBone). In networking parlance, the term *multicast* refers to the simultaneous transmission of information to multiple recipients within a common group. When transporting data, H.323 relies upon T.120, which, in turn, relies upon TCP. Although TCP is ideal for transporting data associated with a videoconference (binary files, whiteboard information, etc.), it is insufficient for transporting the audio/video information.

TCP is a point-to-point protocol that lacks the ability to carry critical, real-time audio/video timing information and that retransmits lost packets. Point-to-point protocols are not designed to support multicasting, a key aspect of multiparty video conferencing. Real-time audio/video must possess accurate timing in order to be properly synchronized and, subsequently, played. Retransmitted packets would wreak havoc upon the sequenced audio/video information being received by destination systems. Although UDP could be used in a multicast environment, it lacks TCP's ability to sequence packets and has no provisions for carrying timing information.

H.323 has provisions to augment the UDP transport protocol with timing and sequencing information via the IETF protocol RTP (Real-time Transfer Protocol). In order to maintain an acceptable QoS (Quality of Service) for the transmitted video and audio, however, a guaranteed sustained data rate must be provided. Such a guarantee is provided by another IETF protocol, *RSVP* (Resource Reservation Protocol). RSVP is used by destination systems to request the reservation of certain resources, such as available link capacity, by all participating nodes en route to the source system.

Video conferencing systems that are based upon H.323 generally consist of computer systems with H.323-compatible clients, an H.323 gateway, a multi-point control unit (MCU), and the underlying network infrastructure (see Figure 8.4). By authorizing and

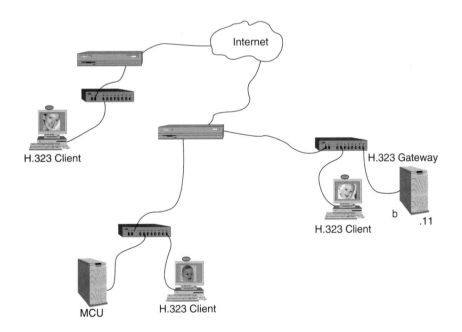

FIGURE 8.4

Basic video conferencing system.

allocating available capacity to incoming calls and controlling the total number of calls, the H.323 gateway essentially behaves as the conference moderator. The MCU is used to control conference channels among multiple end systems.

8.6 IP Telephony

Early Internet PC-to-PC phone calls, were hampered by a number of factors including the unpredictability of the Internet, dynamic IP addresses, client software incompatibilities, and whether the remote system was online.

VocalTec introduced the first successful commercial IP telephony product, the Internet Phone, in 1995. Early Internet PC-to-PC phone calls, however, were hampered by a number of factors, including the unpredictability of the Internet, dynamic IP addresses, client software incompatibilities, and whether the remote system was online. PC-to-Phone and Phone-to-Phone via the Internet were nonexistent. Since those early days, several of these issues have been resolved by the adoption of standards and cooperation among IP telephony manufacturers and telecommunications companies.

Although the digitization, compression, transportation, and decompression of analog signals (images, sensor outputs, voice, etc.) are commonplace, communication via real-time signals, such as voice and video, requires a predictable transportation and delivery infrastructure. The Internet is not such an infrastructure. However, as we discussed in the previous section, protocol standards that add predictability do exist. H.323 was the standard adopted by the Voice over IP (VOIP) forum to provide interoperability among IP telephony-based (voice, faxes, etc.) products. Like video conferencing, IP telephony uses RTP and RSVP for timing, sequencing, and network capacity allocation.

In order to enable PC-to-Phone and Phone-to-Phone conversations via the Internet, IP telephony gateways were created. These gateways convert the format of signals originating from the PSTN (Public Switched Telephone Network) into a sequence of IP packets, and vice versa. Analog signals originating from a customer placing a call from a traditional analog phone to a remote PC are received by the gateway, digitized, compressed, and transmitted to the remote party's IP address. In order to coordinate and manage multiple gateways and provide traditional telephony-like services, such as directory assistance and billing, a computer system, referred to as a *gatekeeper,* is employed.

By strategic location of these gateways, cost-effective Internet-based phone service can be established. Several national and international ISPs are installing IP telephony gateways within their facilities to augment customer service offerings. Such a service provider is generally referred to as an *Internet Telephony Service Provider,* or ITSP.

Summary

SMTP is responsible for transporting e-mail from the originating system to its associated e-mail server and among all intermediate e-mail servers and the recipient's e-mail server.

The two contending protocols responsible for the delivery of messages from the destination e-mail server to the recipient's e-mail client are POP-3 (Post Office Protocol version

3) and IMAP-4 (Internet Message Protocol version 4). POP-3 is a client-side protocol that downloads all of a recipient's messages from the e-mail server before they are read. IMAP-4, on the other hand, is a server-side protocol that allows the recipient to selectively download messages.

Mailing lists are often used in the creation of electronic discussion groups that address common themes, such as becoming an astronaut candidate or preparing sushi. Mailing lists are either moderated (controlled by a list administrator) or unmoderated (unrestricted). The server software that manages the distribution of messages to the members of a list is referred to as a listserv.

USENET is an electronic global forum where thousands of threaded discussions are collected and posted in the form of newsgroups; and mailing lists are generally cross-posted to the appropriate newsgroups. USENET servers are used to manage all aspects of newsgroups including storage, delivery to client programs (referred to as news readers), and distribution to other USENET servers, referred to as a feed. The specific news feeds transmitted to and received from other USENET servers are determined by the administrator of each server.

IRC (Internet Relay Chat) is an Internet service that enables users to converse in cyberspace via their keyboards. Like other Internet services that we have discussed, IRC is also based on client/server technology. IRC servers within an IRC network, such as IRCnet, EFnet, or Undernet, relay conversational information between users participating within a common channel, or topical discussion.

Video conferencing is the real-time exchange of video and audio information via a network to enable two or more parties to meet face to face. Standards-based video conferencing programs are usually augmented by whiteboards, chat windows, binary file exchange, and security features. Video conferencing is based upon the ITU H.323 standard for transporting multimedia traffic over IP-based networks.

The H.323 standard, a modified version of H.320 (video conferencing over ISDN), is comprised of the audio codecs H.263 and H.261; the video codecs H.711, H.722, H.723, and H.728; the channel control protocol H.245; and the signaling protocol Q.931. T.120, on the other hand, is a data conferencing standard that complements H.323 by offering additional services such as whiteboards (T.126), binary file exchange (T.127), and data security and conference management (T.124). H.323 is modified by the RTP and RSVP protocols in order to maintain an acceptable QoS for the transmitted video and audio.

H.323 was also the standard adopted by the Voice over IP (VOIP) forum to provide interoperability between IP telephony-based (voice, faxes, etc.) products. Like video conferencing, IP telephony uses RTP and RSVP for timing, sequencing, and network capacity allocation. In order to enable PC-to-Phone and Phone-to-Phone conversations via the Internet, IP telephony gateways were created.

The Evolving Internet

Chapter Learning Objectives:

- Discuss interactive TV.
- Explore Internet security issues.
- Understand a few of the key developing Internet technologies.
- Discuss the forces shaping the Internet.

"How easy 'tis, when Destiny proves kind, with full-spread sails to run before the wind!"

John Dryer, Astraea Redux

In 1948, the British mathematician and genius Alan Turing wrote a paper entitled "Intelligent Machinery," which describes *connectionism,* or the process of computing with neural-type networks. Thirteen years previously, he conceived of a system referred to as a *universal Turing machine,* which we know as the modern digital computer. It is interesting to note that the likely evolution of the modern digital computer will be based upon neural networking.

Although the "intelligent" nodes that chiefly comprise the Internet do not emulate neurons, they are used to loosely interconnect millions of human minds. In fact, the evolution of the Internet will be driven by several factors, including advances in science and technology, the associated costs, and the need and desire for increasingly complex applications and services. In this chapter, we will briefly explore some of the key services and technologies responsible for the evolution of the Internet.

9.1 Security Issues

Traditional and emerging services, such as corporate and private data exchange and e-commerce, are among the driving forces of well-defined Internet security systems. In this section, we will investigate a few of the salient issues associated with these security systems including encryption, digital signatures, authentication, firewalls, and viruses.

Cryptography

Cryptography is essentially the secure encoding of data using cryptographic algorithms, the behavior of which is uniquely determined by an externally supplied value(s), referred to as a *key*. The two forms of cryptography used in the secure transmission and reception of data are symmetric, known as *secret-key cryptography*, and asymmetric, known as *public-key cryptography*.

●

The two forms of cryptography used in the secure transmission and reception of data are symmetric, known as secret-key cryptography, and asymmetric, known as public-key cryptography.

Although fast computationally, symmetric cryptographic algorithms such as DES (Data Encryption Standard), IDEA (International Data Encryption Algorithm), and RC5 are impractical to deploy because they require that a unique secret key be created for all possible pairs of participating individuals. In other words, if two individuals are exchanging encrypted messages, then two keys are required. However, if N individuals are exchanging encrypted messages, then $N \times (N - 1)/2$ unique keys are required.

Asymmetric cryptographic algorithms such as RSA (Rivest, Shamir, and Adleman) and Diffie-Hellman Key Exchange are relatively slow computationally but are practical in distributed networking environments. Asymmetrical cryptography derives its name from the fact that two similar but different keys are used in the encryption and decryption processes. These two keys, the public and private key, when applied to cryptographic algorithms, behave as the inverse functions of one another. In other words, messages that have been encrypted using one key can be decrypted only using the other.

Everyone who uses public-key cryptography is assigned a private key and a public key. The private key is kept secret at all times, whereas the public key is distributed freely. An individual's collection of public keys is referred to as a *key ring*. To send an encrypted message, he or she encrypts the message using the recipient's public key and then transmits the message. The recipient, in turn, uses his or her private key to decrypt the transmission and recover the original message. Since the recipient is the only one possessing the private key, the sender assumes that no one else read the message.

In the previous exchange, the recipient can be confident that the transmitted message originated from the proclaimed sender if a valid digital signature is included with the message. Algorithms such as Message Digest 5 (MD-5), Digital Signature Standard (DSS), and RSA are used in the creation of digital signatures. RSA, for example, creates a digital signature by passing the original message through a hash function. The output of the hash function is a unique, random code referred to as the *hash code*. Encrypting the hash code with the sender's private key forms the digital signature. The digital signature and original message are encrypted using the recipient's public key, and then they are transmitted.

The recipient decrypts the original message and digital signature with the private key. The digital signature is then further decrypted with the sender's public key to reveal the original hash code. This hash code is then compared to a new hash code generated using the original message. If they match, the recipient has verification of the sender's identity. The only caveat to this approach is the authenticity of the user's keys. In other words, a user's key(s) may have been compromised or revoked. Fortunately, authentication schemes, such as Kerberos and X.509, exist for asymmetrical and symmetrical cryptographic algorithms.

Kerberos, a symmetrical authentication scheme, is based upon a central secret key repository, or *authentication server*. In a typical scenario, a user requests a key from a ticket-granting server. The request is first directed to an authentication server, where the user's account name, password, and privileges are verified. If verification is approved, an encrypted ticket used to access the ticket-granting server is issued. A new key that includes a secret key that can be used to exchange secure messages with other servers is received from the ticket-granting server.

X.509, an asymmetrical authentication scheme, is based on the creation of digital certificates that contain the user's public key and the digital signature of a certification authority (CA). Because the digital signature is created with the CA's private key, anyone possessing a copy of the CA's public key can recover a validated copy of the user's public key.

The length, in bits, of the key(s) used to encrypt a message determines its relative imperviousness. For example, the secret key of a 40-bit DES encrypted message can be one of 2^{40} possible values, whereas the secret key of a 56-bit DES encrypted message can be one of 2^{56} possible values, an approximate difference of 70,000,000,000,000,000 keys! So important is the length of these encryption keys that the U.S. government does not permit the exportation of cryptographic systems that use a key length greater than 40 bits, unless a key escrow (key recovery) system is also employed.

Firewalls

When organizations connect their local area networks to the Internet for purposes of marketing, collaboration, or any other reason, they expose themselves to the possibility of security breaches. Fortunately, systems can be installed to create a network *firewall* that can greatly reduce the type and number of security attacks that the organization might otherwise experience. The installation of a firewall system requires the consideration of several issues including the processing speed of the firewall, the anticipation of the nature of the attacks, the impact on internal users, and the cost.

Generally, the greater the security provided by the firewall, the slower the throughput of data. Among the several types of attack to be considered are denial of service and IP spoofing. A *denial of service attack,* for example, might attempt to overwhelm the firewall by inundating its buffers with excessive messages. Unable to process the incoming

Generally, the greater the security provided by the firewall, the slower the throughput of data.

message, the firewall is either forced to drop its external connection or forward unprocessed data. *IP spoofing* involves the masquerading of an external host as an internal host by using its IP address.

In order to address these security issues, three different categories of firewalls—packet-filtering, application-level gateways (or proxy servers), and circuit-level gateways—have evolved. *Packet-filtering firewalls* are generally routers with certain access lists enabled. These access lists are comprised of a set of rules that either allow or deny packets to be forwarded in either direction. Rules pertain to the fields within IP, TCP, and/or UDP headers.

Suppose, for example, that a network administrator would like to filter all FTP traffic and simultaneously permit all SMTP traffic. Furthermore, all requests from the IP address space $168.28.0.0_{(10)}$ are to be denied, regardless of their nature. The following fictitious access list might be used to accomplish the network administrator's goals:

```
Deny     0.0.0.0       21
Allow    0.0.0.0       25
Deny     168.28.0.0
```

We notice several issues pertaining to our access list. FTP (port 21), for example, was denied to everyone (address 0.0.0.0), whereas all other services, such as Telnet (port 23), were allowed, thus rendering the next line moot. The last line denies all traffic originating from the offending address space.

Application-level gateways behave as go-between agents that relay application-related requests, such as HTTP or Telnet, from one side of the gateway to the other. When a user on one side of the gateway requests access to an application on a remote host on the other side of the gateway, the server asks the user for proper identification and authentication information. Assuming a proper response, the gateway, in turn, contacts the remote host and transmits the necessary information. In addition to managing the application-related traffic, the gateway can also keep logs of all key events.

Circuit-level gateways relay information between two distinct network connections, one between the gateway and the external host and the other between the gateway and the internal host. By allowing or denying the establishment of these circuits, the gateway provides security to the network that it is guarding.

Another often-employed element in an organization's security arsenal is the *bastion host*. A bastion host is essentially a highly secure server that is located externally to the organization's local area network and that typically provides common Internet services, such as DNS and HTTP. Bastion hosts are sometimes configured to be proxy servers. In a sense, a bastion server may be considered part of an organization's firewall, or defensive perimeter.

Firewall products may be a hybrid of two or all three of the firewall technologies in order to provide a more robust security solution. Possible additional features include antivirus software and provisions for network address translation (NAT). NAT enables network administrators to configure the internal network with a bogus address scheme, such as the private address scheme 10.x.y.z.(10) defined in RFC 1918. These addresses can be mapped, via a lookup table, to a legitimate address associated with the external connection of the firewall. External HTTP requests to a corporate, internal web server, for example, would be transmitted to the firewall's IP address, not the actual web server's IP address. If appropriate, the firewall would, in turn, initiate a separate request to the internal web server and then relay the information to the requesting client. Such a process would render the internal web server "invisible."

Viruses

Thus far we have concerned ourselves primarily with the protection of information in transit and the prevention of intrusion from external sources. Some threats, however, might successfully breach external defenses or originate from within the internal network. Viruses, worms, and Trojan horses can be inadvertently, or intentionally, introduced within the network via floppy disks, modems, e-mail attachments, and malicious employees. Internet users have been recently alerted to the W97M_Melissa virus and ExploreZip worm, which are received as e-mail attachments.

Viruses, like Trojan horses, are typically parasitic in nature; in other words, they cannot function independently of a host program. They do, however, often possess an identifying signature or behavior. Both a virus and a Trojan horse are triggered by a specific event, such as the entering of a certain key sequence or the occurrence of a certain date. Viruses differ from Trojan horses in that they replicate, thereby infecting other programs. Other types of viruses include the stealth, polymorphic, and boot sector viruses. *Stealth viruses* are designed to evade detection by appearing not to have altered the infected program. *Polymorphic viruses* change their nature, and therefore signature, every replication. *Boot sector viruses* invade an operating system's master boot record and cause harm during the boot process.

Although they are potentially malicious and replicate like viruses, worms are not dependent upon host programs. Worms propogate from system to system via networks, such as the Internet, searching for means by which to breach the system's security. After infecting the system, they search for information that might indicate the address or services of another system, and the process begins anew. The most infamous worm was released by Robert Morris in 1988.

Antivirus software, firewalls, and internal access restrictions are among the arsenal of tools available to protect systems from attacks by viruses, worms, Trojan horses, or other related maladies. Antivirus software generally operates as a *TSR* (Terminate and Stay Resident), or background program, and/or as a startup program. This type of software is designed to detect, identify, and eradicate viruses. If the virus cannot be identified, and therefore removed from the infected program, users are offered the choice of deleting the program or placing it in quarantine. Because new viruses are generated every day, antivirus programs must be kept current in order to identify new strains.

9.2 A Few Key Technologies
Interactive TV

Embedded
microcontrollers,
lightweight
operating systems
such as
Microsoft's
Windows CE and
Sun's Jini,
advanced access
technologies such
as xDSL and
cable modems,
and IPv6 are
among the
technologies that
will add
interactivity to
everyday
household
objects.

Our modern high-tech culture is about to enter the era of interactivity. Embedded microcontrollers, lightweight operating systems such as Microsoft's Windows CE and Sun's Jini, advanced access technologies such as xDSL and cable modems, and IPv6 are among the technologies that will add interactivity to everyday household objects. Imagine that you are watching your favorite soap opera, when all of the sudden a message appears on your screen: "Would you care for a low-fat snack?"

Using your remote control, you select the menu option: "Yes, what is available?" Your TV queries your refrigerator, which checks its inventory and scans your personal consumption profile in order to generate a menu of choices. You select one of the available TV dinners, and the TV, in turn, sends the requested information to the refrigerator and microwave oven for inventory control and settings configuration, respectively. Of course, you have to physically retrieve the dinner from the refrigerator and insert it into the microwave oven. If this scenario sounds far-fetched, think again. It is already in the works.

We shall limit the current discussion to the interactivity of the most popular home appliance, the television. *Interactive TV,* or ITV, is based upon the concept of blending Internet interactivity and, ultimately, presentations with television broadcast. Surfing will acquire a whole new meaning as users jump between web sites and television shows, or, perhaps, nest one within another using the so-called picture-in-picture feature on their remote control. Users will be able to click a dynamically displayed icon to download the statistics of the next batter, chat with their friends about the handsome knight from the last scene, or order tickets to the upcoming play that was featured in the previous commercial.

The idea of Net TV was actually conceived several years ago. Until recently, however, it has not been able to gain the momentum necessary to attract investors and consumers. The current leading ITV solutions are Microsoft's WebTV and Oracle and NCI's (Network Computer, Inc.) NCTV. Ironically, the current push for ITV is based upon the traditional analog set, not the much-touted High-Definition TV (HDTV), or digital television.

Current technology operates by sending data over a typically unused portion of the analog signal referred to as the *Vertical Blanking Interval,* or VBI. Although the capacity of the VBI (19.2Kbps) is minimal, it is sufficient for transmitting broadcast-synchronized messages. These messages are, in turn, received by an ITV set-top and the consumer's television. When the consumer selects a specific item using the remote control, the selection information is processed by the ITV set-top and transmitted to the Internet via a specific access technology, such as an analog dialup line or cable modem. In the near future, perhaps, Internet and television content will be blended and transmitted within the same stream to our digital televisions, or whatever they might be called.

E-commerce

In the foreseeable future, e-commerce will be one of the key forces driving the Internet evolution. Although the social and cultural implications for buying and selling online are enormous, the technologies that undergird e-commerce will have to be just as trustworthy and convenient as the current system of purchase orders, charge cards, credit cards, debit cards, and cash, prior to being accepted as commonplace.

The traditional system of commerce is deeply ensconced within our culture and, therefore, will not be replaced immediately by e-commerce. In order for such a metamorphosis to occur, several major institutions and organizations (such as the U.S. Treasury, Federal Reserve Banks, other financial institutions, manufacturers, vendors, merchants, and every international equivalent) would have to develop and implement complete digital infrastructures. Therefore, prototypical e-commerce solutions will actually serve to augment our existing practices of commerce.

Although e-commerce encompasses several different relationships, such as business-to-business and business-to-consumer, we shall limit our current discussion to that of business-to-consumer. From a practical perspective, shopping online is virtually identical to shopping offline using mail-order catalogs, forms, shopping carts, checkout counters, and credit cards. The difference, of course, is speed, efficiency, and convenience. One can purchase books, clothes, toys, airplanes, and almost anything else in cyberspace.

This nascent paradigm of commerce is based entirely upon trust. If the consumer feels secure with this new mode of purchasing, then the consumer will eventually adopt it. The U.S. Federal Trade Commission has published several guidelines and tips related to e-commerce and consumer protection. This information can be found online at www.ftc.gov/ftc/consumer.htm.

Currently, the most widely accepted security protocol for e-commerce is the *Secure Electronic Transactions* (SET) protocol. SET is based upon public-key cryptography and is endorsed by several major organizations and institutions including Visa, MasterCard, American Express, Bank of America, VeriFone, VeriSign, Microsoft, CyberCash, and Netscape (acquired by American Online). Although most of the steps involved in an online purchase are transparent to the consumer, a few require active participation. The following is a typical purchase scenario:

1. Consumer acquires a digital certificate from an authorized certification authority such as a bank or credit card issuer. This certificate contains a copy of the consumer's public key and digital signature. Digital certificates are usually kept in one's virtual wallet. Online merchants must also obtain a digital certificate from their financial institution.

2. Consumer directs browser to the merchant's online catalog or virtual storefront via the proper URL.

> The traditional system of commerce is deeply ensconced within our culture and, therefore, will not be replaced immediately by e-commerce.

3. Consumer shops by adding items to a virtual shopping cart or a virtual shopping bag; online forms might also be used, requiring a slight variation on the following transactions.

4. Consumer clicks Submit or Checkout button to send information to the merchant.

5. Merchant sends order form requesting consumer contact, payment, and shipping information and two digital certificates. The first digital certificate verifies the identity of the merchant to the consumer and is used to encrypt the contact and shipping information. The second digital certificate is used to encrypt the payment information.

6. Consumer adds method of payment information and a copy of the digital certificate to the completed order form, and then transmits the entire message to the merchant.

7. Merchant receives the message, extracts the order and encrypted method of payment information, and then verifies the consumer's identification by examining the digital signature. Merchant is able to read order information but not payment information because of the different public keys used in the encryption process.

8. Merchant sends order verification to consumer and authorization request to a payment gateway. The authorization request contains the consumer's credit card number and expiration date, the requested amount, and digital signature.

9. The payment gateway, in turn, sends authorization request to an acquiring bank, which verifies card and authorizes payment.

10. The bank issues an authorization message, which is digitally signed and encrypted by the payment gateway, to the merchant.

11. Merchant ships merchandise to the consumer and sends encrypted payment request to the acquiring bank via the payment gateway.

12. The acquiring bank decrypts the payment request, verifies the merchant's identity, and issues the appropriate funds via the payment gateway.

13. Purchase transaction appears on consumer's monthly bill.

The ability to issue and revoke digital certificates is paramount to the SET protocol. When digital certificates are lost or stolen, intelligent database systems must be able to rapidly suspend or revoke them. The issuance of new digital certificates is similar to applying for a credit card requiring information such as address, phone numbers, credit history, etc.

Although SET is credit card–based, other forms of payment, such as digital dollars and coins, can be purchased and used for anonymous shopping. Purchases of this type are usually referred to as *micropayments*. CyberCash, Inc., for example, sells digital tokens referred to as CyberCoins that can be used for purchases as small as 25 cents or as large as 10 dollars.

XML (eXtensible Markup Language)

In 1998, the W3C completed the XML (eXtensible Markup Language) standard, which defines an entirely new species of tags and the rules that define their context. XML, like HTML, is derived from SGML. XML, however, allows for the definition of multiple markup languages (such as MathML) and employs tags that describe the meaning of the data, not just its format. It also provides a platform for transferring data between disparate applications, supports the Unicode standard (multilingual encoding scheme), and supports multi-entry hyperlinks, referred to as Xlink (XML hyperlink).

XML-compatible browsers parse the Document Type Definition (DTD), interpret the nature of the information being conveyed within the tags, render the information in a stylesheet-defined format via the eXtensible Stylesheet Language (XSL), and perform any specified action. The following sample of source code might be used to declare the use of the fictitious aviation markup language AVML, provide a plethora of aircraft-related information, render the information according to an external style sheet called bluesky.xls, and graphically display the flight characteristics of the selected aircraft:

```
<!doctype xml public "-//w3c//dtd xml 1.0//en">
<xml>
<head>
<link rel=stylesheet type="text/xls" href="http://www.planesRus/bluesky.xls">
</head>
<body>
<aircraft>
        <type>Cessna 152</type>
        <wing_config>high wing</wing_config>
        <engine>single, propeller</engine>
        <flight_characteristics>
            <yaw>Y2</yaw>
            <roll>R7</roll>
            <pitch>P23</pitch>
        </flight_characteristics>
</aircraft>
<aircraft>
        <type>Beachcraft Bonnanza</type>
        <wing_config>low wing</wing_config>
        <engine>twin, propeller</engine>
        <flight_characteristics>
            <yaw>Y3</yaw>
            <roll>R5</roll>
            <pitch>P17</pitch>
        </flight_characteristics>
</aircraft>
<applet code="aircraft_in_flight.class" width=80 height=20>
```

```
<param name="type" value="">
</applet>
</body>
</xml>
```

Unlike CSS, XSL supports several different output formats including Braille, text-only for PCS devices, text-to-speech, and traditional web pages. In fact, the same document can be simultaneously rendered in any or all of these formats. In addition to XSL, the Resource Description Framework (RDF) standard for indexing meta data, which is used to describe the plethora of information generated for the web, augments XML. With the advent of XML, the web is poised to make a quantum leap forward in efficiency, speed, and practicality.

IPv6

Initially referred to as *IPng* (Next Generation), the IETF IPv6 protocol is the progeny of IPv4, the current version. IPv5 was reserved as an experimental protocol. The design of IPv6 exemplifies the modular nature of the OSI model. In other words, IPv6 will replace IPv4 without interrupting the services provided by layers 2 and 4 of the model.

In fact, IPv6 retains several of IPv4's general features including packet fragmentation, connectionless-oriented, and a hop limit field (TTL field in IPv4). Unlike IPv4, however, IPv6 offers several new improvements such as an immense 128-bit address field, automatic address configuration (similar to DHCP), and QoS provisions for real-time audio and video. Whereas the IPv4 header was a single unit of variable length, IPv6 has a base header with optional extension headers that describe the various services offered. The following fields comprise the IPv6 base header:

Version: A 4-bit field the value of which is 6.

Priority: An 8-bit field used to assign routing priority for VBR and CBR traffic conditions.

Flow Label: A 20-bit field used to specify the nature of the traffic and a predefined route to be traveled by the traffic.

Payload Length: A 16-bit field used to define the length of the transported data.

Next Header: An 8-bit field used to identify optional headers that are appended to the base header.

Hop Limit: An 8-bit field used to set the maximum hop count. When this count is reached, the packet is discarded.

Source Address: A 128-bit field used to specify the address of the source system.

Destination Address: A 128-bit field used to specify the address of the destination system.

In addition to the increased address length, IPv6 addresses are usually coded as an eight-word, colon-separated hexadecimal string, referred to as *colon hexadecimal notation.* IPv6 supports three basic address types including unicast, multicast, and anycast. *Unicast addresses* correspond to communication with a single other system, *multicast addresses* correspond to address in a common address group, and *anycast addresses* correspond to a single address within a common set of addresses. Anycast addresses are used to provide concurrent access to systems that offer the same set of services.

VPN (Virtual Private Network)

Although the Internet is merely a best-effort delivery system, many organizations and individuals are using or contemplating using it as a cost-effective, global extension of their internal networks. Corporations, for example, are beginning to implement VPNs (Virtual Private Networks) to provide remote connectivity to mobile workers, telecommuters, branch offices, and business partners. External, Internet-based networks of this type are referred to as *extranets*. Intranets are internal networks that are configured with Internet-based technologies and that are used to provide necessary business functions, such as database access or video conferencing.

VPNs implemented via the Internet are similar in nature to those implemented via switched-based technologies, such as Frame Relay or ATM, in that they both provide a virtual path through which data traverses. When associated with a switched-based network such paths are referred to as *virtual circuits;* however, when associated with the Internet they are referred to as *tunnels.* Packets being transported through these tunnels generally possess authentication information, are encrypted, and are encapsulated within a new IP packet. In other words, the original packet is placed within a new packet with a source and destination address corresponding to the tunnel's two end points.

Router's gateways, and firewalls can be configured to provide VPN services between two or more sites or between a single system and a site. Firewalls that employ NAT, however, could invalidate the authentication information contained within the transported packet. In such scenarios, it is common to position the firewall in parallel with the VPN device. Common protocol standards used by these devices to create VPNs include Microsoft's PPTP (Point-to-Point Tunneling Protocol), L2TP (Layer 2 Tunneling Protocol, a combination of Cisco System's Layer 2 Forwarding Protocol (L2F) and PPTP), and IPSec (IP Security). We shall limit our discussion to the latter.

An integral part of IPv6 and an extension to IPv4, IPSec is the IETF standard designed to address the security deficiencies inherent in IPv4. It is comprised of three main protocols: the Authentication Header Protocol (AH), the Encapsulating Security Payload (ESP), and the Internet Key Association and Key Management Protocol (IKAKMP). AH is used to preserve the integrity of the contents of the transmitted IP packet by providing the recipient VPN device with appropriate authentication information. AH allows for the use of different authentication algorithms, such as keyed Message Digest 5 (MD5) or Hash Message Authentication Code (HMAC), in order to provide compatibility among disparate VPN technologies.

ESP is used to encrypt the IP packet. Similar to AH, it allows for the use of different encryption algorithms, such as Data Encryption Standard (DES) and Triple DES, in order to provide compatibility among disparate VPN technologies. AH and ESP need not necessarily be simultaneously used; rather, their use is predicated upon a specific set of circumstances. IKAKMP, the third protocol, is used in the negotiation of certain security parameters, such as the exchange of necessary keys, among VPN devices.

IPSec operates in one of two modes: transport or tunnel. Transport mode is used between an individual system and a site, whereas tunnel mode is used among two or more sites. Although AH and/or ESP headers are used in both modes, their position varies. In transport mode, they are inserted between the layer 3 and 4 headers. In tunnel mode, they are prepended to the original packet. The whole ensemble, in turn, is encapsulated within a new IP packet.

Summary

Cryptography is the secure encoding of data using cryptographic algorithms, the behavior of which is uniquely determined by an externally supplied value(s), referred to as a key. The two forms of cryptography used in the secure transmission and reception of data are symmetric, known as secret-key cryptography, and asymmetric, known as public-key cryptography.

Although computationally fast, symmetric cryptographic algorithms such as DES (Data Encryption Standard), IDEA (International Data Encryption Algorithm), and RC5 are impractical to deploy because they require that a unique secret key be created for all possible pairs of participating individuals. In other words, if two individuals are exchanging encrypted messages, then two keys are required. However, if N individuals are exchanging encrypted messages, then $N \times (N-1)/2$ unique keys are required.

Asymmetric cryptographic algorithms such as RSA (Rivest, Shamir, and Adleman) and Diffie-Hellman Key Exchange are relatively slow computationally but are very practical in distributed networking environments. Asymmetrical cryptography derives its name from the fact that two similar but different keys are used in the encryption and decryption processes. These two keys, the public and private key when applied to cryptographic algorithms, behave as the inverse functions of one another. In other words, messages that have been encrypted using one key can be decrypted only using the other.

When organizations connect their local area networks to the Internet for purposes of marketing, collaboration, or any other reason, they expose themselves to the possibility of security breaches. Fortunately, systems can be installed to create a network firewall that can greatly reduce the type and number of security attacks. The installation of a firewall system requires the consideration of several issues including the processing speed of the firewall, the anticipation of the nature of the attacks, the impact on internal users, and the cost.

Viruses, like Trojan horses, are typically parasitic in nature. In other words, they cannot function independently of a host program. However, they do often possess a tell-tale signature or behavior. Both are triggered by a specific event, such as the entering of a certain key sequence or the occurrence of a certain date. Viruses differ from Trojan horses in that they replicate, thereby infecting other programs. Although they are potentially malicious and replicate like viruses, worms are not dependent upon host programs. Worms propagate from system to system via networks, such as the Internet, searching for means by which to breach the system's security.

Interactive TV (ITV) is based on the concept of blending Internet interactivity and, ultimately, presentations with television broadcast. Surfing will acquire a whole new meaning as users jump between web sites and television shows, or, perhaps, nest one within another using the so-called picture-in-picture feature on their remote control.

In the foreseeable future, e-commerce will be one of the key forces driving the Internet evolution. Although the social and cultural implications for buying and selling online are enormous, the technologies that undergird e-commerce will have to be just as trustworthy and convenient as the current system of purchase orders, charge cards, credit cards, debit cards, and cash, prior to being accepted as commonplace.

In 1998, the W3C completed the XML (eXtensible Markup Language) standard, which defines an entirely new species of tags and the rules that define their context. XML, like HTML, is derived from SGML. XML, however, allows for the definition of multiple markup languages and employs tags that describe the meaning of the data, not just its format. It also provides a platform for transferring data among disparate applications, supports the Unicode standard (multilingual encoding scheme), and supports multi-entry hyperlinks, referred to as Xlink (XML hyperlink).

Initially referred to as IPng (Next Generation), the IETF IPv6 protocol is the progeny of IPv4, the current version. IPv5 was reserved as an experimental protocol. The design of IPv6 exemplifies the modular nature of the OSI model. In other words, IPv6 will replace IPv4 without interrupting the services provided by layers 2 and 4 of the model.

Although the Internet is merely a best-effort delivery system, many organizations and individuals are using or contemplating using it as a cost-effective, global extension of their internal networks. Corporations, for example, are beginning to implement VPNs (Virtual Private Networks) to provide remote connectivity to mobile workers, telecommuters, branch offices, and business partners. External, Internet-based networks of this type are referred to as *extranets*. Intranets are internal networks that are configured with Internet-based technologies and that are used to provide necessary business functions, such as database access or video conferencing.

The Internet Today

"The present time has one advantage over every other—it is our own."

Charles Caleb Cotton, Lacon

One hundred and fifty years ago electronic messages were conveyed via telegraph lines and encoded in Morse code. Today electronic messages are conveyed via satellites, optical fibers, coaxial cables, phone lines, and several other types of media. Although the encoding scheme for most electronic messages is still the Morse codelike ASCII, the very nature of the message has evolved into a multipart entity, the constituent parts of which are encoded in multiple ways. Advanced communication protocols, such as TCP/IP, are used to transport these messages through the complex web of disparate network technologies.

In addition to messages, other forms of information incessantly speed across the Internet. Such information virtually connects the human mind to cyberspace by providing the content requested from a specific service to a particular user interface, such as a web browser, Braille-rendering device, or digital pager.

Ten years ago, when the Internet was still widely unknown, primitive searching tools, such as Hytelnet and Archie, were used by cyberprospectors to unearth precious nuggets of information in the vast wilderness of cyberspace. Today, the estimated 160 million users who regularly surf the Internet are, at times, overwhelmed by the number of near-accurate search responses and the multitude of online services available. Savvy users customize their Internet experience to receive specific types of information such as stock portfolio updates, sports news, and sale announcements from their favorite online stores. For the novice, the experience can be quite daunting.

In the not too distant future, advanced indexing algorithms will be used to better classify information so that personal software robots, referred to as *mobile agents,* will be able to conduct independent research on behalf of the user. For example, an agent might do comparative shopping for a new pair of shoes, generate a list of the latest medieval-related novels, and send an electronic greeting card to a friend. With such technological advances, the neophyte will instantly attain the rank of advanced surfer.

Major technological developments, such as the web and e-commerce, have spawned a deep cultural awareness of the Internet and the need to be connected. The dawn of a new revolution of connectivity is at hand. Dick Tracy–type wristwatches, with which the user communicates visually and audibly through the watch's face, are already being designed. The Java ring, usually worn on the finger, possesses embedded user identification information that can be scanned and downloaded via an appropriate receiver device for such services as paying for food at a cafeteria or gaining access to a restricted area.

As computing power, virtual reality applications, user interface devices, and access and backbone technologies become sufficiently advanced, users will be able to enter into cyberspace as digital beings and directly interact with other digital beings. Although such an experience, referred to as *tele-immersion,* has tremendous sociological and cultural implications, in many cases physical presence will still be preferred.

The very high-performance *Backbone Network Service* (vBNS) and *Internet2* (I2) are prominent among experimental Internet projects designed to significantly increase network backbone capacities, provide end-to-end QoS guarantees, and provide real-time collaboration and development of advanced, distributed networking applications. The vBNS (www.vbns.net), developed from a cooperative plan between MCI and the NSF, is an ATM- and SONET-based nationwide research network, the backbone capacity of which is OC-12c (622 Mbps), although OC-48c (2.48 Gbps) links are beginning to come online.

Currently, the vBNS has approximately 100 members, including several academic and research institutions and four supercomputer centers. In addition to its provisions and goals, the vBNS supports IPv4, IPv6, and IP multicasting. IPv6 support is provided by IPv6-enabled routers that are connected via ATM PVCs or by encapsulation within IPv4 headers for tunneling through the network. The vBNS also has its own 6bone (an Internet testbed for IPv6) IPv6 address assignment, referred to as a *pTLA* (pseudo Testing Address Allocation), for providing IPv6 connections to other 6bone (www.6bone.net) test sites. IP multicasting sessions are conducted between sites via Protocol-Independent Multicast (PIM) software-enabled vBNS routers. Connections to the MBone are also supported.

The Internet2 project (www.internet2.edu) is a collaborative research and development effort comprised of approximately 150 universities, 20 corporate partners, and 25 affiliate members, which is managed by the University Corporation for Advanced Internet Development (UCAID).

Although the vBNS currently serves as the backbone for testing I2 initiatives, several new, very high-speed communication nodes, referred to as GigaPOPs (billion bit per second Point of Presence), are being designed, implemented, and interconnected to support future I2 data traffic. I2 initiatives bear names such as QBone (QoS Backbone), I2-DSI (I-2 Distributed Storage Infrastructure), and I2-DVN (I2 Digital Video Network). Practical outcomes of these initiatives include digital libraries, wide-scale distance learning, scientific visualization, tele-immersion, and tele-medicine.

As the Internet evolves into a more sophisticated media capable of grasping the attention of humanity, what political, social, and religious ramifications might arise? How have changes in communications and transportation already influenced these spheres? The Internet is a hybrid of communications and transportation and much more. In its current form, the Internet represents one of the seminal principles upon which democracy was conceived—the freedom of information.

Suggested Resources: Periodicals

1. *Network Magazine*
   Address: P.O. Box 58127, Boulder CO 80322-8127
   Phone: (800) 234-9573
   URL: www.networkmagazine.com
   ISSN: 1093-8001

2. *Internet Computing*
   Address: P.O. Box 55458, Boulder CO 80322-5485
   Phone: (800) 933-0484
   URL: www.icomputing.com
   ISSN: 1096-7052

3. *Internet Today*
   Address: Paragon Publishing Ltd., Paragon House, St. Peter's Rd.,
   Bournemouth, BHI 2JS
   Phone: 01202 200200
   URL: www.paragon.co.uk
   ISSN: 1355-5219

4. *Internet World*
   Address: P.O. Box 7461, Red Oak IA 51591-0461
   Phone: (800) 573-3062
   URL: www.iw.com
   ISSN: 1064-3923

5. *Wired*

   Address: P.O. Box 55689, Boulder CO 80322-5689

   Phone: (800) SO WIRED, +1 (415) 276-5000 outside US

   URL: www.wired.com

   ISSN: 1059-1028

6. *New Media*

   Address: P.O. Box 3039, Northbrook IL 60065-3039

   Phone: (800) 253-6641, +1 (847) 291-5225 outside US

   URL: www.newmedia.com

   ISSN: 1060-7188

7. *Web Techniques*

   Address: P.O. Box 1246, Skokie IL 60076-8246

   Phone: (800) 677-2452, +1 (847) 647-5928

   URL: www.webtechniques.com

   ISSN: 1086-556X

8. *PC Magazine*

   Address: P.O. Box 54093, Boulder CO 80322-4093

   Phone: (303) 665-8930, (303) 604-7445 elsewhere

   URL: www.pcmag.com

   ISSN: 0888-8507

9. *BYTE*

   Address: P.O. Box 555, Hightstown NJ 08520

   Phone: (800) 257-9402

   URL: www.byte.com

   ISSN: 0360-5280

10. *Network Computing*

    Address: P.O. Box 1095, Skokie IL 60076

    Phone: (847) 647-6834

    URL: www.networkcomputing.com

    ISSN: 1046-4468

11. *Telecommunications*

    Address: 685 Canton St., Norwood MA 02062

    URL: www.telecoms-mag.com

    ISSN: 0278-4831

12. *Data Communications*

    Address: P.O Box 1290, Skokie IL 60076-8290

    Phone: (800) 577-5356

    URL: www.data.com

    ISSN: 0363-6399

Suggested Resources: URLs

Note: URLs are current at the time of this writing. They are subject to change.

Standards Organizations

www.ieee.org: The Institute for Electrical and Electronics Engineers

www.ietf.org: Internet Engineering Task Force

www.w3.org: The World Wide Web Consortium

www.itu.int: International Telecommunications Union

Governmental Institutions

www.whitehouse.gov: The White House

www.senate.gov: U.S. Senate

www.house.gov: U.S. House of Representatives

www.ftc.gov: Federal Trade Commission (e-commerce, Y2K, and parental guidelines)

www.nih.gov: National Institutes of Health

www.nsf.gov: National Science Foundation

www.nasa.gov: National Aeronautics and Space Administration

www.noaa.gov: National Oceanic and Atmospheric Administration

www.ntia.doc.gov: National Telecommunications and Information Administration

Online Reference

www.loc.gov: Library of Congress

www.nypl.org: New York Public Library

www.cflc.net/refdesk.htm: Central Florida Library Consortium Reference Desk

www.galileo.peachnet.edu: Georgia Library Learning Online

www.britannica.com: Britannica Encyclopedia

www.comptons.com: Compton's Encyclopedia

www.w-b.com: Merriam_Webster Dictionary

Internet Domain Registry and Directories

www.networksolutions.com: Network Solutions, Inc. (domain registry)

ww.nsiregistry.com: Network Solutions, Inc. (Whois search engine)

www.domainsearch.com: DomainSearch.com (Whois search engine)

www.superpages.com: GTE (Yellow Pages)

www.athand.com: At Hand Network (Yellow Pages)

www.thomasregister.com: Thomas Register

Internet Derivatives and Security

www.internet2.org: Internet2

www.vbns.org: vBNS

www.cert.org: Computer Emergency Response Team Coordination Center

Java, ActiveX, and VRML

www.sun.com: Sun Microsystems, Inc. (Java)

www.microsoft.com: Microsoft Corporation (ActiveX)

www.web3d.org/vrml/vrml.html: Web 3D Consortium (The VRML Repository)

Search Engines

www.yahoo.com

www.excite.com

www.lycos.com

www.infoseek.com

www.altavista.com

www.webcrawler.com

www.goto.com

www.hotbot.com

Travel Arrangements

www.travelocity.com: Travelocity.com

www.mapquest.com: MapQuest

www.mapblast.com: MapBlast!

www.leisure-planet.com: Leisureplanet.com

News, Sports, Weather

www.foxnews.com: Fox News

www.abcnews.com: ABC News

www.msnbc.com: MSNBC News

www.cbs.com: CBS News

www.nbc.com: NBC News

www.news.com: CNET News

www.usatoday.com: USA TODAY

www.washingtonpost.com: *The Washington Post*

www.wsj.com: *The Wall Street Journal*

www.nytimes.com: *The New York Times*

www.espn.com: ESPN Sports

www.weather.com: The Weather Channel

Online Investing and Market Analysis

www.schwab.com: Charles Schwab & Co., Inc.

www.etrade.com: E*Trade.com

www.suretrade.com: Suretrade.com

www.fidelity.com: Fidelity Investments

www.smithbarney.com: Solomon Smith Barney, Inc.

www.troweprice.com: T. Rowe Price Associates, Inc.

www.mlol.ml.com: Merrill Lynch Online

www.fool.com: The Motley Fool, Inc.

www.thestreet.com: TheStreet.com

www.dowjones.com: Dow Jones & Co., Inc.

Online Tickets

www.tickets.com: Tickets.com

www.ticketmaster.com: Ticket Master

Online Auctions

www.ebay.com: Ebay.com

www.onsale.com: Onsale.com

Online Books

www.prenhall.com: Prentice Hall, Inc.

www.amazon.com: Amazon.com

www.barnesandnoble.com: Barnes&Noble

www.borders.com: Borders Online, Inc.

www.earbooks.com: Ear Books (audio books)

Online Greeting Cards

www.bluemountain.com: Blue Mountain Arts

www.hallmark.com: Hallmark

Children and Family

www.family.org: Focus on the Family

www.mbusa.net: Mayberry USA

www.nickjr.com: Nick Jr.

www.pbs.org: PBS Online

www.zoogdisney.com: Zoog Disney

www.jumpstart.com: JumpStart Online

www.etoys.com: eToys.com

www.toysrus.com: Toys"R"Us

Online Shopping and Gifts

www.ftd.com: FTD Online

www.autobytel.com: autobytel.com

www.realtor.com: REALTOR.COM

www.century21.com: Century21.com

www.saksincorporated.com: SAKS Incorporated

www.macys.com: Macys.com

www.sears.com: Sears, Roebuck & Co.

www.llbean.com: L.L.Bean, Inc.

www.landsend.com: Lands' End Direct Merchants

www.kmart.com: Kmart Corporation

www.wal-mart.com: Wal-Mart Online

Internet Traffic Analysis

www.internettrafficreport.com: Internet Traffic Report

www.internetweather.com: The Internet Weather Report

Miscellaneous

dart.fine-art.com: The Internet Art Database

www.sciam.com: Scientific American, Inc.

www.discovery.com: Discovery Channel Online

www.tlc.com: TLC

www.realnetworks.com: RealNetworks, Inc.

www.adobe.com: Adobe Systems, Inc.

www.mp3.com: MP3.com

www.broadcast.com: Broadcast.com

Chapter 2

Comer, D. 1999. *Internetworking with TCP/IP.* Vol. II. Prentice-Hall.

Gilster, P. 1995. *The SLIP/PPP Connection: The Essential Guide to Graphical Internet Access.* John Wiley & Sons.

Santifaller, M. 1991. *TCP/IP and NFS: Internetworking in a Unix Environment.* Addison-Wesley.

Chapter 3

Hioki, W. 1998. *Telecommunications.* Third ed. Prentice-Hall.

Rabiner, L.R. 1978. *Digital Processing of Speech Signals.* Prentice-Hall.

Stallings, W. 1993. *Networking Standards: A Guide to OSI, ISDN, LAN, and MAN Standards.* Addison-Wesley.

Stallings, W. 1997. *Local & Metropolitan Area Networks.* Prentice-Hall.

Stark, H. 1994. *Probability, Random Processes, and Estimation Theory for Engineers.* Second ed. Prentice-Hall.

Tanenbaum, A. 1988. *Computer Networks.* Second ed. Prentice-Hall.

Thompson, A. 2000. *Understanding Local Area Networks.* Prentice-Hall.

Chapter 4

Angel, J. 1999. "Satellite-based Networking: Set for Takeoff?" *Network Magazine* 14.6. 44–48.

Couch, L. 1997. *Digital and Analog Communication Systems.* Prentice-Hall.

Comer, D. 1999. *Computer Networks and Internets.* Second ed. Prentice-Hall.

Evans, J. 1998. "New Satellites for Personal Communications." *Scientific American* 278. 70–77.

Hughes, D. 1998. "Spread-Spectrum Radio." *Scientific American* 278. 94–96.

Makris, J. 1998. "Danger: DSL Ahead." *Data Communications* 27.6. 38–52.

Pattan, B. 1998. *Satellite-based Cellular Communications.* McGraw-Hill.

Chapter 6

Hall, M. 1998. *CORE Web Programming*. Prentice-Hall.

Neou, V. 1999. *HTML 4.0 CD with Javascript*. Prentice-Hall.

Wilson, S. 1995. *World Wide Web Design Guide*. Hayden Books.

Chapter 7

Comer, D. 1999. *Computer Networks and Internets*. Second ed. Prentice-Hall.

Frey, A. 1997. "Into ORBit." *Network Computing* 8.4. 51–60.

Hall, M. 1998. *CORE Web Programming*. Prentice-Hall.

Meyer, E. 1999. "What's New in CSS2." *WEBTechniques* 4.1. 42–47.

Neou, V. 1999. *HTML 4.0 CD with Javascript*. Prentice-Hall.

Pesce, M. 1995. *VRML Browsing and Building Cyberspace*. New Riders Publishing.

Savitch, W. 1999. *Java: An Introduction to Computer Science & Programming*. Prentice-Hall.

Chapter 8

Brown, D. 1996. "Bytes, Camera, Actions!" *Network Computing* 7.3. 46–55.

Comer, D. 1999. *Computer Networks and Internets*. Second ed. Prentice-Hall.

Essex, D. 1999. "IP Telephony: What does the future hold?" *Network Magazine* 14.1. 40–44.

Kosiur, D. 1998. "Hiding Your E-mail from Prying Eyes." *Internet Computing* 3.7. 87–89.

Sharda, N. 1999. *Multimedia Information Networking*. Prentice-Hall.

Solari, S. 1997. *Digital Video and Audio Compression*. McGraw-Hill.

Chapter 9

Bosak, J. 1999. *XML and the Second-Generation Web*. Scientific American 280. 89–93.

Bruno, L. 1998. "Certificate Authorities: Who Do You Trust?" *Data Communications* 27.4. 54–63.

Clark, E. 1999. "IPv6: The Ultimate Address Fix?" *Network Magazine* 14.1. 46–50.

Karvé, A. 1999. "Virtual Private Possibilities." *Network Magazine* 14.6. 64–68.

Karvé, A. 1999. "Firewalls for the Rest of Us." *Network Magazine* 14.9. 50–54.

Kosiur, D. 1997. *Understanding Electronic Commerce.* Microsoft Press.

Siyan, K. 1995. *Internet Firewalls and Network Security.* New Riders Publishing.

Stallings, W. 1999. *Cryptography and Network Security: Principles and Practices.*
Second ed. Prentice-Hall.

Zimmerman, P. 1998. "Cryptograph for the Internet." *Scientific American* 279.
110–115.